ANJIN — THE LIFE AND TIMES OF
SAMURAI WILLIAM ADAMS, 1564—1620

A derivative drawing of William Adams, which appears to be based
on a sketch (date unknown) attributed to Dorothy Burningham from
a description given by Malchior von Santvoort – a friend of Adams.
Original drawing is to be found at the Rotterdam Maritime
Museum. This version appears on the
Wikipedia website (source unknown)

¹ANJIN
THE LIFE AND TIMES
OF SAMURAI WILLIAM
ADAMS
AS SEEN THROUGH JAPANESE EYES

BY

HIROMI T. ROGERS

RENAISSANCE BOOKS

ANJIN – THE LIFE AND TIMES OF SAMURAI WILLIAM ADAMS, 1564–1620
AS SEEN THROUGH JAPANESE EYES

First published 2016 by
RENNAISANCE BOOKS
PO Box 219
Folkestone
Kent CT20 2WP

Renaissance Books is an imprint of Global Books Ltd

© Hiromi T. Rogers 2016

ISBN 978-1-898823-22-3 (Hardback)
ISBN 978-1-89882-39-1 (E-book)

British Library Cataloguing in Publication Data
A CIP catalogue entry for this book is available from the British Library

SPECIAL THANKS

The publishers and author are grateful to the Great Britain Sasakawa Foundation for their kind support in the making of this book

Set in Adobe Garamond Pro 11 on 12.5 pt by Dataworks.
Printed in England by CPI Antony Rowe

CONTENTS

૭

「三浦按針はもっと多くの人に知られるべき
歴史上の偉大な人物だ。」― 小泉純一郎

'Miura Anjin should be much more widely known
as a great man in history'

KOIZUMI JUN'ICHIRŌ

小 泉 純 一 郎

Koizumi Jun'ichirō was the fifth longest-serving Prime Minister of
Japan (2001–2006). Like generations of his family before him, he
lives on Miura Peninsula, on land that was part of William Adams'
(Shogun–granted) domain. As Adams would have done some four
hundred years ago, he has looked after the peninsula and its people
with great distinction.

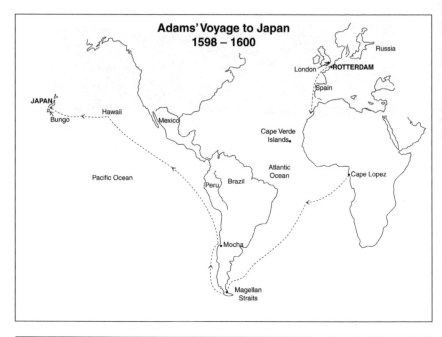

Adams' Voyage to Japan
1598 – 1600

Russia

London ROTTERDAM

Spain

JAPAN

Bungo

Hawaii

Mexico

Cape Verde
Islands.

Atlantic
Ocean

Cape Lopez

Pacific Ocean

Peru

Brazil

Mocha

Magellan
Straits

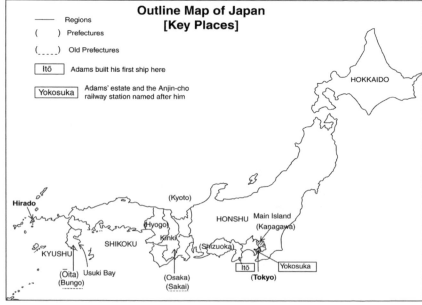

Outline Map of Japan
[Key Places]

—— Regions

( ) Prefectures

(_____) Old Prefectures

Itō — Adams built his first ship here

Yokosuka — Adams' estate and the Anjin-cho railway station named after him

HOKKAIDO

Hirado

(Kyoto)

HONSHU Main Island

(Hyogo)

(Kanagawa)

Kinki

SHIKOKU

(Shizuoka)

KYUSHU

Itō

Yokosuka

(Ōita) Usuki Bay

(Bungo)

(Osaka)

(Tokyo)

(Sakai)

PREFACE

❧

M y interest in William Adams springs from my fascination with seventeenth-century Japanese culture, which began in my student days. This is combined with a desire to recontextualize his story from a Japanese point of view – something that hitherto has been missing from Western literature. Adams, after all, became a fully integrated member of the upper echelons of Japanese society [it has not happened again since] and it was this phenomenon with all its cultural implications that triggered my curiosity to find out more. I might add that as a '*gaijin*' (foreigner) in British society for the last twenty-five years, I have at times felt that I have shared some of Adams' emotions, as he endeavoured to bridge the cultural divide and manage the pain, the presumptions and the paradoxes surrounding him as a foreigner.

My book is an attempt to combine fact and fiction. It is a dangerous route for any author, but yet one that does have honourable precedents, particularly where the 'fiction' is based on the most likely scenarios and, in this case, informed by a native knowledge of culture and context. There will be those who dismiss such an approach as poor or even lazy scholarship. However, I hope there will be others, looking for colour and atmosphere, who will accept my invitation to ride these two horses with me in a spirit of adventure and open-mindedness.

Accepting my responsibility for transparency over this 'two-horse' approach, as far as possible, I have annotated my sources and where this is not the case the reader will understand that I have imagined the dialogue and the context. Where informed imagining expands on a known event to create a likely scenario, the narrative will slip into the present tense, as in the Prologue.

I have of course read the already extensive literature in English on William Adams, from P.G. Rogers' *The First Englishman in Japan* [1956] to Giles Milton's *Samurai William* [2002]. I studied Adams' original logbook and letters, the diary of Richard Cocks [leader of the English East India Company in Japan, 1613–1623], the famous logbook by Richard Hakluyt, the journal of Captain Saris' voyage to Japan and many other European sources which I refer to elsewhere. For the definitive account of the original Dutch voyage to Japan, I am indebted to William de Lange's *Pars Japonica: The First Dutch Expedition to Reach the Shores of Japan* [2006].

I have sought to bring new perspectives to the existing Western literature, but most importantly to draw on respected Japanese sources and accounts not easily accessible to Western scholars with a limited command of the Japanese language, modern and classical. In so doing, I am aware that some Western scholars, who have not seen or been aware of these sources, may find some of my accounts and assumptions problematic. Others will understand that only with the help of Japanese records and accounts, interpreted through Japanese eyes, can we picture and understand what was really going on inside this essentially Japanese story.

My principal Japanese sources can be summarized as follows. Of those originating from the time of Adams' life in Japan, the main sources were *Keicho Kenmon Shu* [the relevant volumes for the early Edo Period], and *Toshogu Gojitsu Ki* [held in the Tokugawa family records]. I consulted later works by respected Japanese historians including Professor Katō Sango [*Miura no Anjin*], Professor Okada Akio [*Chosaku Shu, Miura Anjin*] and Professor Minagawa Saburo [*William Adams Kenkyu*]. Two well-researched twentieth-century biographies by Oshima Masahiro [*Umi no Hayato*] and Noshiyama Toshio [*Aoime no Sodanyaku*] provided new information and many likely scenarios to contemplate and assess.

In addition, I have travelled widely in Japan and in Adams' footsteps – to the sites of his houses, to temples, monuments, castles, universities and museums and consulted those who keep alive the oral tradition, including a descendant of one of his retainers. In my Afterword to this book, I discuss the importance of the extensive handwritten and unpublished records in the personal collections of Japan's great feudal families. They are zealously protected, but to some of them I had privileged access.

My interest in this compelling story extends unashamedly beyond the big historical themes of that period. It is my special hope that my knowledge of Japanese culture and customs in those days has enabled me to flesh out the story by picturing what it must have been like, from the clothes people wore to the food they ate, from the tidy houses and streets to their hairstyles, as well as the great castles, the battles, the executions. It has enabled me to explain some of the local behaviour Adams had to adopt, from never saying 'Thank you' to any of his ninety servants, to the correct use of the miniature towel in a public bath. I have sought to reveal a little more of Adams the man. Alongside his involvement in the great affairs of state, I have been able to describe his domestic life, his love of hot-spring bathing under the stars, the real nature of his 'marriage' to Yuki and his relationships with other women. Adams, it has to be said, revealed very little about himself. However, much can be gleaned from the accounts, official or otherwise, of the people around him – those he impressed and those he did not.

HIROMI ROGERS
Saunton, Devon
Spring 2016

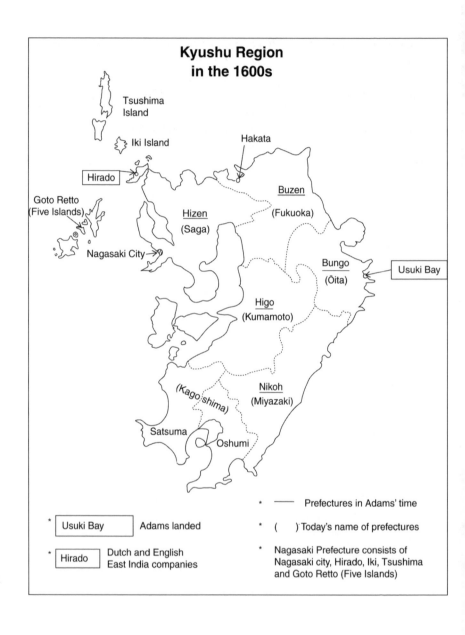

ACKNOWLEDGEMENTS

☙

First and foremost, it is 'hats off', as I have learned to say, to the central character in my book. The achievements of William Adams, or Miura Anjin as we Japanese remember him, has been my inspiration and role model. I feel honoured to be following in the footsteps of authors and scholars such as P.G. Rogers, C.R. Boxer, Richard Thames, Miura Jōshin, Katō Sango, Okada Akio, Etō Iwao, Makino Tadashi, Nishiyama Toshio and Oshima Masahiro. I am deeply grateful to Akira Matsura, the 41st head of the Matsura clan, for research materials and for his support and friendship. I am humbled at the willingness of former Prime Minister Koizumi Jun'ichiro to endorse my book. My thanks also go to Professor Malyn Newitt for sharing his great knowledge of Portuguese history. I am extremely grateful to Sir Hugh Cortazzi for his support and advice, and to Warwick Morris for introducing us.

I will never forget a chance encounter with Tanaka Nobumasa, the first chairman of the Anjin Appreciation Society at Hemi, which took place in front of the Adams memorial statue where he was sweeping the grounds. I thought he was the gardener! I feel Adams' spirit was at work because, at that early stage of my research, Mr Tanaka's help was crucial. My thanks, too, are extended to the second Chairman, Suzuki Mikio and his wife for their warm support and for introducing me to important people. I am grateful to Taguchi Yoshiaki for all his help. I so much respect his walking from Yokosuka to Hirado, retracing the journey made by Adams four hundred years earlier.

I am indebted to the members of the Anjin Appreciation Society, particularly Okada Hidenao, also to the mayor and staff of the Yokosuka City Council, Tsukuda Hiromi, mayor of Ito City, for help with a significant illustration, and chief priest Ōsawa Yūhō at the Ryūkō-in temple for his revelations about the Erasmus figurehead. Kataoka Shin, librarian at Kyūshū University, was efficient and kind, as were the staff of the Sankō Library.

Back in England, I greatly appreciate the support and encouragement from Elizabeth Mitchell, from my mentor Professor Peter Thomson and from Simon Baker of Exeter University Press. Financial support from the Great Britain-Sasakawa Foundation was of critical importance and a source of great encouragement to me. I am forever indebted to Paul Norbury of Renaissance Books for keeping faith in my contribution to the scholarly study of this subject. I am grateful to my neighbours and friends who have helped me through the hard times and to my parents for their love and care. Finally, I give thanks to my husband David for his unwavering support, for his work on polishing my English and for helping me to think internationally.

Those who understand Japanese culture will know I must pray for the spirits of William Adams, Tokugawa Ieyasu, Matsura Shigenobu and other ancestors. With this book, I have embarked on my own voyage of discovery, charting the lives of all those foreigners who had a significant influence on the country of my birth.

LIST OF ILLUSTRATIONS

PROLOGUE

჻

Japan's most celebrated Shogun stoops low to enter his tea house. Tokugawa Ieyasu is dressed not in his usual finery, but in a simple unlined kimono. His silk-decorated sandals or *zōri* are left outside. Shuffling forward on the slippery smooth *tatami* matting, he reaches the *mizuya,* almost silently for such a large man. The *mizuya* is where the tea master keeps his *chadōgu,* or equipment, including the *natsume* or tea caddy. Ieyasu's tea caddy bears the Tokugawa family crest of three hollyhock leaves etched in gold. Otherwise, the equipment is very simple, in tune with the tea ceremony's themes of humility, simplicity and naturalism.

Soon, Ieyasu has his fire lit and as the wood scent fills the small room, a voice calls from outside the guest entrance. It is clearly not a Japanese voice. The Shogun bids his guest enter and the door slides back to reveal a blue-eyed Englishman dressed in kimono and bowing low. Tall and usually bamboo-straight, he too stoops to enter and, as he removes his sandals, Ieyesu notices with silent approval that his guest has remembered to wear the clean white socks or *tabi* for purity.

The Englishman kneels and sits back on his lower legs in the *seiza* style. Ieyasu motions him to the first guest position opposite the tea-master. There is to be no second guest, nor indeed a third. For the first and probably last time a Japanese Shogun has invited his foreign 'prisoner' to the most intimate of his country's ceremonies.

Still kneeling, the Englishman eases himself to the appointed position, his fists clenched so that the knuckles, not the open palm, touch the floor. Through the rising steam from the cooking pot he saw not the all-powerful, ruthless ruler but a short, chubby man comfortable in his own imperfections and intent on a perfect *otemae* or performance of this centuries-old custom. Even to this English mariner, used to the rough life of the sea, the ceremony's guiding principles of harmony, respect, purity and tranquillity are already apparent in that simple room. As he accepts the traditional sweet rice cake, he sees the powdered tea scooped into a bowl and how, before he ladles in the hot water, the Shogun taps the scoop on the bowl's rim twice. Both the scoop and ladle are carved from bamboo and he notices how the Shogun takes his time, seeming to immerse himself in the sound of natural materials. When it comes to using the bamboo whisk or *chasen*, the sound echoes that of the shallow stone-bedded rivers that meander through Japanese formal gardens. The Shogun whisks with intense concentration. It is as though he has set himself the task of emptying his mind of all but the ritual itself.

The pottery bowl has been roughly thrown, its imperfections intended to reflect those of man himself, which the ritual encourages its participants to embrace. So these imperfections are often honoured as denoting the front of the bowl. The Shogun turns the bowl so that its front faces his guest and places it on the *tatami* mat. The Englishman bows and uses both hands to lift the bowl to his lips. The bitter taste contrasts pleasantly with the trace of the rice cake. He compliments his host on the quality of the tea and remembers to turn the bowl round again before returning it to the mat.

At no time does the Shogun drink tea himself. The ceremony demands of its tea-master humility and service. Nor at any time in the conversation that follows does he talk about himself. In the required spirit of harmony the Englishman thanks his host for the simple flower arrangement in the *tokonoma* or alcove. The scroll on the wall behind contains one of the Shogun's own poems. This one is about perseverance and triumphing over adversity, on which subject both men have perforce become experts. These carefully chosen decorations are all the more powerful because they are the only ones.

They talk now of many things, but there are no demands from the Shogun, no hidden agenda, and the Englishman realizes this is not the time to plead again for his release. Instead it seems a special bond is being forged over the glowing embers. After years of dealing with the Portuguese Jesuits, who saw the Japanese as uncivilized, the Shogun has sensed that this foreigner is different. The Englishman will be so much more useful to Japan if he can respect her culture and understand her beliefs. This Shogun's rise to power has taught him not to trust his own countrymen, not even his own son. Perhaps he can place some trust in this straight-talking Englishman, who owes the Shogun his life.

☐

Who, then, was this Englishman, on whom such hope was being placed? His name was William Adams from Gillingham in the county of Kent. He was the first Englishman the Japanese had ever met and he was to become one of the most important foreigners in their history, whose memory is still cherished there today.

Adams was part of a courageous but disastrous Dutch trading adventure in which five ships and nearly 500 men left Rotterdam and only one broken ship and twenty-four men reached their final destination. Of that twenty-four, only six men were still able to stand to greet the samurai boarding party. Then for twenty years William Adams was held 'captive' in Japan, first as a common criminal and eventually as one of the Shogun's most trusted advisers. He was made *hatamoto*, a samurai lord, the only foreigner ever to be so honoured. Anjin, as he was known in Japan, owned great houses and estates and wielded power and influence over Japan's developing relations with the outside world. He built ocean-going ships, trained the Japanese in navigation and ship's cannon and became the Shogun's chief scientific adviser and interpreter in English,

Dutch, Spanish and Portuguese. He died in Japan in 1620, a rich man but almost certainly a sad one, cut off from his English wife and daughter, unrecognized by his native country and disappointed with the English East India Company's base in Japan, which he had done so much to establish.

What kind of a man was he? How close did he become to Japan's most celebrated Shogun and to his own Japanese 'wife' and children? What does his story tell us about European trading ambitions and rivalries in East Asia at that time, about the cautious opening of Japan's window on the Western world or, at another level entirely, about the misadventures of unruly Western sailors in Japanese ports? Why did he not leave Japan when he eventually had the opportunity to return home? Why was he trusted by the Japanese but not his own countrymen? Where did his loyalties really lie?

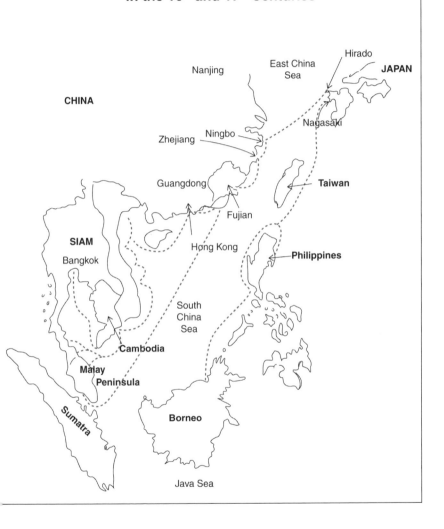

Japanese Trading with Asia in the 16th and 17th Centuries

CHAPTER 1

THE LURE OF THE EAST

୬

We owe to Marco Polo the first European account of Japan, or Cipangu as he called it, although, not having visited the country himself, he was entirely reliant on third-party sources. In the remarkable twenty years he served as ambassador for Khubilai Khan, the fourth Emperor of China and descendant of Chinggis Khan,[1] he visited many neighbouring countries. In *The Travels of Marco Polo*, published in 1298, he describes reports of Japan as a magnificent country, abundant in gold and with white and civilized people, but whose skilful warriors were in constant conflict.

Marco Polo, with his father and uncle, had originally travelled to China overland. In the following century, the expanding Ottoman Empire began imposing heavy taxes on overland travellers, prompting European explorers to look for sea routes that would avoid passing through Islamic territory. The stakes were high. The lure of the East sprang from the pages of Marco Polo's *Travels* – the silk, the gold, the silver, the spices such as pepper, nutmeg, cloves and cinnamon, even the erotic paintings. All were in great demand in Europe. Fortunes were there to be made.

Henry XV of Portugal [1394–1460], known as Henry the Navigator, was particularly keen to solve the sea-route problem and so despatched many of his young explorers with a mission to find an

---

[1] Also commonly known as Genghis Khan.

1

alternative route. The Cape Verde Islands were discovered in 1445 and by 1498 the Portuguese had found an eastern route, around Africa. Columbus, seeking a western route, had found the West Indies and part of South America for Spain. In 1494, the Pope defined what was known as the Tordesillas Line, whereby Spain and Portugal agreed not to interfere in each other's international business on their side of this north-south demarcation line.[2]

The Italian explorer, John Cabot, had also read *The Travels of Marco Polo*. He hoped to reach the East by sailing west, across the Atlantic. He came to England and gained Henry VII's support. In 1497, he sailed for North America and reached Newfoundland, thinking it was Asia. However, his was the first English expedition to reach America. In 1498, he set out again with five ships, but none returned.

In the next century, Ferdinand Magellan and his Portuguese sailors sailed south round America and became the first people to circum-navigate the world. By 1540, the Spaniards Cortés and Pizarro had explored Mexico and much of South America. A French explorer, Jacques Cartier, reached Canada. English merchants too were eager for trade in Asia, but Portugal controlled the south-eastern sea routes round Africa to India, China and Japan, and Spain controlled the south-western route round America and across the Pacific. Apart from the enormous challenges presented by the elements, both routes were beset by danger from pirates and raiders. In 1548, Edward VI's gov-ernment invited John Cabot's son, Sebastian, to England to help. He was a respected geographer and mapmaker. To avoid the Spanish and Portuguese, he recommended a 'Northeast Passage' to Asia, through Arctic waters north of Norway, but Tudor ships were no ice-breakers.

In 1553, with three ships and ninety-five men, Sir Hugh Wil-loughby accompanied by the expert navigator Richard Chancellor set sail from London taking a route around Norway to try to find an ice-free passage to Asia. Their ships were struck by a violent storm and they lost their way in the Arctic ice. After sheltering, Wil-loughby decided not to set out to sea again, but he and his seventy crew members died from cold and starvation. Russian fishermen

---

[2] Revised in 1506.

found their frozen bodies when summer came. On the other hand, Chancellor and his crew were lucky enough to reach the White Sea and an unknown land. Fishermen told them the country was called Russia or Moscovy. They were welcomed by the Russian Emperor, Ivan IV, and English merchants were permitted to trade. In 1554, Chancellor returned home safely, but within two years he had died having failed to discover a north-east passage to Asia. However, he had started a friendship between Russia and England which helped Queen Mary to establish the Muscovy Company in 1555, giving it monopoly control of all trade and discovery in the north.

In the same year, the Muscovy Company sent Stephen Borough to find the north-east passage. He explored to the north-east area of the White Sea, but his voyage was once again blocked by endless ice. Much of the Arctic Ocean was permanently frozen and even in summer it was extremely hazardous because of the unpredictable ice floes and icebergs. Twenty-five years later, the Muscovy Company sent out Arthur Pet and Charles Jackman who tried to find a way through, but the ice hazards also forced them to return. In 1594, a Dutch explorer, Willem Barents, sailed through what became known as the Barents Sea and got as far as the Kara Sea, but he died on his second voyage attempting to explore further. The triumph of discovering and sailing through what is now known as the North-east Passage had to wait until 1879 and the arrival of the Swedish explorer Adolf Erik Nordenskiöld.

In 1576, Sir Martin Frobisher took a different tack. He made an Arctic voyage to try to discover a north-west passage to Asia, but he failed and returned home. In 1578, Sir Humphrey Gilbert also tried, but fared no better. In 1583, he tried again, but this time his ship sank, and he went down with it. The problems with ice on this westerly route were compounded by fog. Between 1585 and 1587, John Davis made three Arctic voyages, but he only reached latitude 73°N, off the coast of Greenland, in what was eventually called Davis Strait.

The sixteenth century, therefore, when William Adams was learning about the world, was a time of fierce competition among explorers to discover the North-east and North-west Passages. As we have seen, it was also a time of great opportunity for adventurers to make their fortune following the newly-established trade routes. One of Adams' childhood inspirations would certainly have been the Devon sailor Francis Drake. For this ambitious and anti-Catholic young sailor, the Spaniards were a natural enemy and he took delight in plundering Spanish ships. Although he was shot in the leg by the Spanish, it only increased his determination. Eventually, he succeeded in capturing £20,000 of Spanish treasure (worth about £20 million today). He returned to Plymouth a hero and a rich one. Drake's next challenge was to explore the Pacific. In 1577, his ships set sail. His voyage proved to be very challenging involving a number of terrible storms, but he survived them and sailed through the Strait of Magellan. During 1579, on raids along the western coast of South America, he plundered £140,000 of silver (worth about £140 million today). He decided not to return via the Magellan Strait for fear of Spanish attacks and sailed north-west towards latitude 48°N. In June his ship landed in what is now Drake's Bay, north of San Francisco. In November 1579, he reached the Moluccas. Then he sailed on westwards, returning home to another hero's reception and a knighthood. At this point, William Adams would have been in his teens.

In the same period that many Europeans were eager for trade with Asia, Japan and China were trading with each other. The main trading port of Japan was the Kobe Port in Hyogo Prefecture, almost at the centre of the main island. Japanese merchant ships, which were no larger than the fishing boats of those days, set sail for Ningbo in China calling in at Hiroshima in western Japan and Fukuoka in the south. At Hakata Port in Fukuoka, they stopped and waited for the autumn north-easterly to speed them on their way to China. They went to trade with Ningbo, Fujian and Guangdong, mainly for silk. Relations between the two countries were strained and trade tightly controlled.[3] They returned home on the spring south-easterly. Later, as commerce in Osaka and Nagasaki

---

[3] It was controlled by the tally stick system called *Kan'ei-fu or Wari-fu*; a wooden tally was divided in half, one half for Japanese and the other for Chinese. When one of their ships was inspected, they had to show the half tally they carried.

developed more than in other areas, the ports of these two prefectures replaced Hyogo and Hakata.

In today's Nagasaki Prefecture, there used to be a port called
Hirado. This is where William Adams was later to make his base.
Hirado became the main centre for maritime traders. It had envi-
ronmental advantages, the right depth of water and was surrounded
by mountains of ideal height to provide good shelter. The Japanese likened its shape to their traditional earthenware oven, sunk
as they were in the ground. Its location at the southernmost tip
of Japan put it closest to the Chinese mainland. Shipbuilding was
also developing in China and soon the Japanese were making ships
with thicker and stronger hulls while also improving the design and
quality of the sails. Consequently, they were no longer confined to
sailing in specific seasons, when a fair wind was blowing, and thus
did not have to stop and wait in Hakata's port in order to pick up
these winds. In time, Hirado Port became a favourite haunt for
pirates, but in those lawless days that was another indication of the
port's status and commercial success.

□

There is little known of William Adams' childhood. What is
recorded is that he was the elder son of an English mariner and
was baptized at St Mary's parish church in Gillingham, Kent, on
24 September 1564. His family was part of an impoverished, Eliza-
bethan underclass, but it is reasonable to assume that he and his
brother Thomas were brought up well, with their imaginations fired
by stories of their father's sea voyages. In the sixteenth century, the
River Medway was very important from both the commercial and
naval points of view with the section of river opposite Gillingham
becoming the harbour for the King's ships. In 1576, when Adams
was twelve years old, his father John Adams died, prompting William to leave home and become an apprentice pilot and shipwright
in Limehouse on the Thames, just outside the walls of the City of
London. In those days Limehouse, unlike the smart riverside flats

of today, was known as the land of the living poor. The many mariners, carpenters and shipwrights who lived there were in constant
danger from street gangs, but it was on these banks of the Thames
that sailors gathered to volunteer for voyages into the unknown.

Adams was trained by the well-known shipwright Nicholas Diggins. He was personally more interested in a career as a pilot than a
shipwright. However, while he was also to prove a keen student of
the new science of navigation – hydrography, astronomy, astrology,
geometry and mathematics – it was his knowledge of how to build
small ships from start to finish, that eventually not only saved his
life but made his fortune.

He completed his apprenticeship in 1588, just in time to go to
war and to take part in the battle against the Spanish armada. His
first assignment, in fact, was on the 120-ton *Richard Duffield*, which
had a crew of twenty-five men, and was a supply ship, responsible
for conveying food and ammunition to the English fleet.

Although Adams' first command was only a modest little vessel,
the fact that he obtained the command at all at such an early age
shows that he must have been a good and diligent apprentice, having earned a first-rate recommendation from the highly-respected
mariner Nicholas Diggins. But Adams had his sights on piloting a
fighting ship, so when, at the age of twenty-four, he was told he was
too young for a command, he resigned from the fleet.

On 20 August 1589, Adams married Mary Hyn Mabel, the
only daughter of Master Saris, a wealthy London merchant. The
ceremony was conducted in the Parish Church of St. Dunstan in
Stepney, just to the east of the Tower of London, but also very near
Execution Dock, where the dead bodies after execution by hanging
could be seen piled up in the water. After tying the knot at such a
macabre place, the bride must surely have been very disappointed
to discover that her husband did not intend to work as a shipwright
in London. He was to be almost continuously at sea – roaming
as far as the west coast of Africa to the south, and the island of
Spitzbergen in the north. Then, one day, poor Mary Hyn, who had
already been left alone so much since her marriage to Adams, was
told by her husband that he had now agreed to be employed in

the English wool trade by the London Company of Barbary Merchants. It was risky work, particularly in the Mediterranean where he could have been caught and hanged by the Turks, but she would have consoled herself that he had sailed to and from North Africa safely for ten years.

During these voyages, Adams had acquired invaluable experience as a mariner and pilot; likewise, the qualities he developed of toughness, determination, ambition and self-reliance were to stand him in good stead later. From 1593 to 1595, Adams had also piloted a voyage of exploration to discover the Northeast Passage to Asia.[4] In the summer of 1595, they reached latitude 82°N, but the frozen Arctic seas forced them to return.

He was also developing his skills at a time of great change at sea. Pilots were now skilled in the science of navigation, rather than just in the experiences of those who had gone before. The pilot who understood astronomy, mathematics and other sciences could qualify as a master pilot, capable of sailing his ship to an unknown horizon, even in the darkest of nights, and reach his destination safely. In fact, Adams was one of the first English apprentices to master the new science of navigation. He was to become the first European to teach it to the Japanese authorities.

In Queen Elizabeth I's reign, the English and Dutch nations shared a common rivalry with the Spaniards. Queen Elizabeth allowed Dutch seamen to sail into the Thames to refit and rest, and towards the end of her reign she actually sent English forces to the Netherlands to help the Dutch in their fight for independence.

Adams had met many Dutch seamen and merchants on his travels and liked them. On one of his voyages, he picked up rumours of a Dutch plan to send a large fleet to the Spice Islands. The word was that five ships were already prepared at Rotterdam. The fleet required experienced pilots, able to navigate safely across both the Atlantic and Pacific Oceans.

---

[4] According to Lucas Waghenaer's *Spieghel der Zeervaert*, 1585, and Adams' letter, he wrote that he, as a pilot, made a voyage to Spitsbergen to try to find the Northeast Passage from 1593-95.

Adams was now thirty-four years old. He had worked for the Barbary Merchants for ten years. He was looking for a change. A long voyage to the East Indies would be high risk, but the potential rewards in spice and gold were enormous. He already had a good understanding of the Dutch, Portuguese and Spanish languages. His nationality presented no difficulties as far as being employed by the Dutch was concerned. He could also take advantage of a connection with his Dutch uncle-in-law. His wife's mother was Dutch and one of her uncles was involved in Dutch trading.[5] So Adams asked him to provide a reference for him to the Dutch East India Company. His wife and daughter, whom they had named Deliverance, reluctantly accepted Adams' decision.[6] As soon as Adams was given the reference from his uncle, he grabbed the opportunity and signed on, along with his brother Thomas.

When the spring of 1598 arrived, without any farewells to his wife and daughter (something he was later to regret), Adams set sail with a little ship to Goedereede Port on Goeree Island, near Rotterdam. The River Thames, Limehouse, the church of St. Dunstan and the town of Gillingham were all gradually lost from sight. His thoughts then were of a triumphant return, not that he would ever see these sights again.

Adams, Thomas and his English crew received a warm welcome from the Dutch organizers of the expedition. Information on the precise purpose of the expedition was harder to obtain. There were rumours in Rotterdam that the Dutch merchants who were financing the fleet had more interest in gold than spice and that they had instructed their captains to copy Francis Drake's tactics and raid Spanish settlements in South America.

The fleet of five ships must have looked very impressive riding at anchor in Goedereede Port, a deep waterway that joined

---

[5] There is a suspicion Adams knew this when he decided to marry, but such calculation was no doubt common enough in those days.

[6] He had another child, but the name and sex of the child are not known. It is believed the child was a boy, who died soon after birth or in babyhood.

Rotterdam with the North Sea. The five ships were the 500 ton *De Hoop* (Hope) with 130 crew, the 320 ton *Het Geloof* (Faith) with 109 crew, the 300 ton *De Liefde* (Love) with 110 crew, the 220 ton *De Trouw* (Fidelity) with 86 crew and the 150 ton *De Blidje Boodschop* (Merry Messenger) with 56 crew (see Plate 5). These names were to prove sadly inappropriate. *Hope* and *Faith* were tested to destruction, *Love* and *Fidelity* wilted under pressure, and when the surviving crew of *De Blidje Boodschop* finally returned home, the messages they brought back were anything but merry.

The admiral of the fleet, Jacob (Jacques) Mahu, asked Adams to join his flagship, *De Hoop*. In certain situations at sea, pilots would carry more responsibility and influence than captains and Adams was to be one of the main pilots for the fleet. He was also lucky to be on the same ship as Timothy Shotten, his best friend, who had already sailed around the world and was a goldmine of advice and information. Adams' brother was placed on *De Trouw* and the other Englishmen were divided between the vessels.

Adams joined his ship at Oudeschild Haven Harbour on Texel Island, at the end of June 1598. The ships had temporarily anchored at this unusually deep harbour to load cargo. For the Londoners, it must have been a surprisingly pastoral location. The ships were laid alongside green fields, watched by curious cattle, and held fast by wooden stakes driven into the banks. Nearby were two top quality wells, from which the ships drew water for their voyage.

Adams took on board the treasures of his trade – his world map, his brass globe, his astrolabe and compass. He would also rely on the knowledge he had built up of the night sky at different latitudes. He and Shotten had discussed the two possible routes to the East. Shotten's experiences on both did not bode well. The westerly route, around the southernmost tip of America, involved a long and lonely crossing of the Pacific Ocean. If they took the easterly route, around Africa's southern cape, they would run into the unpredictable storms that had ended the English explorer James Lancaster's voyage, seven years before. His diary tells how his ship had been hit by hurricanes and struck by lightning. Of his crew, he writes, 'some were stricken blind, others were bruised in their legs and arms, and others in their breasts so that they voided blood two days after'.

When word came that the Dutch fleet's financiers had decided on the westerly route, suspicion increased that their real target was Spanish treasure. Again Shotten's experiences were not encouraging. In 1586 he and his crew had the worst experiences of their lives when they battled through the Strait of Magellan. They had been battered with 'contrary winds and most vile and filthy, foul weather, with such rain and vehement stormy winds…. that hazarded the best cables and anchors that we had'. Finding food and water in this barren land had proved almost impossible. The crew had gone ashore in search of edible plants, but had instead found themselves being eyed up as a tasty meal by savages. 'They were men-eaters', reads the account of the voyage, 'and fed altogether upon raw flesh and other filthie food.' They fought with stone axes, ate rotting fish and looked 'as wild as beasts'. Some were giants with lopsided bones, while others had strangely shaped hands and feet. They actually measured one of their feet; it was eighteen inches long.

Dutch ships were much smaller than those of their enemies, the Portuguese and Spanish, so they needed the fleet for strength in numbers. Adams' subsequent ship, *De Liefde*, remained at anchor at Oudeschild Haven until 23 June 1598, when the four other ships were ready to sail from Goedereede Port on Goeree Island. *De Liefde* had been owned by the Magellan Company, when it was called *Erasmus*. The ship had a carving of Erasmus fixed to its stern (see Plate 3). *De Liefde* sailed from Maas Goereeschegat, Rotterdam, to Goedereede Port where they loaded cargo on 23 June 1598.

According to the records of the Dutch East India Company, the fleet set sail on the morning of 24 June 1598 towards the Bay of Biscay, but the date was deliberately inaccurate because they did not want their enemies to estimate their position. So their departure was actually between 24 and 27 June 1598. Adams expressed frustration that bad weather delayed their departure, as it was now the ideal season for sailing out of Rotterdam. However, they made steady progress through the English Channel and, as Adams noted in his diary, 'departed from the coast of England (the Lizard Peninsula, Cornwall) the fifth July'. As they entered the Atlantic Ocean, fair winds sped them through the often rough seas in the Bay of Biscay.

The first problems encountered were mostly of their own making. Courting popularity perhaps, the vice admiral, Simon de Cordes, had promised the crews 'all necessary provisions' and from the start the sailors could hardly believe their eyes at the size of the food portions. Items they could not eat were squirrelled away in their private chests so that before long the reserves in the ships' holds were running low and the vice admiral had to introduce unpopular restrictions. Sadly, it proved to be a portent of things to come.

Then, after passing the Straits of Gibraltar and running before a steady north-easterly, the fleet came close to disaster. A lookout sighted land and soundings were urgently taken, revealing a depth of only twelve fathoms. When the ships anchored off the lee shore, it was less than four fathoms. If the warning had been much later, the entire expedition would have ended in ignominy off the well charted Barbary Coast. Safely back at sea, an angry Admiral Mahu summoned his officers to the flagship and ordered them to compare their dead reckonings twice a week to avoid a repetition of such a disgraceful error.

Only two months or so into the voyage, Mahu then turned his attention to another problem. Supplies of fish, fruit and meat were exhausted and scurvy was spreading. With rations reduced to half a pound of bread and three cups of wine, by the end of August half the crew on his flagship were too weak to fulfil all their tasks. As the Cape Verde Islands came into view, Mahu faced a difficult decision. The islands were a popular victualling station, the last chance for ships turning west across the Atlantic, but they were a Portuguese colony.

Adams notes in his diary that supplies would have to be taken by force and the Portuguese forts were well positioned to repel landing parties. Later he was to record with frustration the twenty-four days wasted in a literally fruitless battle for the islands' bounty.

The catalogue of misfortunes and misjudgements is well documented in William de Lange's *Pars Japonica*. In what Sir Richard

Hawkins described as 'one of the most unhealthiest climates of the world', the islands were infamous for their 'stagnant and malodorous air'. Today, by contrast, they are an increasingly popular tourist destination for Europeans seeking winter sunshine.

In the September of 1598, after parleying unsuccessfully with local officials, the Dutch invaded Praia Island with 150 men under the command of Captain Van Beuningen. They met little resistance, the Portuguese having made a tactical withdrawal, but they were no closer to securing victuals. The occupation served only to confirm the Portuguese Governor's suspicion that these visitors did not come in peace. So, after several days of tortuous negotiations with intermediaries, when Dutch emissaries finally set out to meet the Governor, he had them ambushed and thrown into prison. They were then only released on condition the whole fleet left the islands immediately. Even that was problematic because a violent storm had separated the fleet as they dragged their anchors and were forced out to sea. It was several more days before the fleet was reunited and fresh water taken on board. Luckily two ships had found a decent supply of corn on one of the islands, together with some 600 eggs only recently laid by two giant turtles.

It was not enough to feed the fleet across the Atlantic so, when it finally left the islands on 15 September, Admiral Mahu set a course for Guinea on the West African coast. It was his last order. The Admiral was taken seriously ill and it was clear to all his officers that he was unlikely to recover. On 22 September a signal was raised on *De Hoop* to call all the captains to the flagship and during the following night the Admiral died. He was only thirty-four.

In spite of Adams' criticism of his dithering in the Cape Verde Islands, Mahu had been a popular leader; 'of a mild and sweet temper, honest, careful, diligent and very kind to seamen', according to one sailor's account. His burial at sea, as recounted in *Pars Japonica*, followed marine tradition with his coffin half filled with rock, covered with a mourning cloth and carried by his captains from the officers' quarters on the rear deck to before the main mast. There it was lowered into the water to the sad sound of drums, trumpets and the wailing of bagpipes.

On the same day, the sealed instructions were opened which stipulated that 'in case Admiral Iacomo Mahu happens to die on the voyage, Vice Admiral Simon de Cordes is to step in his place'. In the new appointments that followed, William Adams was moved from *De Hoop* to *De Liefde* as Pilot Major where, after three months at sea, he was reunited with his brother Thomas.

CHAPTER 2

A PUNISHING PASSAGE

ঙ

The Admiral's death was to be the first of many. His own doctor died from a similar fever soon after his most senior patient, as did the flagship's chief merchant. Scurvy was taking hold on board every ship. On *Het Geloof* over seventy sick men were confined below decks with no sign of recovery. Even with a favourable wind the fleet and its reserves of food were in no state to cross the Atlantic. Mahu had been right. They had no choice but to continue down the West African coast in the hope of finding fresh food and somewhere for the crews to recover.

The plan was to head for a volcanic island in the Gulf of Guinea called Annobon [or Anno Buena] which was well known for its fruit and livestock. However, navigating errors caused the fleet to overshoot the island by some 100 miles. To make matters worse, a caravel they had stolen from the Portuguese carrying their entire supply of corn had disappeared with its crew somewhere along the coast – a mystery never resolved.

On 6 November, anchored in the mouth of a small river north of Cape Lopez, the weary sailors could well have turned their thoughts to travellers' tales about the exotic women of this Cape. The English adventurer William Teverson had found it difficult to hide his fascination. 'They have exceedingly long breasts,' he wrote. 'Some of them will lay the same upon the ground and lie down by them.'[7] He reported that the women 'were given to lust and uncleanness'[8] and enjoyed enticing mariners back to their thatched huts. To Teverson's surprise perhaps, these ladies 'esteemed it to be good fortune to have carnall copulation with a Netherlander' and were seen to 'bragg and boast among themselves'.

For this fleet of Netherlanders, it was not to be. The next few weeks were spent searching the coastline for an opening that would enable them to venture inland. There had been occasional sightings of natives on the beaches and one encounter with a friendly chieftain yielded some supplies...two goats, some poultry and rather a lot of bananas. On this occasion a bottle of the fleet's Spanish wine had lubricated and temporarily suspended the bartering. The chieftain had downed it himself, fallen sound asleep and no-one had dared wake him.

A further attempt was now made to find Annobon and on the afternoon of 16 December 1598 its smoking volcano was spotted and the fleet dropped anchor along its shore (see Plate 2). However, it soon became clear they were not going to be welcome. There was a large force of Portuguese soldiers on the island and if the Dutch wanted food they were going to have to fight for it again. This time they were more successful, although they lost several men in the skirmishes. The Portuguese retreated inland and the Dutch were left to fill their store-rooms with the island's fresh produce and some twenty-seven cows. On the eve of their departure, it was a more cheerful crew that brought in the New Year, even though the island's 'unwholesome air' had taken its toll of their fellows. Thirty men died and were buried on Annobon.

Soon after leaving the island, the fleet picked up a favourable wind and set out across the Atlantic. They reached Ascension Island on 22 January and crossed the Tropic of Capricorn early in February, where in the Southern Hemisphere's midsummer the men would have 'lost' their shadows. They then followed the coast of Brazil south, reaching the Strait of Magellan on 6 April.

---

[7] Wieder, F.C. and Hakluyt, Richard.
[8] Ibid.

During the fleet's three months in the southern Atlantic, the main mast of *Het Geloof* snapped and was lost overboard, the flagship's bowsprit was broken in a great storm with the loss of much rigging, and a sailor on the same ship was hanged for stealing food, his body towed behind the ship as a warning to others. Reduced rations were indeed a major problem. On *De Liefde*, Adams observed how his fellows 'fell into so great weakness and sickness for hunger, that they did eat the calves skinnes, wherewith our ropes were covered'.[9] Barent Potgeiter, the doctor on *Het Geloof*, recorded that 'when the fellows were given mess-food, sentries had to be posted to look on, so that they would eat with manners, for they guzzled with such greed that some burnt their mouths to such a degree that the pieces would fall out'. Adams' own rude health seems to have owed much to his habit of chewing strips of dried penguin meat imported to London from South Africa.

Others were less fortunate. Barent Potgeiter describes some dramatic deaths. A sailor was sitting on a bench when his body suddenly went rigid, 'dropped backwards looking terribly ill, foaming at the mouth. He never spoke and died a few hours later'.[10] Another 'screamed, foamed at the mouth, scratched, kicked and punched'.[11] His speech became delirious and also 'he was so senseless that he could not clean himself or void his excrements in a regular way, and it being very cold, the moisture that was about him freezed and benumbed his flesh, insomuch that they were forced to cut off his legs'.[12] Even that extreme measure was not enough and he died from gangrene a few days later.

However, it was the ever present scurvy that was the greatest scourge, ravaging the body and rendering strong men useless. Ironically, the means to prevent scurvy had been discovered seven years earlier by the English explorer James Lancaster; just three spoonfuls

---

[9] Wieder, F.C. and Hakluyt, Richard.
[10] Ibid.
[11] Ibid.
[12] Wieder, F.C. and Hakluyt, Richard.

of lemon juice to be taken every morning. Somehow his discovery was forgotten for another 160 years.

So it was a severely weakened fleet of men who entered the notoriously dangerous Strait of Magellan on 6 April. The ebb and flow of the waters was treacherous, the passage often narrow, the sea mists thick and the winds changeable. These were a test for the finest of pilots. Moreover, winter was approaching fast so that frozen seas would soon be added to their challenges. Pilot Major Adams seemed to relish such challenges, occasionally recording his frustration at others'[13] caution. 'Many times we have the wind good to go through the Strait, but our General would not.'[14] There were moments of success and satisfaction. On 10 April, the fleet anchored off the Penguin Islands and marvelled at thousands of 'fouls greater than a duck'.[15] That day the hungry sailors clubbed to death more than 1400 penguins. Then in Mussell Bay, the shellfish were 'as much as a span in length' and the flesh 'weighed as much as a pound'.[16]

For the most part, however, Captain De Weert's long list of grievances captured the prevailing mood: 'rain, wind, snow, hail, hunger, losses of anchors, spoils of ship and tackling, sickness, savages, want of store and store of wants conspired a fulness of miseries'.[17]

The first encounter with savages came on 7 May on the Charles Islands. Vice Admiral Van Beuningen had taken two boatloads of men in search of seals when they came under attack from natives hurling stones. 'Ten or eleven feet high, reddish of colour, with hair down to their shoulders,'[18] these savages retreated after some were hit by Van Beuningen's guns. On 26 May, a small group of sailors foraging for food and firewood were again ambushed by natives. This time, five were captured and three killed before a rescue mission could be mounted. On that day, the physician Potgeiter had been present and he described how the savages 'went altogether

---

[13-18] Ibid.

naked,[19] with the exception of one, who had an old seal skin tied around his neck that covered his back and shoulders'.[20] Their weapons were long spears which they threw 'very fiercely and straight'. At the top of the spear were teeth like a saw or harpoon, making it hard for the physician to extract the tip from the wounded man. In a few cases he had no option but to 'push some right through, since they were lodged so deep in the body'.[21]

The fleet were to have one more encounter with the Strait's inhospitable inhabitants. On 23 August, the ships left the bay where they had sheltered from the winter storms and ice. By the end of the next day, they had made good progress westward, passing the Carlos III Islands and into the narrowest part of the whole Strait. Admiral de Cordes decided it was high time for a bit of pageantry to lift the spirits of his men and steel them for the perils of the Pacific. All the able-bodied men assembled on shore where the admiral announced that he had decided to erect a monument 'of so Glorious a Dutch fleet, having passed here with such effort, with such trouble, and amid such danger'. The monument was to bear the names of himself and his five captains, who he then had sworn with great ceremony into a lifelong fraternity, the Brotherhood of the Unfettered Lion, dedicated 'to plant the Dutch Coat of Arms in those provinces from where the King of Spain gathers the riches with which he has sustained his war against the Netherlands'. He then renamed the bay where they were anchored Ridders [or Knights] Bay and the pillar-like monument was raised at its entrance.

Then further down the Strait they came across a promontory which de Cordes felt would be a better place for his monument. So Captain de Weert was despatched to retrieve the pillar. He found its location occupied by about eight natives and wisely decided to return when they had moved on. When he did so, with more men, they were faced with a scene of absolute horror.

---

[19] Wieder, F.C. and Hakluyt, Richard.
[20] Ibid.
[21] Ibid.

'The natives had exhumed the remains of the dead that had been interred on the bay's shore. The remains of the admiral's physician, found floating face-down in the shallows, had been severely disfigured. The grave of another had also been desecrated, although his remains could not be found.'[22] All a search party could find was 'a fragment of the memorial plaque, which had been smashed to pieces'.[23]

Finally, on the morning of 2 September, the fleet reached the Pacific Ocean. They had been the first to overwinter in the Strait and the extreme weather had taken its toll. In all, 120 men had died. Captain de Weert's ship *Het Geloof* was the worst hit. Of his original complement of 110 'there were left but eight and thirtie'.

The Pacific's welcome belied its name. Adams wrote: 'We came into the South Sea and were six or seven days after in a greater storm.'[24] Before long, all the careful repairs undertaken while at anchor in the Strait were being tested to the limit. *De Blijde Boodschop* lost her bowsprit and some sails and signalled for help. In the rescue operation that followed, other ships were damaged and, as fog descended, the fleet drifted apart with only *Het Geloof* and *De Trouw* still together, but driven back into the Strait by the wind. One of the smaller ships *De Postillon* was never seen again and *De Blidje Boodschop* was hit again by a great wave and drifted for weeks before capture by the Spanish.

After all their trials and tribulations, the separation of the fleet and the loss of some ships broke the spirit of many mariners. The crew of *Het Geloof* had had enough. They turned round, re-entered the Strait and eventually limped back to Rotterdam, arriving in July 1600.

The crew of *De Trouw*, on the other hand, decided on one last gamble. After some reckless skirmishes with the Spanish in pursuit of gold, they turned westward and struck off for the East Indies on

---

[22] Wieder, F.C. and Hakluyt, Richard.
[23] Ibid.
[24] Adams, William.

their own. They did make it to the Spice Islands, but were quickly imprisoned or executed by the Portuguese.

Meanwhile, *De Liefde* too had been driven off course by the southerly winds, but she eventually resumed progress up the coast of Chile to the island rendezvous of Santa Maria, agreed upon earlier should the fleet become dispersed. In fact, Captain Van Beuningen had misunderstood the rendezvous to be at 46 degrees south rather than 36 degrees south and waited for twenty-eight days at the wrong place. It was a lucky mistake as the natives were friendly and willing to barter for their sheep and potatoes. Having waited, not surprisingly in vain, for the rest of the fleet, *De Liefde* left her sheltered anchorage and sailed on up the coast until low rations forced them to look for a landing just south of the rendezvous island of Santa Maria. At first, after a show of strength, the Dutch bartered successfully for local wine, potatoes and fruit, with the natives encouraging them to return the next day for more.

That evening, the ship's council agreed to proceed cautiously 'to go to the waterside but not to land more than two or three men at the most',[25] since the natives were 'wilde, not to be trusted'.[26] The next morning, Van Beuningen and twenty-seven men approached the shore. Adams, from the deck of *De Liefde*, saw what happened:

> The people of the country made signs that they [our men] should come a land....the people not coming near unto our boats, our captain, with the rest, resolved to land, contrary to that which was concluded aboard our ship before....At length three and twenty men landed with muskets and marched upwards towards four or five houses, and when they were about a musket shot from the boats, more than a thousand Indians, which lay in ambush, immediately fell upon our men with such weapons as they had, and slew them all to our knowledge. So our boats did long wait to see if any of them did come again: but being all slain, our boats returned, which

---

[25] Wieder, F.C. and Hakluyt, Richard.
[26] Ibid.

sorrowful news of all our mens deaths was very much lamented of us all.

Among the men slain was Adams' own brother Thomas.

To Adams' surprise, Jacob Quaeckernaeck took over as captain of *De Liefde*, an able seaman but with little experience of leadership. His first decision was to sail on to the island of Santa Maria to seek victuals. There, on 8 November, an excited lookout spotted *De Hoop* riding at anchor. 'We found our Admiral',[27] Adams wrote and, still reeling no doubt from the loss of his brother, 'our hearts were somewhat comforted'.[28] However, hopes were dashed when they boarded the flagship. *De Hoop* had in fact lost its admiral, Simon de Cordes, one of twenty-eight men killed on the island of Mocha.

Now, of the 130 men that had set sail on *De Hoop*, only thirty-three remained. On *De Liefde*, there were only twenty-eight. It was a dire situation that the Dutch tried to hide during successful negotiations for victuals with Santa Maria's Spanish officials, distracted by their own war with the local Indians. However, even with enough provisions to continue their expedition, the situation remained dire. Newly appointed to the ships' council, the two pilots, Adams and his friend Timothy Shotten, recommended 'to take all things out of one ship, and to burn the other'.[29] But 'the captains that were made new….could not agree to leave the one or the other',[30] so the remaining men were split equally between the two ships. It was an odd decision when each ship, in Adams' words, would have 'scarce so many men left as could wind up our anchor'[31] and be much more vulnerable to attack.

The next decision was more straightforward. With no gold to barter for spice and a cargo of broadcloth and rough wool, which

---

[27] Adams, William.
[28] Ibid.
[29] Wieder, F.C. and Hakluyt, Richard.
[30] Ibid.
[31] Ibid.

would be of little use in the tropics, there was not much point in heading for the Spice Islands. On the other hand, they might find a market for their goods in China. On the way, suggested one of the crew who had sailed there with the Portuguese, they could stop off in Japan, a country then unknown to the other crew members.

So, on 27 November 1599, the two ships with their skeleton crews set off to an unknown country across an unknown ocean. At first, with a fair wind, they made good progress with both ships able to keep within sight of each other. However, fear and foreboding still hung over the crews, so it was perhaps no surprise that when they reached islands at 16 degrees north, probably the Guam Islands, eight men from *De Hoop* stole a pinnace and escaped ashore. For them, taking their chances with natives likely to be man-eaters must have seemed like better odds than continuing their journey. In a way they were proved right, for on 23 February Adams is recording 'a wondrous storm of wind as ever I was in'. The next day *De Hoop* lost its battle with the elements and sank with all hands on board.

As the storm abated, it is hard to imagine what the crew of *De Liefde* now felt. Their bodies were weakened by scurvy and dysentery and their minds ever fearful of the same fate as their flagship. Even the stoical Adams was losing confidence. 'We proceeded on our former intention for Japan,' he wrote, 'but found it not, by reason that it lieth false in all the charts. Great was the misery which we were in, having no more but nine or ten able men to go or creep upon their knees.....our captain and all the rest looking every hour to die.'[32]

Adams was now effectively in charge of *De Liefde* and its fate. On 24 March, he had a stroke of luck when he sighted an island called Una Colona. The island with its distinctive column shape was on his charts and he could now tell his ailing captain and crew that they were less than 600 miles from their goal. Even then, with a damaged ship, a broken crew and inadequate charts, it was more by luck than judgement that *De Liefde* reached Japanese waters.

---

[32] Adams, William.

Adams had actually fallen asleep with exhaustion when at 35.30 degrees north his ship drifted within sight of Usuki Bay, Bungo, in today's Ōita Prefecture.

On 19 April 1600, Adams awoke to a miracle. Against a clear, dark sky jewelled with countless stars, he would have seen the outline of a mountain range. Gradually as indistinct shapes would have become trees, temples and houses, he realized it was not a dream. Steering as best he could, Adams brought *De Liefde* to its journey's end. 'So we, in safety, let fall our anchor,' he wrote later; words that do not begin to capture the relief he must have felt.

After twenty-two months out of Rotterdam and from the fleet's original complement of 491 crew, twenty-four survivors had reached Japan. Of these pitiful wretches, Adams was one of only six still able to stand, to survey their surroundings and greet what Fate would throw at them now.

CHAPTER 3

LIFE OR DEATH

~

The country to which Fate had brought them was the Land of the Rising Sun, born it is said when the sun first rose above the earth. The country was originally ruled by an emperor, the self-styled 'Lord of Heaven'. In 1192, a new government position, the 'Shogun' or 'greatest warrior', was established as the emperor's protector, although in fact it was a manipulative role. He had complete political and military power over the whole of Japan, made up at that time of three principal islands; Main (Honshu), Eastern and Western (Shikoku), Southern (Kyushu) .

For Japan, the sixteenth and seventeenth centuries were a golden age, in which some unique Japanese cultures were created. There was exquisite calligraphy and painting on scrolls, lacquer art, and delicate textiles for kimomo. Poetry, Kabuki and Noh lyric dramas, all flourished. Yet it was also a terrible era of feudalism and civil wars.

In 1600, and fortunately for Adams, the emerging 'power behind the throne' Tokugawa Ieyasu was a particularly enlightened leader. A master of the art of patronage, he was greatly to increase the number of feudal lords in the provinces (about 280 in all) to ensure control over the whole of Japan. Usuki Bay, Bungo, where Adams and his crew landed, belonged to Kyushu province. The feudal lord of Bungo was Fukuhara Nobutaka. However, he relied for advice on the former lord, Ōtomo Yoshimune, whose title and estate had been confiscated by the Shogun because of his disloyalty in a civil war. Yoshimune was a son of Lord Ōtomo Yoshishige, one of the first Japanese warlords to be involved with Portuguese missionaries and later their merchants.

The first Portuguese had arrived in Tanega-shima, Kyushu, in 1543. Six years later, on 15 August 1549, the first Portuguese Jesuit, Francis Xavier, landed on the island of Kagoshima, Kyushu. He was actually Spanish but worked for the Portuguese Compâgnia de Iesus. He had met a Japanese refugee, Anjiro, during his missions in Malacca and was encouraged by Anjiro to go to Japan. Six years later, the first Portuguese merchant ship sailed into the port of Hirado, Nagasaki. With Chinese merchants suspicious of Japanese aggression, the Portuguese were able to take advantage and act as a middle-man. The Japanese craved Chinese silk. The Chinese wanted Japanese silver. It was an enormously profitable business.

As a young prince, Yoshishige persuaded the Jesuit authorities to organize some Portuguese merchants to settle in his port and trade silk with his local merchants. Around the year 1555, the prince was also presented with a gun by a senior Portuguese Jesuit called Fernão Mendes Pinto. In Japan, samurai warriors still fought with swords, daggers, spears and halberds, so Yoshishige was understandably excited at the prospect of firing such a powerful weapon. However, the first time he tried to use it, he was severely injured and lost his thumb. Afterwards, those responsible for the prince's safety accused Pinto of causing the accident and he was sentenced to death by execution. However, mindful of Pinto's value, the prince stopped the execution and instead challenged Pinto to heal his wounds with Portuguese medicine. In twenty days, the prince recovered (albeit without his thumb) and on Pinto's second visit to Japan in 1556, the prince received him with honour and converted to Christianity.

When the story about Pinto's 'miracle cure'[33] spread over southern Japan, many Japanese converted to Christianity. In 1562, the lord of Nagasaki, Ōmura Sumitada, became the first

---

[33] Boxer, C.R.

Christian *daimyo* or lord to be baptized, with the name of Dom Bartholomew. In Nagasaki, Yokoseura, he gave a warm welcome to Portuguese merchants from Macao.

In 1571, he ordered that bands of Jesuits should be accompanied everywhere by a strong guard. Within seven months, 20,000 people had been baptized by monks from some sixty Japanese monasteries.

So, before Adams made land in Bungo, foreign influence was already a monopoly of the Portuguese Jesuits, who had lived there for almost sixty years.

□

In that early evening of April 1600 in the small bay of Usuki, local fishermen would have been scraping the flesh out of abalone shells. When one of them got up to stretch a tired leg, it is easy to imagine how his face must have frozen with amazement. An ocean-going vessel, of the kind only ever seen in large ports, was drifting into view. The mysterious foreign vessel was certainly entering the bay, through the narrows that marked an important border-line between Iyo and Bungo Prefectures. The fishermen might immediately have assumed that the Chinese were invading, but they would soon have realized she was a wrecked ship beyond the control of her captain. Two of her three masts had gone and the remaining one stuck out like the beak of a spearfish. Its shredded sail, hung from the beam, was trembling like a Japanese rope curtain. The vessel was listing heavily to starboard and her broadside was caked with seaweed and barnacles. The life-size statue fixed to her stern looked battered by countless rough seas. As the ship drifted closer, the fishermen realized she was manned when her anchor was thrown in with a splash. There was also somebody standing at her stern looking through a telescope. A flash of reflected sunlight on the glass of the telescope sent the fishermen scurrying back to load the buckets of shells into their boats and run like rabbits to spread the news to their village.

Through the round eye-piece of his early 'telescope',[34] Adams would have seen the fishermen running away and, as the news spread, in a short while the bay became a swarming mass of agitated men and women of every age. The men all wore white loin cloths and rough short jackets, the women simple kimono rolled up to their knees. For Adams, his deep concern and worries were over, at least for the moment. He had reached his goal. As he put down the telescope, his rough reddish-brown hair fell low over his eyebrows and over his shoulders, which were probably shaking with relief. Tears must have welled up in his sunken eyes and flowed down his cheeks and his over-grown beard. But that moment would not have lasted long, there were important duties to attend to. He looked round his badly damaged ship, but several times he dropped to his knees with exhaustion. He called his crew to give them the good news, but he had almost lost his voice.

Slowly and painfully his men assembled, tottering, holding on to the side of the ship or supported by their oars. Some would have been crawling. Nobody was able to walk properly. Their yellowy-brown faces and bodies were covered with blood and most of their teeth had fallen out – all symptoms of scurvy. Adams managed to stand, stiff and still, to make his important announcement; their ship was now in Japan. Jan Joosten van Lodensteyn, in a hint of the developing rivalry between the two men, was suspicious. When Adams expressed his confidence, Jan Joosten crossed himself and said 'Thank you God for blessing us. *De Liefde* has indeed been blessed with good luck.'[35] The sight of the crew all crossing themselves was too much for Adams. 'That's one of the

---

[34] Before the first known 'telescope' was invented by Hans Lippershey in the Netherlands in 1608, the principles of the telescope were understood in the late sixteenth century. There is some documentary evidence of this, but no surviving designs or physical evidence. Writings by John Dee and Thomas Digges in England in 1570 and 1571 respectively ascribe the use of both reflecting and refracting telescopes to Thomas' father Leonard Digges, and it is independently confirmed by a report by William Bourne in approximately 1580. These may have been experimental devices and were never widely reported or reproduced.

[35] Translated by the author from Oshima, Masahiro.

reasons,'[36] Adams interrupted 'but our achievement was mostly from our skills and endeavours and with the right instruments such as a map and compass.'[37] The atmosphere was spoiled. They all realized he was praising himself, but nobody argued with him because they knew well his belief that God only helps those who help themselves.

Adams reminded his men that, to the Japanese, De Liefde would look like a wrecked ship, easy pickings for plunderers. They should prepare for the worst. 'How many men can stand up?' Adams asked. Including Adams, the able men were only seven, Jan Joosten van Lodensteyn, Melchior van Santvo, Gisbert de Coning, Dirck Gerritszoon, Jan Cousynen and Jan van Oudewater. Adams wrote 'six besides myself, that could stand up his feet'. He had thought the survivors numbered twenty-six, but he was told by Jan Joosten that two men had just died. Thus only twenty-four men out of De Liefde's original complement of one hundred and ten were left. 'Why does God give us such hardship?'[38] exclaimed Jan Joosten. Although Adams felt the same, he ignored the sentiment and concentrated on a strategy to protect the ship's cargo. He knew that some of the crew held him responsible for the decision not to return to Rotterdam, that it was his stubborn ambition that had caused the tragedy. It was why several saw him as cold-hearted.

In the Captain's cabin, which reeked with foul smells, Captain Quaecknaeck was dying. The good news of their arrival was no comfort to this dejected man. When Adams told him, there were tears but not tears of joy: the Captain never opened his eyes. When Adams asked him to allow him to take charge of De Liefde, he feebly nodded his assent. It was an appointment not everyone welcomed. There was some anxiety about Adams' tough and direct style. He knew that saving lives was the most important goal, but saving the cargo was also important, not just out of loyalty to their company, but to bargain for the survival of his men and himself.

---

[36] Ibid
[37] Author's words
[38] Wieder, F.C.

They also needed to build up their strength. Adams ordered his crew to cut and bring leather rope to catch any rats and to collect barnacles, seaweed or anything edible to make a soup with their stored rain water.

Meanwhile on the shore, as the sun set over Usuki Bay, the twinkling of many lanterns revealed some commotion. Government officials had rushed to the bay, noisily clearing the crowds to get a good view of the invader. Even the local officials had probably never seen anything like this before.

Before sunrise *De Liefde* was surrounded by many fishing boats. One boat was ordered to get closer. Several fishermen, wearing headbands and armed with hatchets or the Samurai swords called *Wakizashi*, slung their hooks over both sides of *De Liefde* and clambered expertly up the ropes. They gripped their swords and looked cautiously in. What they saw were not aggressive Chinese armed to the teeth, but several groaning Western men on the verge of death. The samurai swords stayed in their sheaths. When the fishermen saw the ship's cargo of woollen items, they must have concluded that these 'invaders' had come to trade. Adams had hidden the cannon much earlier.

Mustering a smile of welcome and probably with more confidence than he felt, Adams greets the Japanese in Dutch:

> Goedenmorgen, japan vrien aagenaam kennis te maken! (Good morning, Japanese friends. How nice of you to come!) We are the crew of *De Liefde* sailed from the Netherlands. Unfortunately we have been through severe storms. We do not intend to harm you, so we expect no harm from you in return. As you can see, here is our load of trading items for you. We would like you to exchange them for water, vegetables, fish or other food please.

While he speaks, he takes out one piece of woollen cloth and enacts a trade. Taking their cue from Adams, his crew point to one cloth after another with one hand and make gestures of eating and drinking with the other. None of the Japanese understand Dutch, but a few understand that these foreigners might need food. They take out the bamboo water bottles attached to their waists and rice cakes in straw bags from their inside breast pocket. 'Do you need these things?' they say in Japanese.

Adams later writes with relief in his log book 'The people offered us no hurt.' Adams himself makes the first trade. When a fisherman inches forward with a water bottle and rice cakes, Adams takes the items and hands him a few pieces of woollen cloth. However, when the fisherman shows off the luxurious cloth, the others are envious and agitated. One of them raises his hatchet and shouts, 'Let's take the cargo off them!'[39] His whirling hatchet singles out the unfortunate Gisbert de Coning who panics and surrenders the woollen cloth he is holding. In vain, Adams orders him to stand firm, but Coning collapses, crying. Encouraged, the Japanese break out into wholesale pillage. Adams and his crew are pushed out of the way. While they are stumbling towards the safety of the stern, Adams lifts up Coning, who is crawling, and they watch helplessly as the pillaging is conducted with great thoroughness. Adams later writes, 'they stole all things they could steal'.[40] The hesitant fishermen have morphed into a mob. They swear at each other and rush to an open hatch. Their footsteps reverberate down the stairs, but they are blundering about in the dark inside. All the cabin doors have been left open invitingly, although it has been a long time since most of the cabins have shown signs of life. The corridors are littered with old clothes, pieces of paper and the everyday debris of a sailor's life. The mob burst into the cabins and take everything they can. Adams is particularly sad at losing most of his sea-charts and navigational equipment.

When nothing is left on deck, one fisherman shouts, 'There must be more below stairs,'[41] so a search for stairs begins. Suddenly they hear somebody screaming in a corridor towards the stern, where a pile of dead bodies are hiding some of the ship's instruments and ropes. All the bodies are naked and rotten. Their pupils are dilated

---

[39] Translated by the author from Miura Joshin.
[40] Adams, William.
[41] Translated by the author from Oshima Masahiro.

and their faces frozen in agony. One fisherman pushes past his shocked countrymen and shouts, 'These are only bodies. Get rid of them,'[42] but as soon as he touches the bodies, his knees crumple and he collapses, screaming. Some of the bodies are swarming with hungry rats. Quite unafraid of the fishermen, the rats continue their meal, nibbling the flesh and bones with a noise that would haunt any man who heard it.

The shaken fishermen return to deck and climb the stern watchtower, but they find nothing to steal there. So they return to threaten Adams with their hatchets and demand, 'Where have you hidden the cargo?'[43] Adams keeps silent. Suddenly, it is all over. One fisherman sees five boats approaching with government officials on board and sounds the alarm. The fishermen rush to throw the stolen items into their own boats and slide back down the ropes. The boats are away in an instant.

Adams went down to the corridor where the pile of bodies were and called out for his Captain. A hand rose feebly from among the dead bodies. Captain Quaeckernaeck was struggling to stand up. Adams was relieved to see him safe. Quaeckernaeck was not so sure. 'I was lucky not to be nibbled by rats,' he said 'otherwise I would have found it hard not to scream.'[44] Adams smiled. 'But the plan worked,'[45] he said. Covering the trap door to the ship's secret stores with a pile of dead bodies had been Adams' last resort. Somehow he had persuaded all the sick and the dying to lie down with the dead. Thanks to them and the hungry rats, the cannon, ammunition, Adam's prized world map and a few of the ship's instruments remained undiscovered.

Meanwhile, two Portuguese Jesuit priests who had taken up residence in Usuki town saw *De Liefde* and came to try to rescue her crew, but as soon as they realized that the vessel was their enemy, they turned back.

---

[42] Translated by the author from Oshima Masahiro.
[43] Ibid.
[44] Author's words.
[45] Ibid.

Adams reported to his 'dead'[46] men that the mob had gone, but the bad news was that they were to stay where they were, as Japanese Government officials were approaching. He also had to tell them that three more of their fellow mariners had died. When Adams went back on deck and leaned over the side of the vessel, he saw the officials calling up. They clearly wanted to come aboard and he immediately ordered his men to hang out a rope ladder for them.

For Adams and his crew this was the first time they had seen Japanese samurai. They were certainly unlike the savages they had encountered elsewhere on their voyage; warrior-like but short and slim, fit, tidy, elegantly dressed and wearing a strange topknot over a bald patch on top of their heads. Their top hair was in fact plucked with tweezers to leave their skin smooth and shiny with the knot tied at the back. They wore fine, silky robes, 'after the fashion of a nightgown',[47] and their swords were gracefully curved.

By now, Adams and his crew were desperate for food and fresh water, but they were unable to communicate that to the officials. They just shouted back in an unknown language. Adams tried to have a conversation with them in English, Dutch, Portuguese and Spanish, but they looked at him with blank eyes and barked something back in Japanese. He eventually gave up, as he wrote later 'neither of us both understanding the one the other'.[48] The only word he could make out was 'Bungo'.[49]

From Japanese sources we know the leader of the Japanese warriors asked Adams and his crew who they were and why they had landed there, but received incomprehensible replies. It was only when Adams tried physical gestures that the Japanese understood they needed water and food. When they signalled reassurance that they would rescue and feed his crew, Adams understood and was seen to show great relief.

The warriors returned to their boats and sailed quietly back to shore. A senior official, Isogai, reported to Lord Ōta Shigemasa,

---

[46] Adams, William.
[47] Alessandro Valignano's quote in Moran, J. E.
[48] Adams, William.
[49] Ibid.

the lord of Usuki castle, all the things they had seen. It must have crossed the calculating and devious mind of this dark-skinned lord that he could order another search for valuable things on *De Liefde*, but as the feudal lord, he had to take the first step according to the rules. Nevertheless, he was not sure how to deal with this exceptional situation. So in a Japanese version of pass-the-parcel he asked Lord Fukuhara Naotaka, but the lord of Bungo was not sure either. Lord Fukuhara urgently sent a message to former Lord Ōtomo Yoshimune, who still wielded political power around Bungo and had experience of foreign affairs.

Although Yoshimune had no idea from which country Adams' ship hailed, he assumed it had come for trade and had been shipwrecked around Bungo. He advised Lord Fukuhara to welcome and look after Adams and his crew for a while and then take them to Osaka to be questioned by the Council of Regents.

Accordingly, a boat was sent back to *De Liefde*, loaded with fresh food, fruits, clean water and a generous supply of *sake* or Japanese rice wine. From being prisoners in their own ship, Adams and his crew suddenly found themselves receiving the hospitality and friendship that Lord Ōta normally reserved for visiting samurai warriors. With the food and drink devoured, their spirits quickly revived.

Half an hour later, *De Liefde* was being pulled by five fishing boats, each rowed by eight boatmen, calling out their strokes rhythmically as they cut through the waves. Soon a large town came into view, in the centre of which stood a castle on a hill, its tower constructed with three-tiered roofs like a wedding cake and surrounded by enormous single-roofed buildings. Adams pointed to the town to enquire if this was where they were going. From their reply, he understood the town was called Usuki and he would meet the lord of the castle.

The five fishing boats halted some 100 yards offshore and untied their ropes from *De Liefde*, which was ordered to drop anchor. Adams wrote: 'our ship was brought into a good harbour'.[50] Then

---

[50] Adams, William.

an extraordinary thing happened. About twenty boatmen climbed aboard the ship and, carrying all the sick Dutchmen on their shoulders, climbed back down the ropes to their boats. Then each of the three dead bodies was wrapped in straw matting and carried carefully down to the boats the same way. Adams was the last to leave, having reassured himself that *De Liefde* was being guarded by security boats.

Adams and his men were brought to dry land at last. Those first few steps on terra firma must have been a joy after what they had endured at sea. A large crowd of Japanese would have gathered to stare at these strange foreigners. But Adams did not sense any hostility, just curiosity as the officials cleared a way for them to pass. Each member of the crew was allocated a basket palanquin and carried away by two minders. They had no idea where they were being taken and could see nothing through the sides of the close-knit basket. However, they had been treated with great courtesy and remained optimistic they would be taken to a comfortable and safe place.

Soon, they arrived at a little house on the foreshore, inside the grounds of a Buddhist temple. It was a tight fit for twenty-one large European men, but decent, well-prepared accommodation with three or four rooms. They noticed the house was built with wood and mud and had paper partitions and a floor laid with the straw mat called *tatami*. They acted out how they might manage without chairs, beds, dining-table and other Western furniture. One of the men seemed to call out as though for today's room service, but the Japanese could not of course understand what he said. They were too polite to laugh, but we can imagine the Japanese found the sight of these large men fooling around in their unfamiliar surroundings very funny.

In the country where cleanliness *is* godliness, the Japanese officials were shocked at the dreadful smell and state of the newcomers. They beckoned Adams first and took him to the bathroom. Adams saw duck-boards laid down, several wooden buckets and a large wooden steaming bath. Much to his surprise young and not-so-young female servants were waiting to wash their strange guests.

Kneeling, with a towel in their outstretched hands, they would have seemed a vision of gentleness, but once all members of the crew were undressed, the servants scrubbed their bodies vigorously with a rough flannel. 'We are treated like horses!'[51] one said and the others laughed. However, once they were in the bath everybody's spirits were lifted and their energy restored.

In the evening they were brought to the kitchen, where rice porridge was prepared. One Japanese official showed them how to eat the unfamiliar food. As was the custom, he even tasted the porridge before offering it to them. The surviving crew members started to warm to their new home. Adams settled a little uncomfortably on the straw mat for the first time and began, if somewhat awkwardly, to use chopsticks.

After the hot bath, a decent meal and more *sake,* the crew must have had no difficulty falling sound asleep. Except, perhaps, William Adams; at least, not for a while. Woken by his habitual tension and sensitivity to his surroundings, he slides open a paper door and sees several Japanese guards padding around the house. Their cloth shoes are silent, it is their bamboo spears that are making a slight noise. Adams lies back down to a chorus of grunts and snores from his crew. Are they having nightmares or just comfortable in the fresh, cotton-padded bedclothes? With painful clarity, he realizes that all their lives are now his responsibility. Wide awake, he starts going over the day's events. The gentle and friendly officials seem to be getting used to dealing with foreigners, in spite of the difficulty in communication. He has noticed several of them wearing exquisite silk robes, presumably a badge of authority, and Adams turns over in his mind how they can help him open up trade. He is aware that his hosts have sent for interpreters, but he is worried about their nationality and whether that will make them hostile to Dutch interests. That could put all their lives at risk and he is unable to go back to sleep.

In the morning, Adams found that four of the weakest men, including Captain Quaeckernaeck, were so seriously ill they were

---

[51] Translated by the author from Nishiyama Toshio

now unable to eat. Their bodies were little more than skeletons, except for their stomachs swollen from malnutrition over such a long time. They were carefully transferred to a separate room and nursed until a doctor could be fetched, probably from Nagasaki.

Two days later, the doctor arrived. There was consternation when he treated Captain Quaeckernaeck with moxa clay – his crew assuming from his cries that their captain was being murdered. However, it became clear that moxa clay[52] was standard Japanese medication and they gradually became fascinated by many other aspects of the oriental life-style and culture. The fascination was clearly helping Adams in particular to focus on the future and to forget all the unspeakable hardship he had experienced on the voyage.

Despite the doctor's help and care, of his four patients only Captain Quaeckernaeck survived. Adams was given permission to bury the three bodies at a corner of the cemetery managed by the Buddhist temple. This is the first recording in Japan of Christian bodies being buried in a Buddhist temple.

After five days, the senior official, Isogai, brought two European men to meet Adams and his crew. They were escorted by many high-ranking samurai warriors. When Adams and his crew realized these men were interpreters, they were relieved. Adams had spotted his Japanese hosts showing some irritation at the limitations of communicating by physical gesture alone and he feared his gestures might offend them by mistake one day. However, as these European men came closer, Adams' relief turned to fear. It was clear from their dark hair and black robes that the men were Jesuit priests and Adams saw his roller-coaster life taking another dip. It was actually worse than Adams realized. These Jesuits came from a stronghold of Portuguese priests, who had spent many years promoting their faith and their trading monopoly in southern Japan.

---

[52] Moxa clay is made with Japanese mugwort mingled with another green herb, which after drying is made into little matches to burn a person's body–legs, arms or any part where they feel pain. It was often done in place of letting blood and was believed to have had positive and speedy outcomes.

One of the priests asked, '*Tem alguen que entende o poutugues?*'[53] (Is there anybody who can speak Portuguese?), and Adams answered that he could. The priest was assuming *De Liefde* to be a Portuguese or Spanish vessel, perhaps blown off course by a storm en route from Nova España to the Philippines. It was too early in the year for a vessel to come over from China or the Philippines before the south-west monsoon began to blow. 'You must be of my brotherhood,' he said, 'of course you are all welcome'[54] and held out his hand in friendship. When Adams explained who they were and how they had got there, the priest withdrew his hand and changed his expression. Suddenly, he and the other priest were raining abuse on them, calling them heretics and pirates. Adams and one priest nearly came to blows, grabbing each other's collar, spitting and swearing at each other. Isogai and the other Japanese looked on in amazement. One of the priests turned away to say something to Isogai in Japanese; it was clear the 'heretics' were not getting a good report. There was nothing much they could do and Adams resigned himself to his fate. As Isogai listened to the priest's report, he looked suspicious and angry, but occasionally laughed. He stared hard at Adams for a while and Adams hoped he would look again at *De Liefde*'s cargo and believe his story. However, for the moment Isogai issued a short order to his lieges to confine the *De Liefde* crew to the house.

Meanwhile, the Jesuits were busy persuading the Japanese authorities that the arrival of an unauthorized ship was a serious matter; the crew were clearly pirates, intent on theft and murder, and it was therefore imperative that they should be killed immediately. The Jesuits had never explained to the Japanese that Western Christendom was deeply divided into Catholics and Protestants. Adams prayed that the samurai lords would believe that his vessel came for trade when they found a great number of woollen cloth, corals, glass beads, mirrors and spectacles.

Every day, the Jesuits came to the house and threatened *De Liefde*'s crew with their certain fate. Adams called them 'our

<hr>

[53] Translated by the author from Oshima Masahiro
[54] Ibid

deadly enemies'.[55] He and his men learned that they had recommended to the Japanese authorities that they should all be crucified, which was the customary punishment for piracy in Japan. It was the most extraordinarily painful death. The cross was laid on the ground and the body of the condemned man stretched out and fixed to it. Iron manacles were nailed to the wood of the cross and then clasped round the wrists, neck and ankles. Then the cross was quickly raised and its foot planted in a hole made for the purpose. Two executioners pierced the sufferer's body with a spear, thrusting it up into the right side through the heart and out above the left shoulder, thus passing through the whole body from one side to the other. Then, not infrequently, the two executioners returned, each with his lance, one piercing one side, and one the other, as much as sixteen times, so that the spears crossed one another and both points appeared above the shoulders without piercing a single organ. Death speedily followed. And if, as occasionally happened, the sufferers did not die as the result of these spear wounds, their throat or heart was stabbed to put an end to them.

Two of the *De Liefde* crew, Gisbert de Coning and Jan van Oudewater, were so intimidated by 'the threat of being crucified alive'[56] that they betrayed their fellows and went over to the Portuguese side, 'on assurances that in doing so their lives would be spared'.[57] Adams wrote: '(These) traitors sought all manner of ways to get the ship's goods into their hands, and made known unto them all things that had passed in our voyage.'[58] Both Dutchmen disappeared from the house soon after and Joãao Rodrigues, the head of the local Jesuit mission, recorded everything they had told him and without the knowledge of Lord Ōta.

---

[55] Adams, William.
[56] Adams, William.
[57] Ibid.
[58] Ibid.

Rodrigues then reported his findings to Alessandro Valignano, his superior in Nagasaki. Found in *De Liefde*'s cargo were eleven great chests of coarse woollen cloth, a box containing four hundred branches of coral and as many of amber, a great chest of glass beads of various colours, some mirrors and spectacles, many children's pan pipes, two thousand *cruzades* in reals, but more to the point, he was able to add triumphantly, nineteen large bronze cannon and other smaller ones, five hundred muskets, and five thousand cannon balls of cast-iron, three hundred chain-shot, fifty quintals of gun powder, three great chests of coats of mail, three-quarters having breastplates and pectorals of steel, three hundred and fifty-five darts, a great quantity of iron nails, hammers, scythes and mattocks and other tools.

Valignano immediately took this important information to Terazawa Hirotaka, Nagasaki's governor and the Council of Regents' highest representative on the island. Terazawa had converted to the Catholic faith, mainly to facilitate trade with the Portuguese and Spanish. So when Valignano introduced the arrival of 'the Lutheran Pirates' as a dangerous threat to the Japanese and that the Dutch were enemies of the Portuguese and all Christians, he was sure of a sympathetic hearing. Valignano urged his fellow Christians that the heretics should be expelled from Japan or crucified.

Before the Governor received Valignano's report, he had already received several missives from Lord Ōta confirming that the contents of *De Liefde* had been secured and Lord Ōta was awaiting further instructions. The evidence was persuasive, but Governor Terazawa saw an opportunity to increase his personal power amongst the warring feudal lords by confiscating the ship's weapons. For this he would need the Dutchmen alive, because none of his Japanese warriors had any idea how to use them. Now was not the time for crucifixion or expulsion, but there was no longer any need to treat them as honoured guests. In the meantime it would be wise to follow protocol and send a messenger to the Council of Regents in Osaka, for formal advice on how to deal with this unexpected arrival in Japanese waters.

Back in their house, Adams and his men were seized and tied up by Lord Ôta's men. They were thrown into the palanquins, which this time were firmly tied with rope from the outside, resisting all attempts to break out. When they reached the Japanese prison, they were horrified at the conditions. The inmates were held in dark cells with thick wooden grilles, damp walls, water on the ground and an unspeakable stench. The prisoners were naked except for a loin cloth and were forbidden to wash. There was a bucket for their excrement, but many were so weak with dysentery that they were unable to move. They lay in their own filth. They were rarely fed or given water. A prisoner's dead body would corrupt within seven hours and become so swollen and hideous that the very sight of it caused some prisoners to vomit.

The worst humiliation for the *De Liefde* crew was that every day their agony was observed through the thick grilles by passers-by, as if they were freaks or animals. Adams hoped every day to die. He was unable to write his diary during this torture because all his possessions had been taken away, but other crew members were able to write about their traumatic stories. We know from these and from Adams' later accounts that he attempted suicide several times because he lost all sense of dignity, but thoughts of his responsibilities to his wife and daughter rallied his spirits. Many times he regretted he had ever set sail on this fateful voyage. The prison officers were barbarians, who treated all prisoners with the same contempt. The samurai lords were not interested in what the prison was like; it was just a place to dump their enemies.

CHAPTER 4

THE SHOGUN DECIDES

ॐ

Nine days after the *De Liefde* crew were imprisoned, four large junks arrived at the Usuki harbour. An envoy from the Council of Regents had instructions to bring the captain of *De Liefde* to Osaka for questioning. However, Captain Quaeckernaeck was still critically ill, so Adams, as the next most senior officer, represented him. He was allowed to attend with one other and chose the ship's merchant, Jan Joosten van Lodenstey. Both men departed the next morning. Adams wrote, 'The great king of the land sent for me to come unto him.'[59] He did not know where Osaka was, nor how long it would take to reach there, but he had heard from the Jesuits about this great king, so he was aware that this voyage would decide his and his crew's fate.

The fleet of five boats spent several days on the Inland Sea, which separates the main island of Honshu from Shikoku. They sailed its full two-hundred-mile length before they arrived at the seaport of Sakai. During the voyage Adams was untied and given good food and drink. He would have found it strange to receive this hospitality and must have assumed it was like the last meal of a condemned man. He was pleased at being released from the dreadful prison, even if it proved temporary. Spring had come. The ocean was calm and sparkling like purple crystal. Salty scents were borne on soft

---

[59] Adams, William.

breezes. Adams was no longer afraid of whatever might happen to him. He would accept God's will.

On the voyage, Adams and Jan Joosten met a friendly Japanese officer who could speak some Portuguese. He asked both men where they came from and introduced himself as a Catholic, born in Manila in the Philippines. When he learned their nationalities, he said that that must make them enemies of the King of Spain. Adams countered, 'Japan is an enemy to the King, too.'[60] The officer nodded and said that some of his friends who had ceased to be Catholic had told him the same thing. It was his mother who had persuaded him to be Catholic, but he had doubts about the religion. It was already well known among Japanese Catholics that the two local Societies of Jesus (the Spanish one, which Francisco de Xavier had established in Manila, and the other for the Portuguese and Italians in Goa and Macau) did not see eye to eye. The officer told Adams and Jan Joosten how four years earlier the Spanish vessel, *San Phellieppe*, had drifted into the Bay of Tosa, Shikoku, on its way from Manila to Mexico. The Kanpaku or governor-general, Toyotomi Hideyoshi, was not interested in their religion, but was certainly interested in their cargo. But the message Hideyoshi received from the Spanish Admiral, Francisco Olandia, was not very diplomatic. He showed a world map to Hideyoshi's two messengers and pointed out how much of the world the King of Spain occupied and how rich he already was. He said that his King did not trade or barter. He invaded the countries he wanted, in order to expand his kingdom. The message infuriated Hideyoshi and quickly spread all over Japan. In less than a year, six Spanish and twenty Japanese Jesuits were crucified.

Adams wondered aloud why he was being told this story. He asked the officer whether Tokugawa Ieyasu had summoned him to be crucified. The officer said that much of the common knowledge about conflict between Spanish and Portuguese Jesuits and the religious wars between Catholic and Protestant had been kept from Ieyasu. The officer looked Adams full in the eye and said that

---

[60] Ibid.

Ieyasu would ask him about the Society of Jesus. He advised him to be honest and give Ieyasu clear answers and certainly to inform him that the Netherlands and England were in a religious war with the Spanish and Portuguese. In time, Adams would appreciate this valuable advice.

The fleet sailed slowly and arrived at its destination in thirteen or fourteen days, on 12 May 1600 (29 May by the lunar calendar). The officer came up to shake hands with Adams and guided him to the horses which would take them to Osaka Castle.

Osaka was a huge and impressive city several dozen times larger than Usuki, with a river 'as wide as the Thames'. Adams and Jan Joosten arrived shortly after a great battle between rival lords and had to pick their way through the battle remains, then through the city towards the massive and elegant Osaka Castle. Adams noticed many more sophisticated and richly-dressed people than he had seen in Usuki. There would have been loud conversation and laughter; it was a city vibrant with life. Adams probably assumed it was the capital of Japan.

The castle was surrounded by several moats and built with high stone walls that spoke of great military power. Adams was also impressed by the harmony in the architecture, with black pillars and white walls and layer upon layer of sparkling roofs, eight in all, decorated with a tremendous amount of gold and silver. Inside the walls were Nature's miracles in miniature. The four seasons of the year had been depicted with 'rocks, trees, shrubs, greenery and many other natural things'.[61] 'A lot of money and years of work must have been spent on creating such an exquisite, sophisticated garden and its decorative ponds and miniature waterfalls.'[62] Adams realized that he had come to a civilized country, certainly not a barbarian one, and must have imagined the king of the country to be a man of considerable dignity. After dismounting, Adams and Jan Joosten were carried in a palanquin up to the castle's great entrance. Once inside, servants opened each of the doors as they walked nervously forward. The cor-

---

[61] Joâo Rodrigues.
[62] Cooper, Michael and Boxer, C.R.

ridor was wide, but they turned so many corners it was like a maze, with no hope of finding their way back. The people who passed by Adams and Jan Joosten seemed to be used to foreign visitors. They were obviously of a higher class than those Adams had seen in the city. They wore the *hakama*, a loose jacket and matching pantaloon, richly coloured in silk or satin and which had the effect of making their bodies look bigger and more imposing. Each one of them held a long sword in the right hand and wore a short sword on the waist.

The interior of the castle was constructed of wood and hand-made paper, but looked more luxurious with some exquisite and ingenious handicrafts. Adams and Jan Joosten were led deep inside the castle until they reached the audience chamber. When the sliding doors of the waiting-room were opened, both men would have looked at each other in amazement. Although there was not much furniture, the walls and ceiling were sparkling. Adams wrote later 'a wonderful costly house gilded with gold in abundance'.[63] What he saw was like a gallery of the exotic art so prized in the great houses of Europe. The ceiling was made up of square wooden panels covered in gold, each one painted with a scene depicting one of the four seasons. He saw flowers, fruits, trees, birds, leaves, the moon and lakes; delicate pink-coloured cherry blossoms in spring, bright purple-blue bellflowers in summer, a crescent moon above Japanese pampas grass in autumn and austere trees in a snowy winter. The sliding doors through which Adams and Jan Joosten entered were similarly decorated. Adams imagined again this great king must cut a masterly or even haughty figure. The last sliding doors were opened, the guards dropped to the floor in obeisance. The Englishman from humble Limehouse came face to face with....... an enormously stout man with large eyes, long eyelashes and a wispy beard, wearing sober-coloured robes, which Adams found in sharp contrast[64] to such an extravagant castle. He immediately warmed to this gentle-looking man, who seemed around sixty years old, with

---

[63] Adams, William.

[64] It was well known that Ieyasu projected a certain humility, but was generous with hospitality to his important visitors.

wrinkles on his plump cheeks and round his eyes. He was resting one arm casually on a lacquered armrest. This was Tokugawa Ieyasu.

Tokugawa Ieyasu was not meant to be Shogun or king, the third to be so titled since the Genji Family took all power away from the Emperor in the twelfth century. When he first received Adams at Osaka Castle he was in fact just one member of two groups of five elders[65] sworn to govern the country until the son of Toyotomi, the previous governor-general, came of age. He was supposed to be equal in status to the other members of the regency, who included members of Toyotomi's family, but he was very different from the others. He had natural authority – he was fearless, sharp-witted, worldly, hard-working and a brilliant strategist in battle.

Ieyasu was born into a family of provincial warriors. He had formed a small but highly efficient army, which re-established the boundaries of his family's feudal territories until he became a force to be reckoned with. He was certainly ruthless. His path to power was littered with plots against rival lords, assassination, including by poisoning, and false accusations that led to a rival's suicide. However, he was just as likely to persuade people by letters written in his own hand. In 1600, before the decisive battle of Sekigahara in October of that year, he wrote over a hundred-and-fifty letters to prospective allies. His enemies included several powerful samurai families loyal to the young son of governor-general Toyotomi, but even they recognized that Ieyasu wielded enormous power in most of Japan.

Before Adams arrived, Ieyasu was already fascinated by the outside world. He made it clear to his staff that he wanted to meet people from other countries. Once, he summoned a Jesuit monk and asked him to persuade the Spanish in the Philippines to come to his land. His purpose was not for friendship, but to persuade their master shipwrights to help him build vessels that would carry his

---

[65] One of the groups of five called *Go Tairo/Council of Five Elders* were new, powerful warriors including Ieyasu. The other called *Go Bugyo/Five Commissioners* were all hereditary retainers of the former Kampaku/Imperial Regent or governor-general, Hideyoshi.

countrymen safely as far as Mexico and the East Indies. The Spanish refused to help because it was effectively giving the Japanese the very means they needed to invade the Philippines.

The only people granted an audience with Ieyasu were the richest and most powerful warlords, called the *Rōjū*, accompanied by their eight retainers. They were expected to bring a large quantity of presents worth at least £9000 in today's money, which had to be put a hundred steps away from the Shogun's throne. They wore the most formal of dress called *Sokutai*: these were extraordinary costumes, which Adams described as 'long pantaloons trailing about 20 inches behind them on the floor, so it was impossible to see their feet'.[66] Then they and their retainers all had to make the deepest of bows from a kneeling position. Adams thought that they were required to kiss the floor, although it was sufficient for their heads to stop just short.

Although Adams had no knowledge of this kind of courtly etiquette, he was received warmly by Ieyasu. He felt very honoured. Ieyasu had immediately realized that Adams and Jan Joosten, with their blue eyes and reddish hair and beards, were a different race from the Latins, with whom he was now familiar. He was pleased to meet someone from a completely unknown country, particularly ones who subsequently made it clear they saw the Portuguese and Spanish as an enemy. He was used to seeing people scared or nervous in front of him and avoiding his eyes, so he was impressed at Adams' calm aloofness and reticent manner, sitting back firmly on his heels. His clothes were rough, but somehow he retained a certain dignity. Ieyasu declared later that this dignity had reminded him of the leading samurai, the brave and proud lords of his own troops. He wagered that this captain must have a number of important secrets to reveal. By contrast, he was displeased at the Portuguese Jesuit acting as his interpreter, who had thrown Adams and Jan Joosten a look of fierce hatred, quite unlike a religious believer, and whose legs were sprawled out despite his having several years' experience of service at the castle.

---

[66] Adams, William.

For Adams, there was some frustration at the limits on conversation with no common language. He wrote: 'He made many signs unto me. Some of which I understood, and some I did not.'[67] But he felt that the king 'viewed him well, and seemed to be wonderfully favourable'.[68]

Ieyasu then ordered a prominent merchant called Suminokura Ryōi , who was sitting by him and spoke a little Portuguese, to tell the Jesuit to interpret very precisely everything that Adams would answer to his questions. Ieyasu started by quizzing Adams on his homeland and the purpose of his voyage. The Jesuit reluctantly interpreted the questions. Adams had brought with him some of the sea charts on board *De Liefde*; 'I showed unto him the name of our country'[69] on the opposite side of the globe and 'explained that our land had long sought out the East Indies, and desired friendship with all kings and potentates in way of merchandise'.[70] England and the Low Countries, he added, 'produce diverse commodities, such as woollen cloth, glass goblets, coral and others which Japan had not, and also wished to buy such merchandise in this country, which our country had not'.[71]

While the sharp-eyed Ieyasu had recognized the hostility between Adams and the Portuguese, it had surprised him because the Jesuits had always impressed on him that Europe was united in both faith and rule. He asked Adams whether his country had wars. Adams thought for a moment whether a true answer would be a wise move. He remembered the advice from the Japanese officer he had met on the boat from Usuki. He should tell the truth: 'Yes, with the Spanish and Portuguese, being in peace with all other nations,'[72] he said. Ieyasu was intrigued and asked both about the cause of these wars and various other questions about religion. The questions now came so thick and fast that Adams' diary left off recording them all. Adams wrote: 'It was tedious and I felt tired.'[73]

Ieyasu's next line of questioning was about the trading goods that *De Liefde* was carrying. It had been reported to him that much

[67–72]Adams,William.

[73] Adams, William.

of what was discovered in her cargo did not seem like merchandise for trade. Adams answered that 'many of them had been inside the crew's belly'.[74] Ieyasu wondered what he meant. Adams explained they had taken one year and ten months on the voyage from the Netherlands and had to trade the merchandise for food in countries where they anchored. Ieyasu was astonished to hear of a voyage of nearly two years. He learned the route *De Liefde* had taken to Japan was different from the usual Portuguese route round the Cape of Good Hope. Adams showed Ieyasu his world chart. He pointed out the Strait of Magellan and said that he had piloted *De Liefde* through this channel, but Ieyasu had his suspicions that Adams was lying.

Adams' audience continued until midnight, by which time Ieyasu too was weary. Before being ushered out, Adams asked Ieyasu whether he and his crew could be granted the same trading privileges as had long been granted to the Portuguese. Ieyasu answered before his visitors left the chamber, but Adams did not understand what had been said. He felt optimistic because the king had appeared pleased to meet his first English and Dutch guests and had showed them some favour. He was soon to realize it is easy to misjudge the Japanese face; words or face are not the same as actual intentions. Hope of mercy would evaporate.

After the long audience Ieyasu remained silent, weighing his suspicions. Wasn't Adams' demeanour too dignified to have gone through the hardship he claimed? Yet, to a samurai, his composure was familiar and attractive. He had thought carefully before replying; he had not revealed emotion; his concern for the well-being of his crew had appeared more important than his own life. However, when Ieyasu finally declared himself unconvinced by Adams' story, the high-ranking warlords hurried to agree with him. The Portuguese interpreter said he was in no doubt *De Liefde*'s crew were pirates. Ieyasu rose and commanded that Adams and his men remain in prison.

---

[74] Ibid.

The Osaka prison, in which Adams and Jan Joosten were now put, was much better than the previous prison. It was a decent room, they were well fed and their guards were civilized. But the uncertainty was getting to Adams. He was desperate to help his crew, who were still in the Usuki prison, and about whom he had had no news for over five weeks. He feared daily that he and his men would be crucified as, he now knew, was the custom with Japanese justice at that time.

Two days later, Adams and Jan Joosten were summoned again by Ieyasu and were asked the same questions they had been asked before. It was the test of consistency for Adams' story. When Ieyasu commanded that both men be taken back to prison, Adams probably thought that this would be a dreadful prison before execution. Surprisingly the prison cell was even better than before. The food was better, with grilled fish, boiled and seasoned vegetables and green tea. They were also allowed, under close guard, to take a bath. Both men were wonderfully relieved and dared again to believe the king would not execute them.

During the long imprisonment, the Portuguese Jesuits had been hard at work producing evidence against Adams and his crew and in Adams' words 'procuring friends to hasten my death'. They told Ieyasu that they were 'thieves and robbers of all nations'[75] and 'if they were suffered to live, it should be against the profit of His Highness and of his country'.[76] They demanded that the heretics should be immediately tried or expelled so that the rest of that nation 'without doubt should fear and not come here any more'.[77]

☐

In fact, Ieyasu gave little thought to crucifying Adams or any of De Liefde's crew. He was far more absorbed in political strat-

---

[75] Adams, William.
[76] Ibid.
[77] Ibid.

egy and how at this moment he might use their military skills and weaponry. His bearer had passed him an unwelcome letter. It was a reply to his letter to Lord Uesugi Kagekatsu, one of the group of five *Go Bugyo* and a former loyal retainer of Hideyoshi. After Hideyoshi died, the ruling groups, *Go Tairo* and *Go Bugyo*, had exchanged a number of oaths with each other. Lord Uesugi had accepted responsibility for restoring Osaka Castle and gathering prisoners and armour. If he had any trouble, he was to report to Ieyasu. He had also promised to present Ieyasu with one hostage from his blood relations, both of which pledges he was to confirm personally to Ieyasu. In his letter, Ieyasu had demanded that Uesugi fulfill these pledges, but Uesugi believed his status as a lord to be the same as Ieyasu's and he ignored all Ieyasu's demands, taunting him that his rustic and vulgar manner came from his low-ranking samurai background. Unusually, Ieyasu gave vent to his fury and flung the letter away.

Ieyasu realized that this reply was nothing less than a declaration of war. He sensed that all the members of *Go Bugyo* might be turning against him. First of all, Lord Uesugi would probably try to lure Ieyasu to fight against him up in Aizu, approximately 700 miles away from Osaka in the north-east corner of the mainland. During this battle, Ishida Mitsunari, the leader of *Go Bugyo*, and his troops would march to Osaka Castle and occupy it. When Ieyasu calmed down, he saw that Mitsunari's aggression against Osaka Castle could be part of his own strategy. He knew that Mitsunari was ambitious to conquer the whole of Japan, but if he raised an army against Mitsunari, it would be judged a personal attack and few warlords would support him. So Ieyasu gathered the Osaka resident warlords, held a council meeting and wrote to all his allies in *Go Tairo* throughout Japan to assure them that he would subdue 'the enemies of Hideyoshi and our enemies' who had broken the official pledges, but that he needed their support. Soon after, he received letters of agreement from more than thirty respectable warlords, so he was confident of having over 90,000 elite forces under his command.

Meanwhile, according to the contemporary record *Keicho-Kenmon-Shu*, Suminokura Ryōi, who Adams had met in the audience chamber of Osaka Castle, came to see him. He avoided the prison guards, stood close to the lattice door of the prison cell and in a low voice told Adams he could arrange his release. However, there would be a condition. If he agreed to support Ieyasu in war, with the cannon they had discovered inside *De Liefde*, he could be free right now. Adams wondered what kind of war and why the king would want one. Suminokura explained that Ieyasu was not the king yet. The current king was an infant prince of the late governor-general and some loyal retainers of the prince had always been hostile to Ieyasu and eventually had provoked him to start a war. It would be a decisive war between the eastern and the western provinces of Japan.

Adams initially refused to be involved in a war that was nothing to do with him or his country. Suminokura insisted that if Ieyasu were victorious, he would be the king of Japan, with all military and political power. He would agree to trade with England and Adams and his crew would be permitted to return home. The wealth and honour of which Adams dreamed would be his. However, if Ieyasu were defeated, Adams and his men would fall into the enemy's hands. The enemy was very close to the Portuguese and Spanish Jesuits, because they made great profits by trading through them. Adams asked Suminokura what Ieyasu thought of the Catholics. Suminokura answered that Ieyasu hated them because they would not help the Japanese with trade unless they were willing to be converted to the Catholic faith. Many warlords in the western provinces had become Christians and some of them had even given part of their domains to the Catholics. Ieyasu was concerned that the whole of Japan might eventually be occupied by the Portuguese and Spanish.

Adams realized that *De Liefde* had arrived at a turning point for this country. He did not completely trust Suminokura's honeyed words, but he readily understood why Ieyasu was after nineteen-calibre guns and cannon. Was this gamble too risky? Could he perhaps be the kingmaker? Although this cautious pilot had never thought of taking sides in a war in an unknown country, he must have realized he was being given no choice. Even if Ieyasu were defeated and consequently he and his crew died on the cross, all the seamen must accept their common destiny. To die as a failed king-maker, rather than just a prisoner, would surely have more hon-our. He held out his hand in a gesture of agreement. Suminokura expressed pleasure at the reply and yet again had reason to admire Ieyasu's foresight. He told Adams that Ieyasu had been impressed at his calm detachment in describing the unbelievable voyage and horrors he had experienced, and that he planned to make him a close ally.

After this secret negotiation, it seemed that fortune again smiled kindly on the man from Limehouse. Ieyasu rejected the Jesuits' plea for crucifixion and made it clear that Adams and his men had done no harm or damage to his country, and 'therefore it was against reason and justice to put them to death'. The Jesuits had been sharply snubbed and, like an earthquake tremor, they felt the ground shifting a little under them. On 22 June 1600, Ieyasu had another meeting with Adams. This time he quizzed him more about living standards and the general condition of Adams' country, 'of wars and peace, of beasts and cattle of all sorts, of the heavens'. He was convinced by all he learned and released Adams and Jan Joosten. Both men were now lodged in a secure house in Osaka. Over the week since his first meeting with Adams, Ieyasu had come to two important decisions. He would detain *De Liefde*'s crew in a reasonable condition, but he would forbid them to leave Japan. Ieyasu was ambitious to develop Japan's shipbuilding and to upgrade the skills of her pilots and he was sure that these resil-ient adventurers could be put to good use. He was also enthusi-astic about enhancing the technology in his country's silver mines and he hoped *De Liefde*'s crew might possess the skills that were needed.

Adams' and Jan Joosten's period of detention was to last a further six weeks before being once again summoned by Ieyasu. This time, Adams was given the good news that if he wanted to see his men aboard *De Liefde*, Ieyasu would arrange it.

For fifty days, including the travelling time from Usuki, Adams had heard no news of his men in the dreadful Usuki prison. He feared they had died or been executed. However, they were all alive and had sailed *De Liefde* to the Osaka Port, where Adams and Jan Joosten were now reunited with their men. Adams was joyful at finding Captain Quaeckernaeck and the rest fully recovered from their illnesses. When Adams walked aboard *De Liefde* again, it must have been an emotional moment for them all. The crew thought Adams had been executed a long time ago, because the Jesuits had come to threaten them in the Usuki prison and told them that Ieyasu had sentenced Adams to death and that the rest of them would soon be crucified as well. In fact, soon after Adams left Usuki, the crew had been taken to Osaka. The next day, high-ranking officers had come aboard *De Liefde* and inspected the guns, gun-powder, cannons and all other weapons. From that time, although the crew were in detention, they had been taken to a decent house, given a doctor and had been well looked after.

His crew reported to Adams that when more than ten Japanese shipwrights had come to repair *De Liefde*, they had assumed that Ieyasu would permit them to return home. Now, with the news from Adams and Jan Joosten, their minds were clouded. Adams encouraged them to stay and work for Ieyasu for a few more months, with high hopes of returning home and obtaining permission to trade with Japan in the future.

After the joy of reunion, it gradually dawned on the *De Liefde* crew that they were actually destitute. Their vessel had been completely stripped of her contents. For the ship's merchant Jan Joosten, this was a loss hard to bear. The loss for Adams was not as bad, but he was frustrated that, except for the charts which he had taken with him to Osaka, all his marine instruments and records had been taken, 'so that the clothes which I took with me on my back I only had'. When they appealed to Ieyasu for help, he immediately ordered that all the goods stolen from *De Liefde* be returned and on his personal orders a grant of 50,000 Portuguese reals was delivered to the *De Liefde* crew in compensation. Adams records that the grant was 'in the hands of one that was made our governor,[78] who kept them in his hands to distribute them unto us as we had need'.

De Liefde's crew were held at anchor in Sakai's harbour for thirty days. During this time, the grant was enough for major repairs and restocking with fresh victuals. On 23 July, they received an order from Ieyasu that *De Liefde* should be brought to the Kanto region, farther east along the coast. First, however, they were to call at the port of Anotsu, in the Bay of Ise, where they were to load timber, which they were to carry all the way up to the port of Uraga (Kanagawa Prefecture), on the tip of the Miura Peninsula, guarding the mouth of Edo Bay. Once there, the timber was to be transferred to smaller vessels and carried to Edo[79] (today's Tokyo). Edo was where Ieyasu had his permanent residence, the Edo castle.

Edo was 576 km from Osaka and, as Adams recorded, a similar sea journey as London to Cornwall. They encountered strong winds and it took several weeks to arrive at their destination. Adams was concerned about the shortage of money to buy enough rations and other supplies for their vessel to leave Japan. He would also need money to discover where Dutch merchants might trade. He tried to gain permission to sell their remaining cargo, but his pleas were ignored. He tried bribery, offering large sums of money to Ieyasu's retainers, but this failed. Within a few weeks, they had spent most of the money that was given to them.

When *De Liefde* arrived at the Uraga Port in mid-August 1600, Ieyasu was already there. He had come up on 5 August, but had had no time to attend to Adams and his men. The crew were led to a guest residence alongside the Uraga Port, which belonged to Mukai Shōgen Tadakatsu, Commander-in-Chief of the Navy of Uraga, under the order of Tokugawa Ieyasu. Adams alone was taken to stay in Honda Masazumi's mansion nearby the Sumida River in central Edo.

A few days later, several fishermen brought fresh fish to Mukai in his mansion. He asked the fishermen to take Adams back to the

---

[78] Terasawa Hirotaka, Nagasaki governor.
[79] Edo was the *de facto* capital of Japan after Ieyasu became the Shogun.

guest residence at the Uraga Port, where Adams could see his men again. When Mukai introduced Adams, the fishermen thought he was one of the Dutchmen. Mukai said, 'His name is William Adams and he is an Englishman.' Sukeji, a thirteen-year–old boy, could not stop staring at Adams. It was the first time he had been close to a foreigner, so tall with shoulder-length brown hair. Sukeji was particularly scared by the strange blue eyes dashed with green. While Adams was aboard the fishermen's boat, the boy kept silent and sat at the foot of a mast, with his knees drawn up uneasily in loose-fitting trousers and an anorak-like jacket with gold buttons. When they arrived at their destination, all the fishermen guided Adams to the guest residence. Adams thanked them and then bent down to hold Sukeji's hand and said 'Arigato'[80] meaning 'thank you' in Japanese. This time, the blue eyes seemed rather kind.

In a few days, Sukeji heard a rumour that a cannon would be shot on the shore. He describes in his memoir how he went and saw a black cannon, which had been carried from a Dutch ship, being laid down on the beach. Many of Mukai's retainers and ten Dutch and Englishmen, including Adams, were gathered round. At the request of Ieyasu, Adams was training the Japanese samurai how to use the cannon.

After the shooting practice, Adams and Sukeji met each other again. This time, Adams offered his hand and they shook hands in the European way. Adams asked Sukeji in his limited Japanese in which 'mansion'[81] he lived? Sukeji was confused at this question because he lived in a humble fisherman's hut, but he soon real-ized what Adams meant and invited Adams to come to his home. Sukeji's parents and grandmother had all died, so he lived with his grandfather. His great aunt (the grandfather's elder sister) came over daily from next door to manage the housekeeping. In the lane on the way to Sukeji's hut, Adams ignored his superior status and walked beside Sukeji as equals. When they arrived, Sukeji's grand-father was too shy to shake hands with Adams. The grand aunt,

---

[80] Translated by the author from Nishiyama Toshio.
[81] Ibid.

watching from a safe distance, was clearly frightened. When the grandfather introduced her to Adams as a Dutchman, she could only nod, but she soon spread a mat on the earth floor and started talking away to herself. Adams understood that she was trying to be hospitable and lowered his tall frame onto the mat. Soon afterwards she was serving slices of fresh cool watermelon and Adams was teaching Sukeji the words 'ship', 'boat' and 'thank you'[82] in English.

From that day, Adams made time occasionally to visit 'My Little Friend'[83] Sukeji. The grandfather had always been proud of Sukeji's intelligence and he encouraged him to learn foreign languages from Adams and also to teach Adams Japanese. So, on their long walks to the mountains, the seaside and several other places, the tall Englishman and his little friend 'traded' one language for another and Sukeji's dark eyes would have opened wide at the stories of Adams' voyage from Rotterdam.

One day, Sukeji describes in his memoir finding Adams at the Uraga Port, watching the sea alone. He guessed his friend was thinking of his wife and daughter and their believing that he must have drowned in an unknown sea. As he watched the seagulls hovering above, he might be wishing he, too, could have flown home. Suddenly, Adams was called by the Buddhist priest, his interpreter. It startled him out of his mood. He was being summoned to a council meeting with Mukai. At the meeting, all councillors agreed that, as Ieyasu would accept no failure, it would be safer to march and convey the cannons and guns to Edo by road rather than sea.

Two days later, over 200 troops led by Mukai set out from Uraga. Along the road they would march through Ōtsu, Shioiri, Jūsan-Tōge and Hodogaya to reach Edo. It was tough going, through dense forests and up steep rocky paths. On the way, under the flaming sun the troops stopped at Jūsan-Tōge [thirteenth pass] to take a rest in the shade of trees. Adams had his first view of Hemi Village

---

82   Ibid.
83   Ibid.

from the peak of the pass. He was impressed at the magnificent view, with the village looking resplendant surrounded by the sea and mountain ranges. Little did he know that this plot of land and stretch of sea would soon be where he was to settle in his own permanent home.

CHAPTER 5

THE BATTLE OF SEKIGAHARA

చ్

Mukai's troops eventually arrived in Edo. When Adams saw how seedy Edo Castle looked compared with Osaka Castle, he was disappointed. It was not defended by stone walls, just surrounded by low and long mounds of earth with fortifications atop. The fortifications were also made of earth and covered with bamboo and weeds. Inside these fortifications there was the main castle and a smaller one, both low buildings constructed with *hinoki* (Japanese cypress – high quality, rot resistant), with their roofs covered with moss and weeds. They looked like the huts of bandits. There was a new small house with white walls and roof tiles, which looked like a sort of castle. If this humble house was Ieyasu's stronghold, Adams doubted Ieyasu would be the future king. When he asked Suminokura Ryōi, whether it was perhaps Ieyasu's second home, Suminokura smiled at Adams and answered 'it is his stronghold'.

Suminokura then began to explain why Ieyasu's stronghold was so humble. In 1590, governor-general Toyotomi Hideyoshi had given Ieyasu *Kantō hasshū* [eight districts of the Kantō] in the East of Japan. These districts were Sagami, Musashi, Awa, Kazusa, Shimosa, Hitachi, Kouzuke and Shimotsuke. The first Edo Castle in Musashi district had been built by Ōta Dōkan in 1457. Since then, it had been occupied by successive Uesugi Sadamasa and Hōjō Ujitsuna lords. When Ieyasu became the lord of the castle, he was advised by his loyal retainers to build a new castle, but he ignored their advice and instead pioneered a canal between the castle and the Hirakawa estuary in Edo Bay. He wanted the canal to transport weapons from the sea. At the same time, he recovered land from the sea, using the earth excavated during the canal construction. On this land he built three new towns called Zaimoku-cho, a wood dealers' town, Funa-cho, a seafaring town and Yokka-ichi-cho, a market town. In a move of which the modern-day town planner would approve, a separate residential area for the townspeople was created with views over the man-made lagoons. There was no good water in the reclaimed ground, so Ieyasu set up the waterworks that channelled and purified the water from Inogashira, in the western part of Edo. In time-honoured fashion, Ieyasu had given estates to his most loyal retainers; higher-ranking lords were to reside in the hilly section and low-ranking lords were to reside near his castle. All these lords were pledged to defend his castle from any enemy.

Adams realized that Ieyasu's ambition was on a far bigger scale than he had thought. Ieyasu was set on establishing a new capital in the East of Japan, something that no leader had attempted before. This is how today's Tokyo became the capital of Japan. Ieyasu's plan was to build a new castle after defeating Mitsunari. Adams saw Edo already vibrant with life and realized that, in preparing the land for industry before raising his own castle, Ieyasu was doing the same as great kings had done in his own country. His respect for Ieyasu was growing.

As Adams entered this new and humble castle, Ieyasu was there to meet him with a warm welcome. Adams found Ieyasu very cheerful, in contrast to their meeting at Osaka Castle. Next day, Adams was summoned to a Council meeting and told that Ieyasu's force would depart from the Edo Castle for Gifu, in the western part of midland Japan, in a few weeks' time. Adams was curious about how the Japanese waged war, particularly on land. He was nervous but excited and probably spent a sleepless night wondering whether Ieyasu's victory and revolution for Japan might be in his own hands.

Next morning, Adams and his men gathered at the Hibiya beach to perform a firing test. All the weapons from *De Liefde* had been loaded onto carts. Some soil had been put in place to check the cannon's recoil. Ieyasu ordered Adams to fire all nineteen cannon at the marker boat, floating close to a mile out to sea. Adams gave the signal to Jan Joosten to fire the first cannon from the right. One after another the cannon were fired and cannonballs sped out to sea. All hit the target.

The ground shook and the cannon rumbled back against the piles of soil. As the silence returned and the smoke cleared away, Ieyasu and all his retainers stood blinking in amazement. Then a great cheer rang out. Ieyasu was clearly impressed, remarking to his aides that he had never seen such accurate firing before. Ironically the person who was most surprised was Adams. He had had no experience of firing on land before and found it much easier than he expected. However, and perhaps with not a flicker of relief on his face, he said they were ready to do it again! Here was a great opportunity to impress Ieyasu and other Japanese authorities with his and his men's skills.

□

A major battle, one of the turning points in Japanese history, was about to begin. It was late summer 1600. In the Sawayama Castle, Mitsunari pondered a confidential letter, handed to him by Ōta Shigemasa, who had secretly betrayed Ieyasu and leaked the announcement made at the Council meeting. Mitsunari was not surprised to hear that Ieyasu's army was to march into his territory, but he was surprised by the letter's description of nineteen cannon, guns, five thousand bullets and many other weapons from *De Liefde's* cargo, as he was sure that he had been informed earlier that only three cannon had been found. Next day, Mitsunari was informed that during her anchorage in Usuki, Ieyasu had been aboard *De Liefde* to investigate her cargo and had been helped by Lord Terasawa Hirotaka, who had been one of Hideyoshi's loyal retainers. Mitsunari now understood why Terasawa had never supported him and, although he had done the same thing with Ōta, he was infuriated at their conspiracy.[84] Ieyasu's growing power and popularity was worrying. It was time to talk to the Portuguese Jesuits about obtaining more cannon.

Ieyasu then divided his own forces in two. His son Hidetada was to lead a force of 38,000 warriors along the Nakasendō, the main inland route north, leaving on 21 August. Another force of 32,000 warriors led by Ieyasu was to set out for Aizu, a north-eastern province of Japan, six days later. Adams was ordered to join Ieyasu's force. All these warriors were extremely skilful and elite samurai. Mounted on their horses they were a feast of colour, their armour gold, red and purple. The *Ashigaru* or foot soldiers held colourful banners several yards high. The elegantly curved swords of the samurai warriors awaited battle. These swords could slice their enemies to pieces. Adams describes Japanese sword skills as graceful, but the end result as horrifyingly brutal.

Adams had no idea what Aizu would be like or indeed why they were going north and not west. Sweating from the late summer heat, he struggled to keep pace with the other foot soldiers as the rice fields turned from green to beige. Finally, after crossing the great Ōmori River, they were reunited with Hidetada's force on 30 August. In the evening, Ieyasu was eating rice porridge when the messenger he had long expected arrived and reported that Mitsunari had formed alliances with the four other members of *Go Bugyo* in the western provinces. He had persuaded them to promote Hideyori as Hideyoshi's rightful successor and to contrive a confrontation with Ieyasu's forces. He now commanded 85,000 troops as the leader of the West Forces and on 23 August his army had set off from Kyoto for the Kantō eastern region confident that, as planned, Lord Uesugi would engage and hold Ieyasu's forces in Aizu.

---

[84] Conspiracies of this kind were commonplace during this period of Japanese history. Samurai lords lived in constant anxiety that they would be betrayed by trusted allies.

Ieyasu gave a sigh of relief. 'I was tired of waiting for this news,'[85] he said. He had been going to chance a move against Uesugi the next day. If he had, he would have lost many of his troops in a one-sided battle.

Meanwhile, Mitsunari's army had laid siege to Fushimi Castle, Ieyasu's official residence just south of Kyoto. Although the castle was defended stoutly by Ieyasu's lieges, it fell on 8 September, after ten days of fierce fighting.

However, Ieyasu, the master of strategy, monitored Mitsunari's actions calmly. He was now confident of the loyalty of a large number of warriors and of the many weapons confiscated from *De Liefde*. He believed particularly that the nineteen cannon would prove decisive. At the beginning of September, Ieyasu withdrew from Aizu to draw in Uesugi's forces. He had persuaded a number of northern warlords to keep an eye on Uesugi and attack him from the north. He could now leave them to fight it out and by 11 September, before Mitsunari reached Kantō, Ieyasu and his forces had returned to the Edo Castle, unharmed and intact.

Adams still did not realize that the expedition to Aizu was part of Ieyasu's strategy to tempt Mitsunari to make the first move. He wondered why, with so many troops, Ieyasu had marched them up and marched them back without a fight. Adams' interpreter explained that the battlefield had changed now, to the west. Adams assumed that he would have to go west next, but he was instructed to take one of his men and go to Utsunomiya, 207 km from Aizu where he would join 8,000 troops led by Lord Kamou Ujisato of Utsunomiya Castle. Adams' duty was to fire cannon as often as possible for half a month or until Ieyasu reached Kyoto to fight Mitsunari. Ieyasu knew that when Uesugi heard that Ieyasu was on his way west, he would gather his forces and threaten Ieyasu from the rear. Utsunomiya was on their way, so Adams would have to give Uesugi a reason to think again.

The thud of Adam's cannon was heard for miles. Volley after volley of fire rang out in the Nikko Mountain ranges. Each time

---

[85] Translated by the author from Oshima Masahiro.

a tree was ripped up, mountain rock cracked or a hillside went up in flames. For Lord Kamou, watching every morning and evening from his castle, this was great entertainment. As a result of Adams' efforts, Uesugi's force never appeared and Lord Kamou was permitted to return to Edo at the beginning of October.

When Adams arrived at the Edo Castle, he heard that three days before all his Dutch colleagues had joined Hidetada's force and left for the west, conveying ten cannon. He suspected that this force would launch an attack on Mitsunari's force soon and the result would be decisive. Although he had often thought that *De Liefde* had arrived in this country at the worst of times, he was now keen to test his skills and ability in battle.

In a private room in the castle, Ieyasu, with his adviser Suminokura, congratulated Adams on the success of his efforts in Utsunomiya. He now wanted Adams to serve in the war in the West. Adams immediately accepted and asked him what service he needed, firing at an enemy castle or on the battlefield, or into forests to threaten the enemy as he had done in Utsunomiya. If Ieyasu wanted him to fire on the battlefield, Adams suggested that the carts for the cannon should have bigger wheels. The carts were designed for the deck of a ship, so the wheels were too small to move freely on the battlefield. He had struggled with them in Utsunomiya. Ieyasu answered that he had no idea where his forces would confront the enemy and hoped Adams would be able to fire at both their castles and on the battlefield. In which case, Adams advised much bigger wheels should be prepared because it would also be much easier for horses to pull the cannon from Edo to the West. 'You are quite a capable man,'[86] Ieyasu said, and in an aside to the interpreter he wondered why Adams, still a prisoner, was so active and ambitious for another's cause. Once Adams was dismissed, Suminokura said he understood that people in the Low Countries and England were used to trading not only goods but also their skills with other nationalities, unless they were the enemy. Thus Adams, the Englishman, was employed by the Dutch East India Company. So when

---

[86] Translated by the author from Oshima Masahiro

Ieyasu gave Adams a grant of 50,000 Portuguese reals, this English-man might have thought that the future king of Japan put a high value on his skills and ability. Ieyasu realized he had much to learn about things outside Japan.

For a moment Ieyasu remained silent. The word 'prisoner' might have prompted a memory of loneliness that haunted him from the thirteen years he spent as a hostage in his childhood. His family was of minor samurai lords. As part of the custom whereby a major lord held a hostage from a minor lord's family as security, Ieyasu was given as a hostage to Lord Oda's family when he was only six years old. Then from the age of eight to nineteen he was held in Lord Imagawa's family, during which time his life was threatened several times. However, he had realized that lamenting his misfortune would do nothing for him, so he treated the hardship as a test and a motivation to triumph in the future. He had never given up hope and now fate had rewarded his patience on several fronts. Lord Imagawa Yoshimoto had been defeated by Lord Oda in Okehazama in 1560 and Lord Oda forced to commit suicide by his enemy, Akechi Mitsuhide, in 1582. Governor-general Hideyoshi, another block to Ieyasu's rise to power, had died in 1598.

Ieyasu would have seen some parallels in Adams' life. After a terrible voyage, he had become a prisoner among strangers and was now involved in their war. Most people would lament these misfortunes, but he, too, was treating them as motivation for his future triumph. In spite of their different nationalities, as human beings, he felt a close affinity with Adams. They were both tough adventurers, but they were both scholars. However, he was careful not to reveal sentiment or sound too sympathetic in front of his interpreter: 'I will work Adams hard because he is a prisoner,'[87] he said, as he dismissed Suminokura and concentrated on writing more letters.

The confidential letters were to the allies of his enemy. Ieyasu was trying to tempt them to come over to his side, playing on their hopes for a large reward. He knew that martial arts were not the

---

[87] Author's words.

only means to victory in a war: the dark arts of persuasion, deception and bribery were important too. He had written over 150 confidential letters. The main reason why Uesugi had been riveted to Aizu was because he had to keep a wary eye on the forces of Lord Date and Lord Mogami, both allies of Ieyasu's and both recipients of his letters.

On 7 October (1 September in the Japanese calendar), Ieyasu put down his brush pen and headed west along the Tōkai-dō, at the head of 30,000 troops. Adams and Santvoort brought up the rear with nine cannon on carts that now had larger wheels, a yard in diameter. As Adams had predicted, and despite the great clunking and clanking, the horses were making light work of their heavy loads.

On their steady progress through Hakone, Odawara and Mishima, messenger after messenger urged Ieyasu to hurry up to reach Mino Akasaka, in Gifu Prefecture, which was some 200 miles away from Edo. Ieyasu had other ideas. He stopped off at the Sunpu, Shimada, Kakegawa and Hamamatsu castles and leisurely took refreshments. In Maizaka he took a boat-trip and enjoyed fishing in the Hamana Lake. He was allowing time for some other high-ranking fish to rise to his bait.

At last, on 21 October, Ieyasu arrived at Mino Akasaka and pitched the main camp at the confluence of two rivers. He was handed fourteen confidential letters from lords Kikkawa Hiroie, Kobayakawa Hideaki, Wakisaka Yasuhuru, Kutsuki and ten other major lords. They had all agreed to come over to his side. It was also reported that, on 17 October, his loyal retainers had crossed the Kiso River and taken the Gifu Castle, where Lord Hidenobu Oda, Mitsunari's ally, was staying. After Lord Oda surrendered the castle, he too went over to Ieyasu's side.

Mitsunari, who was in the Ōgaki Castle, in the south-western part of Gifu, was now worried. After Gifu Castle, the Inuyama and Takenohana castles had also fallen to the enemy. These castles were the ones he had planned to use for his defence. He assumed that Ieyasu's troops would attack the Ōgaki Castle next. He rallied his allies and waited for Ieyasu's next move.

At the council meeting of Ieyasu's forces, opinions were divided. The lords of Ikeda and Ii were both for attacking Mitsunari in the Ōgaki Castle, but the lords of Fukushima and Honda insisted on attacking the Osaka Castle, the ultimate prize. Ieyasu listened to both sides, but he wanted to entice the enemy out into a battle-field and play to his own strengths. When he had looked at a map, Sekigahara had caught his eye.

Sekigahara was in a valley with the Ibuki Mountains ranging down from the north and the Suzuka Mountains ranging down from the south. It was also close to the Nangū Mountains in the east and the Imasu mountains in the west. Through it ran the Tōzan-dō road and the other main highways that lead to Kyoto and Osaka. In 672, the valley had proved an ideal battleground for the well-known Prince of Oama in the Jinshin War and was the border between the east and the west on the Japanese main-land.

Ieyasu decided to entice the enemy onto his favoured battlefield. His strategy was to pretend to attack the Sawayama Castle, where Mitsunari's father and brother were staying, and which was on the way to Osaka. On the assumption that Mitsunari would come to the aid of his relatives, Ieyasu's forces would be able to execute a lightning strike against the enemy when they entered Sekigahara. At Ieyasu's command, Adams and his cannon, supported by 5000 of Lord Honda's troops, headed for the Sawayama Castle. Adams was instructed to make a great show of the cannon in broad day-light.

The news soon reached Mitsunari in Ōgaki Castle. When he heard about the two foreign men, he guessed them to be the crew members of De Liefde. He knew full well the dangers that he would face and he regretted that, although he had been able to acquire five cannon[88] from the Portuguese Jesuits, he had left them all in Osaka Castle, on the assumption that Ieyasu would attack there first. If

---

[88] At that time most Portuguese merchants had returned home. Thus the Jesuits were unable to provide many cannon, but Mitsunari thought five would be enough.

the Sawayama Castle fell, surely Osaka Castle would be the next target. So Mitsunari concluded that his forces must stop Ieyasu's forces in Sekigahara. However, the lords of Shimazu Iehisa and Ukita Hideie, his elite retainers, disagreed. They saw that his forces could be caught in a trap. They insisted he suppress his concern for his relatives and launch a surprise attack on Ieyasu's camp at midnight, when Ieyasu's troops would be weary. A calm and determined Mitsunari did not listen to them and insisted they march their troops to Sekigahara where, with their superior numbers, they would surely all taste victory.

At 7 o'clock on the rainy evening of 20 October, Mitsunari, at the head of 30,000 men, set off for the Sawayama Castle. To be undetected, they had put out their torch-lights, bound up the horses' mouths and kept their voices low. Only the moon cast long shadows on the castle walls as the troops gradually disappeared into the darkness.

At 2 o'clock on the morning of 21 October, Ieyasu was informed of the enemy's move and immediately commanded Hidetada's forces to head west along the Tōzan-dō road carrying lighted torches. He also sent an urgent message to Lord Honda, whose troops had pretended to head for the Sawayama Castle and had been waiting for the command they expected to change direction for Sekigahara.

Lord Honda passed the command to Adams, who had been in the shade of a tree sheltering from the rain, to prepare for battle. Adams felt the thrill at having played an important part in the deception of Ieyasu's enemy. He had never met Ishida Mitsunari and bore him no malice, but the pilot had set his course and, in the cold rain, he focused on fulfilling the expectations of Ieyasu.

At 4 o'clock the same morning, the forces of the West came together at Sekigahara, some 85,000 in all. Intending to surround the enemy, they formed a long line, with the Sasao, Tenman and Matsuo mountains on the south eastern flank of the valley behind them. The lead troops of the forces of the East arrived there at 5 o'clock, covered with mud. The rain was easing, but one of this valley's heavy fogs had descended on the battlefield. The last of Ieyasu's forces arrived at 6 o'clock. They erected their main camp on the Momokubari Mountain and, as was the custom, raised the Buddhist banner seeking forgiveness for the sin of violence and a safe haven in the after-life. The valley of Sekigahara was now jam-packed with some 120,000 men, their weapons and their horses.

Mitsunari in his main camp on the Sasao Mountain realized he had been caught in Ieyasu's trap. When he heard there had been no siege of Sawayama Castle, he regretted he had not attacked Ieyasu at midnight. However, he was still determined to confront the enemy, believing his forces were larger and stronger. Two things worried him; that some of his allies might go over to Ieyasu, who would certainly have tried to entice them, and that the five cannon which he had commanded Lord Mōri to convey from Osaka Castle had not yet arrived. He feared that just one unanswered round of cannon fire would have a profound effect on his troops. Why was there no message? With mounting irritation, he peered into the thickening fog.

On the slopes of Momokubari, Ieyasu was also agitated about two things. His son Hidetada's 38,000 troops including ten can-non, marching along the Tōzan-dō road, had not arrived. If they did not arrive in time for the decisive phase of the battle, his forces would be severely weakened. To make matters worse, Lord Honda's troops, including Adams, starting out from Tarei only 2.5 miles away, had not arrived either. Ieyasu had sent messen-gers, but there was no news. He sensed something was wrong and feared they might have been captured and killed. He didn't want the captured cannon used against his own men. It was more an angry soldier than a future Shogun who spat on the ground many times.

Despite Ieyasu's anxiety, at 8 o'clock in the morning, one of his closest relatives, Lord Ii, chose this moment to challenge the decision to have Lord Fukushima Masanori's troops lead off in the battle. Seizing an opportunity, he launched a surprise attack on Lord Shimazu's troops. The stirring sight of his rival's red-armoured cavalry provoked Lord Fukushima to attack Lord Ukita's troops. Soon the forces of Lord Kuroda Nagamasa, Hosokawa Tadaoki and Katō Kiyomasa were engaged too. Mitsunari's forces fought back ferociously. Unplanned and uncoordinated, the battle was well and truly joined and on a much larger scale than Ieyasu wanted.

Mitsunari was fortunate to be served by Shima Sakon, a samurai master of the martial arts; more fortunate than he deserved, many believed. To stop any advance by the East forces, Shima had his guns in three defensive lines and he himself, wielding a spear, would be the first into the fray. Meanwhile Ukita's and Fukushima's troops were locked in deadly combat. As Fukushima's troop met with a setback, Lord Fukushima swore profusely and railed against the driving rain. He urged his men forward, but they were driven back. While the fighting see-sawed endlessly, suddenly a thundery volley of shots rang out from Shima's defensive lines. Lord Terasawa saw his opportunity to join in and help reinforce Ukita's troops. Lord Ōtani, a recipient of one of Ieyasu's letters, saw the dangers in this move and attacked the rear of Terasawa's troops. In the dense fog, the warriors of both forces could see very little and were slipping in the mud. It was only 11 o'clock in the morning.

Meanwhile on the Momokubari Mountain, Ieyasu raised his hand to his eyes to screen them from the rain and ground his teeth in anger. The enemy had a definite advantage and his forces seemed to be flagging. He badly needed Lords Kobayakawa, Wakisaka and Kikkawa, who had promised to come over to his forces, to make their move. But nothing had happened. He began to suspect these lords might be hedging their bets. He was now nervous and continually pacing around his main camp.

At that very moment, a stir swept round the camp. Lord Honda's troops had finally arrived. Ieyasu exploded, 'How useless you all are! Where have you been?'[89] He did not recognize their individual faces; they were completely covered with mud. Lord Honda apologized and he and Suminokura threw themselves at Ieyasu's feet, grovelling like frogs. The road down which they had marched was very muddy from the heavy rains. Their carts had sunk so deeply under the weight of the cannon that the horses couldn't move at all. Reluctantly, the soldiers had waded hip-deep

---

[89] Translated by the author from Oshima Masahiro.

into the muddy morass and had moved the cartwheels. They had heard the sound of shooting and had hurried to reach the camp, but their strength was limited. Ieyasu shouted 'Prepare the cannon, Anjin!'[90] but Adams had already started work. To Adams, in the confusion of battle, the forces of East and West were indistinguishable, but he realized from Ieyasu's countenance that things were not going well. 'Where is the target?'[91] Adams asked. Ieyasu replied testily, 'Mitsunari's main camp.'[92] Adams asked, 'Where is it?'[93] 'Over there,'[94] Ieyasu answered, pointing out the Sasao Mountain in the west with his whip. Adams saw the camp, marked out with the traditional white cloth, just visible through the mist. Then he looked through his telescope to determine the precise position. Soon after, the fog closed in over the mountain. Adams took out paper and pen and began to draw a triangle. 'What are you doing? We have no time to lose. How can you take a sighting in such a fog?'[95] Ieyasu blurted out. 'This is why I am using geometry,'[96] Adams answered. Calmly Adams continued to calculate, while Ieyasu fumed. Geometry was of course essential knowledge for both a voyage and gunnery in the thick fog that often shrouded English coastal waters.

After Adams had finished calculating, he instructed Santvoort to set the cannon to the correct position and shooting-angle and ordered him to pack in extra gunpowder for a bombardment. Ieyasu asked whether Adams was sure that the fire would not hit his own forces, but when Adams said, 'The target is 2,700 yards beyond the front of your forces,'[97] Ieyasu permitted him to fire. Seconds later, an overwhelmingly loud explosion rang out and echoed round the mountains. The amazing sound, which nobody had heard before, was as if a hundred thunderclaps had hit Sekigahara at the same time. Everyone was confused. Mitsunari's forces froze in terror. They dropped to the ground and saw that their tents had been ripped apart, their banners flattened and their horses were screaming in panic. The trees surrounding the main camp had been

---

[90] Author's words.
[91-97] Translated by the author from Oshima Masahiro.

uprooted or their trunks and branches blown to pieces. Mitsunari felt his confidence draining away. This enemy's power was beyond anything he could have imagined.

Ieyasu could see the battle swinging his way. Pointing to the Matsuo Mountain, in the southwest, he ordered Adams, 'The next target is over there.' His intention was to persuade Lord Kobayakawa, who had been slow to commit his forces, to make up his mind. Adams found Kobayakawa's troops to be widely distributed, so he instructed Santvoort to fire five cannon in quick succession. The onslaught was a bolt from the blue to Kobayakawa.[98] His troops were being decimated by cannonballs coming out of the fog. When he learned from his close retainers that the firing was from Ieyasu's troops, he decided to take the remains of his army to the front in support of Lord Ōtani's troops, who had promised to support

---

[98] There is, in fact, no official record until the late seventeenth century of samurai using cannon or muskets. Under the *Bushi-do*, samurai had to fight with swords, spears and arrows to demonstrate their superior traditional skills. If they use other weapons, it dishonours them. All samurai authorities, including Tokugawa Ieyasu, would have discouraged any official record of cannon. Their use at Sekigahara and later at the siege of Osaka castle is generally accepted. Less accepted is the involvement of Adams in firing cannon at Sekigahara, which is self-evidently not something we would expect to see celebrated. And yet we know from Dutch (F.C. Wieder), Spanish and Japanese (Keicho Kenmon Shû) sources that Ieyasu confiscated the Dutch cannon with a view to putting them 'to good use'. We know from Dutch, English, Portuguese and Japanese sources that Adams was ordered to teach gunnery to Ieyasu's retainers. Ieyasu knew Mitsunari had cannon from the Portuguese. A Spanish missionary's account (*They Came to Japan 1549-1640*) records that Ieyasu employed at Sekigahara '12 cannons, 500 cannon balls, 500 chainshot balls and 500 musket' and that 'they were fired continually into the enemy ranks'. Finally from a Japanese primary source *Keicho Kenmon Shû* we have Miura Joshin recalling a word of mouth report that Adams and his crew had been involved in that battle. We know too that Adams was in the charge of Honda Masazumi, under the Japanese system of submission and loyalty to a feudal lord, and that Honda Masazumi and his retainers played a leading role in the battle, for which he was richly rewarded by Ieyasu. You do not need all the pieces of the jigsaw puzzle to get the picture and, for such an important battle, the assumption made is that Ieyasu would not risk his newly-trained gunners acting alone when Adams was available to supervise them.

Ieyasu but had been stopped by an unexpected attack from the rear. Then Wakisaka and other fence-sitting lords Kutsuki, Ogawa and Akaza launched attacks on the West forces. Ieyasu's forces sensed victory and soon Mitsunari's forces were in full retreat. It was getting dark in the west at 2 o'clock in the afternoon when a loud call 'Ei-Ei-Ohhh!'[99] rang out from Ieyasu's forces. Adams realized it was the war cry of triumph and he and Santvoort felt the relief and satisfaction of comrades in arms.

As if to cleanse the battlefield, rain now poured down on over 10,000 bodies of both the East and West forces and on a mass of banners and broken poles. Thousands of riderless horses were galloping around aimlessly. At Ieyasu's main camp, the decapitation of prisoners had begun. It was the custom for samurai warriors to present the heads of enemy combatants to their victorious leader, as proof of their prowess and in the hope of reward. Adams turned away in horror at the sight of these pale and severed heads, imagining that if Ieyasu's forces had been defeated, this would have been his fate.

It wasn't until 25 October that Hidetada's forces finally arrived at Sekigahara. They had been held up by Lord Sanada's troops in Shinshū, at a junction on the Tōkai-dō road. The battle over, all they could do was grovel before Ieyasu, but Ieyasu was deeply offended by his son's ineffectiveness and expressed no sympathy to them.

Meanwhile, Adams received some sad news from Jan Joosten. His Dutch fellow, Hertszoon, had been hit by a stray bullet and had died in the battle. His last words were that he wished he could have died in Holland. His body was buried in a mass grave at the foot of an unknown mountain, alongside many Japanese warriors. Adams was handed his ring and necklace crucifix as relics. He had been just about to announce to his men that, with Ieyasu triumphant, they might be permitted now to return home, but it was not the right moment. Clasping Hertszoon's relics, he mourned his friend's death.

☐

---

[99] Oshima Masahiro.

Ieyasu's victory opened a new era in Japanese history. Although the infant Hideyori Toyotomi was still alive and still the appointed successor of governor-general Hideyoshi, nobody believed that Ieyasu would accept his becoming the next leader of Japan. On 30 October, Lord Mōri, who was protecting Hideyori in the Osaka Castle, surrendered the castle to Ieyasu. On 2 November, Ieyasu rode in triumph into the castle, where he had a symbolic meeting with the eight-year-old Hideyori. He did accept the hereditary rights of the Toyotomi family at that time, in order to avoid a rebellion by Fukushima, Kuroda, Kotō and many other lords, who still supported the family. He judged it best that Mitsunari should be the only one blamed for this outbreak of war.

Mitsunari, Yukinaga and Eki were captured in full flight. The day chosen for their decapitation was 7 November. They were robed all in white (the Buddhist colour for death), their arms were put behind their backs, and the whole of their bodies were bound up firmly with rope. Mitsunari closed his eyes and Adams noticed him calmly preparing for death. He also noticed one samurai, Yukinaga, was wearing a crucifix round his neck. Yukinaga was first ordered to commit *seppuku*, but he begged to be decapitated because suicide was against his Christian principles. Many warriors of the West forces had converted to Christianity. Shortly after, the Kogi-Kaishaku-nin (or Chief Executioner) stepped forward, a skilled samurai trained to despatch high-ranking lords with the minimum loss of dignity or suffering, and the three men were decapitated.

Legend has it Mitsunari's head was reduced to a skull and then painted with gold by an artist. The sparkling gold head was laid on a small wooden table for presentation to Ieyasu. A servant carried the head into the chamber when Ieyasu was having dinner and set it down just a couple of paces from him. Ieyasu studied it like a work of art, in between mouthfuls of rice, then expressed his satisfaction and ordered it to be displayed in his castle as a symbol of his triumph.

In mid-November, Ieyasu reorganized fiefdoms and confiscated land to a total of 4,160,000 koku (1 koku equals 0.28 of a square yard) from eighty-eight of the lords who had remained loyal to the West forces. He also confiscated 2,160,000 koku by reducing the land of the lords who, in failing to support his forces, had sat on the fence. Together with his original land, 2,500,000 koku in the Kanto, he was now in possession of half of Japan. He had turned sixty (Japanese age), but this was the moment for which he had long planned. He could now ask the Emperor to pronounce him 'Sei-i-Tai Shogun', the Generalissimo.

CHAPTER 6

THE SHOGUN'S ADVISER

With his newly-won power, one of Ieyasu's first acts was to reward his allies with the confiscated lands. He greatly increased the estates of the lords of Fukushima, Ikeda, Kuroda, Kobayakawa,[100] Terasawa, Ii, Honda and others and ordered them to establish their residences in the new capital and regularly to attend formal occasions in Edo Castle. Every other year, they were permitted to return to their fiefdoms, where their wives and children were to reside as custodians of the estates. At the same time, Ieyasu confiscated all Lord Ōta's land and forced him into an itinerant life on the outer edges of the country. He also dramatically reduced to 700,000 koku the land of Hideyori, in the clearest signal that the would-be successor's star was waning. Hidetada, his own son, received nothing. Ieyasu gave Adams a reward of 10,000 reals, his men a total of 10,000 reals and condolence money of 5,000 reals for a departed soul. Sadly for them, the most important announcement never came. Ieyasu did not allow Adams and his men to return home. Adams decided he must appeal directly to Ieyasu.

---

[100] Kobayakawa later turned against his Shogun, breaking the samurai code in valuing his own life above his family's honour. For centuries his family had to live with this disgrace and even today people link his name with *uragiri*, meaning the act of treachery.

A few days later, Adams was taken to a reed field surrounded with sparse trees in the Kyoto suburb of Fushimi, where Ieyasu had been enjoying falconry every day since his victory. Stepping out of the *jin-chi* or tent, which normally hid great men from public gaze and on which the hollyhock trefoil coat of arms of the Tokugawa clan was now embroidered (see Plate 7), Ieyasu welcomed Adams warmly. 'You come here to ask me why I don't permit *De Liefde*'s crew to return home, do you not?' Ieyasu said, as if he had prepared for Adams' visit. He tried to explain the reason to Adams, but struggled to recall the word 'geometry'. Eventually, Adams understood that Ieyasu was deeply fascinated by a science which made it possible to find accurate distances and angles for gun fire, even in a fog. He also had a strong desire to learn about navigation, astronomy, mathematics and much else from Europe. Adams suggested a deal. He would provide this knowledge, Ieyasu would permit *De Liefde*'s crew to leave Japan, and Adams would delay their departure for one more year. Ieyasu was not doing deals. As the wind rose, so did Adams' anger and sense of powerlessness. If he raised his eyes to the skies and watched a falcon return, he must have realized that he too was one of these birds, destined always to return to the master.

It was now the year 1601 and *De Liefde*'s crew were still billeted in Mukai's guest house at the Uraga Port. They were becoming frustrated and obsessed with their own troubles. Four or five mariners had rebelled against Captain Quaeckernaeck and Adams and decided to try their luck elsewhere. The rest chose to remain in the house, but soon others became tired of the endless waiting and joined the rebels. The captain and Adams struggled to contain the revolt. For Adams, embarrassed about failing to obtain permission for them to set sail from Japan, it must have been a relief when his superiors finally agreed to give them the remaining money allocated by Ieyasu. It was divided between them and 'every one took his way'[101] with 3,000 reals each.

Ieyasu was not surprised to learn of the disintegration of *De Liefde*'s crew. He promised to support them with a more generous

---

[101] Adams, William.

arrangement. Every man would be given a rice allowance of two pounds in weight a day, which was more than enough to ensure their survival. Rice was often used as a reward in Japan, because it could easily be exchanged for money. Wealthy warlords, therefore, owned large rice fields.

However, Ieyasu's generosity came with a condition. The men must work as hard as his falcons. Some of the crew gave gunnery lessons to samurai trainers; some worked on Ieyasu's estate and his fishing boats and some taught foreign languages. William Adams was given a particularly important position as special adviser to the Shogun on geography, geometry, mathematics and navigation and was also his personal interpreter. The crew members' annual wage was the equivalent of £4.95–5.40 (£985.00 - £1,075.00 in today's money) compared at that time with the average annual wage for a Japanese labourer of almost half that amount.[102] They all moved to another of Mukai's houses in Edo and some married Japanese women.

Ieyasu's rejection of Adam's request to return home hit him hard. Feelings of homesickness for his wife and daughter, a sense of guilt towards his men and resentment and hatred of Ieyasu, all assailed him. Nevertheless, he subsequently came to the view that these negative emotions were essentially self-pity. He reminded himself that he had chosen to become a marine pilot. He had learned he was unable to control the weather and that Lady Luck often came to the rescue. He convinced himself that he was anchored in Japan as just part of an extensive voyage. During his anchorage, he would learn Japanese to be able to communicate with Ieyasu directly. He had mastered Dutch, Spanish and Portuguese, so he was confident of learning this new language. He would ask his interpreter to teach him to speak, write and read Japanese.

---

[102] According to *Dai Nihon Siryō* and *Jidai Kōshō* Jiten, the average annual wage for Japanese maid-servants was 1 ryō. Currency equivalance calculations are based throughout on the Purchasing Power Calculator at www.measuring-worth.com and on the assumptions used by the Currency Museum Bank of Japan which puts 1 ryō between 120,000 – 130,000 yen in today's value. The sterling equivalent is £577.50.

Meanwhile, in Fushimi Castle, Ieyasu was completing the form-ing of his government and administration. In November 1601, Adams was summoned by Ieyasu, who by then had returned to Edo Castle. They had not met each other for two months. '*Okaeri Nah-sare-mase*,' said Adams, surprising Ieyasu with his odd accent but confident inflection. A Japanese greeting should fade away, head bowed in diffidence or deference, particularly to one of great rank. His interpreter said to Ieyasu, 'Adams greeted you sir, saying *Okaeri Nah-sare-mase*, welcome back.'[103] Ieyasu threw his head back and his hearty laugh reverberated round the room.

Ieyasu was now ready for his first geometry lesson. He showed Adams a drawing he had prepared of his forces and the enemy's posi-tions, with a wide river between. The river current was too rapid for anyone to cross and measure, so how, Ieyasu asked, could Adams measure the distance between the positions and direct his fire on the other's forces. Adams confidently replied that trigonometry, the rules of triangles, would provide the answer. He borrowed Ieyasu's brush and drew a line from the left side of Ieyasu's forces [the first point] to Ieyasu's own position [the second point] directly opposite, and therefore at a right angle to, the enemy's position. By measuring the distance between those two points, together with the angle between that line and the one from the first point to the enemy's position, he was able to calculate the distance between Ieyasu and the enemy.

Ieyasu was fascinated, but was quick to ask how forces could defend themselves from the enemy if their range was so easily found. Although Adams then described for Ieyasu something of the origin and development of cannon, he had to concede the point. Geometry had not been developed for battle, but had been used for both attack and defence in European wars.

Ieyasu then set his eyes on the tallest Japanese cedar in the gar-den. It was over 300 years old and looked more than eighteen yards high. Ieyasu asked Adams whether he could find the height of the tree by the same method. Adams erected a ten-yard pole along-side the tree and measured the length of the shadows cast by both.

---

[103] Miura Joshin.

Then with those three measurements he was able to draw his two triangles and, knowing that the angles would be the same in each, establish his ratios and work out the missing measurement. Within a few minutes he announced that the height of the tree was twenty-five yards. Ieyasu looked dubious and ordered a gardener to climb the tree with a rope marked to scale. When the somewhat nervous gardener finally reached the top, another gardener, holding the bottom of the rope, read off the measurements. Adams was correct and Ieyasu broke into a broad smile.

From that day and for one year, Adams came to teach Ieyasu the elements of geometry, mathematics, astronomy and navigation. The lessons ranged more widely, as Ieyasu was very interested in world affairs and particularly the antagonism between Catholics and Protestants. Adams explained how the split in Western Christianity had occurred with the Reformation in the sixteenth century, but he admitted the main reason England had become a Protestant country was because King Henry VIII did not want the Pope forbidding his divorce and re-marriage. Ieyasu leaned forward in surprise. Adams explained that the King wanted to divorce Queen Catherine, who had not produced a boy, and to re-marry her lady-in-waiting, Anne Boleyn. 'Why did he need permission from the Pope only to find a woman who could produce a boy?'[104] asked Ieyasu. 'I can have many mistresses to produce boys and then choose the most brilliant among them to succeed to the throne.'[105] While recognizing this was a very practical solution, Adams explained that, in Christianity, that son would be called a bastard and could not ascend to the throne. So Henry VIII had established his own church in England and arranged for it to annul the first of his many marriages.

Adams also explained how, some fifty years earlier, the Society of Jesus had been formed in Spain to support the orthodox Catholic faith against heresy and to mount foreign missions to convert people in Asia and South America. Its organization was military and

---

[104] Author's words – according to Morrill, John and other texts.
[105] Author's words – according to Miura Joshin and Nakamura Koya.

autocratic and many believed the missionaries' main purpose was not to preach their religious principles, but to help Spain and Portugal to increase their trade and influence in foreign countries. He believed the Jesuit missionaries in Japan were part of that plot. 'Isn't that a slander?'[106] Ieyasu said and reminded Adams that his accusation was serious and had better be correct. 'I swear' Adams replied, 'the Jesuits believe that not only Protestants, but the followers of all other religions are heathens, Japanese Buddhism included.'[107] Their ultimate goal, he believed, was to put all countries in the world under Spanish and Portuguese control and that this was already happening to countries in the south of the New Continent (South America).

Adams became aware Ieyasu was looking anxious with his arms folded, so he stopped talking. There was silence for a while and then Ieyasu went out into the garden. He stood by a pond, arms still folded. The rain began to fall, disturbing the surface of the pond. Ieyasu's mind was also disturbed. He foresaw trouble with the Jesuits.

Long before Adams' warning, Ieyasu remembered that he had often been offended by the Jesuits and had been concerned at the scale of their mission in Japan. His predecessors, governors-general Oda and Toyotomi, had tolerated their mission because of the good returns from trade with the Portuguese and Spanish. However, they had become increasingly anxious at the sheer number of Japanese converting to Christianity, including many samurai lords, and in 1587 governor-general Toyotomi issued a rather ineffective decree forbidding Christian conversion. Ieyasu also remembered how in the Sekigahara Battle, a Jesuit called João Rodriguez, realizing that Lord Konishi, his Catholic patron, was about to lose, had visited Ieyasu with lavish presents to congratulate him on his victory. Ieyasu also noticed that the Jesuits had stopped criticizing Adams. He could issue a stronger decree forbidding Christianity, but he too did not want to give up the good returns from trade and he was not yet in the right official position to issue such a decree. Practically,

---

[106] Author's words – according to Adams' diary.
[107] Ibid.

he had gained total power in Japan, but he had not been officially announced as Shogun. So he hesitated to grant Adams his wish and permit the Dutch and English to trade with Japan; he did not want his country drawn into the battle between Catholics and Protestants.

Ieyasu noticed that Adams had come out into the garden and wanted to say something. Before he could speak, Ieyasu said dismissively, 'I can do nothing about trading with the Dutch and English.'[108] Adams made bold to convince Ieyasu that his country had been losing out in such exclusive trading with the Portuguese and Spanish. He explained that many countries had already adopted free trading, because they were able to choose the best deal from a number of countries. The Portuguese and Spanish traders were taking unfair advantage in selling goods to Japanese merchants at prices as high as they wished. 'You still want my country to trade with Protestants?'[109] Ieyasu asked wearily. Adams asked him why the Japanese merchants did not go overseas to purchase goods and sell Japanese products themselves. In that way, Adams suggested, it would act as a brake on Portuguese monopoly trading. 'Do you mean the *Shuin-sen* trader?'[110] Ieyasu asked. The *Shuin-sen* trader, or Red-seal ship, was the Japanese trader governor-general Toyotomi had permitted to go to foreign countries in 1592. However, after Toyotomi dispatched troops to Korea, the relationships between Japan and foreign countries had deteriorated and Japanese traders had withdrawn from foreign countries.

Ieyasu had actually been planning to revive the *Shuin-sen* trader, but again had been waiting until he became Shogun. He began to see good reasons to revive the trader sooner rather than later. He would try to reconcile relationships with hostile neighbours and put the brakes on Portuguese and Spanish traders. As a result of his victory, Ieyasu now owned a large number of gold and silver mines in Iwami, Tajima, Sado, Izu and many other prefectures; he was

---

[108] Author's words.
[109] Ibid.
[110] Ibid.

confident of extracting abundant gold and silver which could be exchanged for foreign products. Portugal had been the first nation to refine silver. According to a Portuguese record in 1601, the Japanese silver bars that the Portuguese Great Ship brought from Nagasaki to Macao, three or four times in an average year, were worth a million bars of Chinese gold. The ship also brought Chinese silk, porcelain and other commodities, only a small proportion of which would be re-exported from Macao and Goa. So silver was always in great demand at that time. When Adams looked keen on helping Ieyasu with this project, Ieyasu asked him, 'Have you given up returning home?'[111] Adams answered, 'I am still your prisoner.'[112]

In 1601, aged sixty-one, Ieyasu had reached his *Kan'reki* or year of retirement. Tradition dictated he be dressed in a red sleeveless jacket and hood, as worn by babies, to signify his rebirth. Instead, Ieyasu announced the rebirth of *Shuin-sen*, Red-seal ship, the government official trader system. He gave the certificate to Suminokura, the merchant Chaya Shirojirō, Lord Shimazu in Satsuma, Lord Katō in Higo, Lord Matsura in Hirado in the South and other powerful lords in the West. They all arranged for trading ships to sail for Taiwan, Annam (Vietnam), (Siam) Thailand and Luzon (the Philippines). Following Adams' advice, they loaded gold, silver, copper, sulphur, camphor, rice, pottery, Japanese lacquer and brought back raw silk, silk fabrics, cotton, deer skin, wool, shark skin and much else.

Adams, who had become one of Ieyasu's favourite advisers, now had to contend with severe criticism from his own men. They saw the continuing delay in obtaining permission to return home as partly his fault. As Adams could only agree with his men, he did not argue with them. His thoughts were complicated. He now felt some kinship with Ieyasu and his ambitions. He would of course be honoured if his knowledge and skills were appreciated and respected by the authorities of any country, but this time he felt instinctively he was involved in something big. While his men languished in

---

[111] Ibid.
[112] Ibid.

aimless frustration, he was hoping to be put in charge of trading between Japan and England and Holland. Only then would he be able to improve the fortunes of his men.

Contemplating his plan, Adams was determined to avoid making the same mistake as the Portuguese. He intended to deal with religion and trade quite separately. When the Portuguese learnt that Adams had become one of Ieyasu's favourites, they were infuriated and their hatred towards him increased. Once they thought of assassinating him, but realized that would weaken their position with Ieyasu. So when they met Adams, they masked their feelings in formal and reluctant courtesy.

In 1602, Sukeji was told by his grandfather that all the Dutchmen were rumoured to be leaving Japan soon. Sukeji was very sad at having to say goodbye to his close friend. However, he soon heard another rumour that Adams alone would remain in Mukai's house, to be available occasionally to Ieyasu. At the end of 1602, Sukeji's grandfather died. He had now lost all his direct relations. At the funeral for his grandfather, Sukeji saw Adams among the mourners. Adams put a little earth on the coffin and said a prayer in English. Sukeji understood only the word 'amen'. Adams consoled Sukeji with many kind words and told him the most painful story of how his close brother, Thomas, had been brutally killed by savages during their voyage to Japan. Sukeji was so shocked and sad for Adams that for a moment he could forget his own grief. He asked Adams more about this loss and the other deaths on the voyage, to try to understand Adams' feelings. Many years separated Adams and Sukeji in age, but grief had brought them closer together.

□

In November 1602, to prepare for his inauguration ceremony as Shogun, Ieyasu headed for the capital, Kyoto, with 30,000 troops. Alone in his black-lacquered palanquin, behind the bamboo curtains with their orange silk tassels, Ieyasu's feelings must have been hard to describe. He had come so far, but there was so much more to do. Adams was there, mounted on a horse among the troops and beside Suminokura. This time, he knew where he was going and would have felt a secret sense of pride at his own contribution to placing the man in the palanquin on the throne of Japan.

Adams was amazed at the tremendous improvements to the Tōkai-dō road, where he had found such difficulty in pulling the cannon during the Sekigahara Battle. Just one year after his victory, Ieyasu had started a project to convert 300 miles of the wild road between Edo and Kyoto to nine-yard-wide gravel, thereby making it much easier for walking and transportation. He also converted some village houses to staging points interspersed along the road. There were thirty-six horses in each of the houses to convey people and luggage. The project was all part of Ieyasu's careful preparations to move the capital to Edo once he was pronounced Shogun.

As they rode together, Suminokura wondered aloud whether Hideyori in Osaka would really agree to Ieyasu's inauguration as Shogun. Hideyori was now just one of many lords, but there were still lords who supported him as the rightful successor to his father Hideyoshi. Considering the short distance between Osaka and Kyoto, now would be a great opportunity for them to mount a counter-attack against Ieyasu. Adams agreed with his companion. Hideyori was like a thorn on which Ieyasu had pricked his finger. He would have to remove the thorn if he was not to be poisoned. 'What is Ieyasu planning to do?'[113] Adams asked. Suminokura answered: 'I have no idea, but we don't have to worry. We should just trust the Great Leader.'[114] Something in the nodding of his head told Adams Suminokura knew exactly what would be happening.

Ieyasu arrived at the Fushimi Castle in Kyoto before the New Year. He was already planning another deception. He ordered his retainer lords to present their New Year greetings to Hideyori in Osaka on 1 January (the date that denoted the greatest respect) and to him on 2 January. It was thus believed that Ieyasu was express-

---

[113] Translated by the author from Oshima Masahiro.
[114] Ibid.

ing his respect to Hideyori. Moreover, in February, Ieyasu himself presented New Year greetings to Hideyori and promised him, as he had promised his father, that he would offer Princess Sen, the daughter of his son Hidetada, in marriage to Hideyori. Ieyasu also hinted that his shogunate would be only for one generation and that after he died, power should return to the Toyotomi family. The family was relieved and immediately sent Ieyasu a congratulatory message on his inauguration as Shogun.

The news worries Adams. It is obvious that he will be affected if the Toyotomi family regain power. He imagines Portuguese priests dancing in triumph and so he goes to ask Suminokura again what he thinks will happen. He pats Adams on the shoulder and answers: 'Who can easily give up the power that he has craved for so long and gained at last? Adams, you have a worrying nature.'[115]

The twelfth of February 1603 was a chilly and rainy day. The Emperor's important councillors, Hirohashi, Karasumaru Mitsuhiro, Kokawa and others, arrived at the Fushimi Castle and gathered in the banquet hall for the inauguration ceremony. They announced many appointments, from the Shogun himself to his guards and servants. There were also various new posts for lords, priests, chancellors, governors, directors, curators and others, far more than in any previous period. Every time a councillor announced an appointment, Ieyasu handed the person a leather pouch full of gold dust. Although the sixty-two-year-old Ieyasu looked tense with flushed cheeks and mouth held tight, his proud bearing revealed his satisfaction and pride. All the former high-ranking lords at the ceremony were confronted with the fact, staring them in the face, that one of the lower-ranking lords was now the Shogun, for the first time in Japan's history. Power transforms and, as they looked up to the proud Tokugawa Ieyasu, they saw a different man.

The rest of the ceremony went off smoothly. Before all the councillors left the hall, the rain had stopped. The hall was brightened by the gentle spring light. After Ieyasu saw off the Emperor's

---

[115] Author's words.

councillors, he returned to the seat of honour. All those attending looked up to their new leader, then knelt and bowed down, head and back parallel to the floor, in a gesture of the greatest respect and submission.

In the afternoon of the same day, Ieyasu was presented at the Imperial Court to the Goyōzei Emperor[116] and swore the solemn oath to protect the country and its people.

In the same year, on the other side of the world and unknown to Adams, his own Queen, Elizabeth I, died and James I succeeded to the English throne.

At the end of March, Ieyasu finished the construction of the magnificent Nijō Castle. With its five layers of elegant roofs and a look-out tower, it was located almost in the centre of Kyoto, near the Imperial Palace. Ieyasu's purpose was to stay there when he came up to Kyoto, but also to put the Imperial Court under close observation. A few days after he moved in, he organized a presentation at the Court to express his thanks for the inauguration ceremony and the New Year's greetings. Ieyasu arrived at the Court with his servants and guards, who carried a large quantity of presents. He presented one thousand pieces of silver as his thanks for the ceremony; for the New Year greetings, he presented one hundred bales of cotton and one hundred pieces of silver. In April, Ieyasu held a grand entertainment for the members of the Court. It included a Noh drama appreciated by the Japanese upper class. It was the first play Adams had seen in Japan and he was by no means the last foreigner to find it slow and incomprehensible, but he did his best to fit in with the festivities.

The new castle then witnessed a daily procession of lords seeking an audience with Ieyasu to present their gifts and curry his favour. When May came, Adams was summoned by Ieyasu. At the entrance to the audience chamber, Adams said to Ieyasu in fluent, if a little

---

[116] Although powerless, Emperors in Japan at that time played some useful roles. One was to confer legitimacy on the lord chosen by his fellow samurai as Shogun. Another, from their base in Kyoto, was to encourage traditional arts and culture.

too familiar, Japanese, 'Congratulations on becoming Shogun!'[117]
Ieyasu welcomed Adams with a smile and beckoned him in. The
guards left and Ieyasu and Adams were alone. Adams said: 'Please
forgive me for presenting no gift; although I was thinking of something with which to congratulate you, I have nothing with me, I
am afraid.'[118] He bowed low, as an apology. He had thought of a
telescope, a compass, a nautical chart or pencils, but these were all
used goods, not worthy to be presented to the Great Leader. 'Do
not worry,'[119] Ieyasu said, waving the thought away.

He explained that Adams had given him enough presents, with
the priceless knowledge of geometry, mathematics and other things
hitherto unknown in Japan. The reason why he had summoned
Adams this time was rather because he wanted to express his thanks
for Adams' efforts and to give him a reward. 'A reward for me?'[120]
Adams was surprised. Ieyasu answered, 'Yes, a mansion in Edo.'[121]
He was concerned that Adams was finding it uncomfortable to
dwell in a terraced house for so long with its shared kitchen, bathroom and toilet, so he had prepared a mansion for his use, close by
Nihon Bashi in the Odawara-machi Town with male and female
housekeepers, a monthly allowance of 50 Ryō[122] and one kilo of
rice per day. *De Liefde*'s crew would receive the same amount of rice
as Adams, some allowances and be permitted to live in a small but
decent house in the grounds of the estate.

'*Arigato gozaimasu*',[123] Adams said, thanking him in Japanese,
and he bowed his head down on the *tatami* mat floor. Although
Adams wished it could have been permission to return to his country, the scale of the reward was more than he expected. He felt honoured that his knowledge and skills were so appreciated, so when

---

[117] Translated by the author from Miura Joshin.
[118] Translated by the author from Oshima Masahiro.
[119] Author's words.
[120] Translated by the author from Miura Joshin.
[121] Translated by the author from Oshima Masahiro.
[122] Around £40,000 today. This sum was to run the estate, which actually
belonged to Lord Honda Masanobu.
[123] Author's words – according to Miura Joshin.

Ieyasu asked him whether he was pleased, he answered 'Heartily.'[124]
Ieyasu was relieved and allowed Adams to return to Edo.

In the middle of May, Adams arrived back in Edo and was amazed
at the enormous improvements made in only half a year. According
to Ieyasu's plan, the large-scale construction of a new fortified town
had started below his Edo Castle. Before he became Shogun, Ieyasu
had paid the construction expenses, but now he ordered seventy
powerful lords to bear the cost by providing one labourer per 1000
koku of land they owned. A total of 40,000 labourers were now
employed. The most remarkable project was the levelling of Kanda
Mountain to the north of the Edo Castle. With the earth and sand
from the mountain, the plan was to create a commercial area down
by the estuary. From dawn to dusk, a long line of labourers shoul-
dering rope baskets full of earth snaked down to the sea. Various
country accents from the north to the south filled the air. The sky
was covered with earth dust as if veiled with a spring haze out of
season. However, the Edo Castle itself remained modest. Adams
realized the great power Ieyasu now wielded and identified with his
order of priorities.

Those members of *De Liefde*'s crew that had stayed together were
delighted to hear that Adams was to be given use of a mansion and
that their living conditions would also improve. In a move that
brought pride and delight to his orphan friend, Adams asked Sukeji
to live with him and become his right-hand man.

☐

In a procession that must have puzzled onlookers, Sukeji, Adams
and his men were led to the mansion by one of Ieyasu's civil
servants. As they walked alongside the Horikawa River trench
on the eastern side of the Edo Castle, they saw a newly-built
bridge sixty-eight yards in length and eight yards in width. The
original bridge, in poor condition, had been made with just two

---

[124] Translated by the author from Miura Joshin.

logs. Two logs is *Nihon* in Japanese. Many labourers from all over Japan had gathered to make the bridge, *Nihon* also means Japan. A bridge is *Hashi or Bashi* in Japanese. Therefore, the bridge was named *Nihon Bashi*; it still exists as a central part of modern Tokyo. At one end of the southern side of the bridge stood a sign listing social and shipping rules, typical of what was mandatory in Japan's strict, feudal society. At the northern side of the riverbank, there were several fish shops, selling the fresh plaice and mackerel that were plentiful in those days in the sea around Edo. The official walking with Adams explained that the riverbank was called Odawara riverbank and the town around it Odawara-machi..

They walked down a path and turned right. Then Adams stopped; the officer was pointing to a mansion. It was much larger than he expected. It was surrounded with a high wall of earth and wooden gates embossed with an iron crest. After passing through the gates, Adams and his men saw two magnificent single-storey houses, joined to each other by a covered walkway . The main house with ten rooms was for Adams and the annex for his men. There was even a stable at the back of the garden. *De Liefde*'s crew and Sukeji all burst into cheers.

'I was looking forward to meeting you all;'[125] they were being greeted by a middle-aged man with dark and bushy eyebrows and wearing a kimono with a formal crest. As Adams guessed, he was not a samurai but the mayor of Odawara-machi . His name was Magome Kageyū. His surname, Magome, means ostler and he was responsible for Ieyasu's horses.

Adams took a walk around his new estate which was heavy with the scent of cedar. When he saw that some of the incomplete garden was still as beautiful as the garden of Edo Castle and how easy it was to go down to the sea, he appreciated Ieyasu's kindness. *De Liefde*'s crew initially complained about the difference between Adams' living conditions and theirs, but soon they abandoned that complaint.

---

125 Author's words.

As soon as Adams and his men returned to the main room, several housekeepers, carrying tea cups, appeared. They were instructed by one young woman to serve the tea to Adams and his men. Magome said, 'They are your housekeepers from today,' and introduced senior housekeepers Matsuzo and his wife first, then Taka and other males Tasuke, Gonzo, Yasu and a female, Kiyo. The woman he introduced last was his daughter Yuki. She would be their local guide and their link to him. She would come to see them a couple of times every month. In Japanese, Yuki means snow and her snow-white cheeks would very likely have blushed a delicate pink as she bowed to Adams and his men. Then all the nervous housekeepers followed Yuki in bowing low and Adams and his men bowed to them.

Afterwards, Magome introduced Adams to a bold, stout man. His name was Miura Joshin. He was a rice merchant and he would deliver their rice, provided by the government, from Ise-machi, the town next to Odawara-machi, where he lived. He was also a writer, a commentator on the ways of the world. As he had a lot of knowledge about Japanese ways, Magome suggested politely that Adams might take his advice from time to time. Joshin greeted Adams jovially: 'I will deliver the best quality rice for you,' he said, 'and don't hesitate to ask me to help you at any time.'[126]

After all the introductions, the person who was found to be actually in charge of Adams' estate was Orito Chūhei, one of the senior retainers of Lord Honda Masanobu who was himself close to Ieyasu. Since Sukeji was now part of Adams' household, he was adopted by Orito Chūhei and started being privately educated as a son of a samurai. Adams was at last surrounded by kind and helpful people. In turn, they found him quite unlike the stern and aloof lords of the manor. He treated all his housekeepers as good friends and continued to teach Sukeji English and to entertain him with stories about his sea voyages.

Near to his residence, different bells would have marked the passing of time, melodiously from the Catholic Church, sono-

---

[126] Translated by the author from Miura Joshin.

rously from the Buddhist temple. One summer evening, Captain Quaeckerneack and Melchior van Santvoort unexpectedly visited Adams. They came to discuss how to return home. Adams was very pleased to see them and to make plans. He offered to put them up in his residence for a while. They both gave Sukeji Dutch language lessons, so that Sukeji was probably learning some English, Portuguese and Dutch every day. Santvoort, who had been in charge of ship's victuals in *De Liefde*, was a good cook and a good buyer of groceries. The female housekeepers would have been glad to have his help. European food was served every day and the residence became a cosy and lively home with these pleasant people.

However, finding enough meat to eat proved difficult. Hideyoshi's government (1585–1598) had forbidden the breeding of horses and cattle for meat. The Japanese had suffered a shortage of these animals since the Spanish and Portuguese started killing them for food. Horses were important for samurai warriors and cattle were needed for pulling carts loaded with wood, water, food and even equipment into battle. The Japanese did not drink milk. They were disgusted by the taste, as if it was fresh blood. To the frustration of many Western residents, the prohibition was continued by the Ieyasu government. However, the charming and resourceful Santvoort found a black market for meat by the Sensō-Ji Temple. He managed to buy rabbit, wild boar, venison and even beef. He also went regularly to a huge market nearby to get groceries such as cereal, vegetables, fish, oil, farming implements, carpentry tools, pottery, cloth, thread, bamboo-work and others. He was likely to have been the only Westerner there!

CHAPTER 7

AN EXCEPTIONAL HONOUR

か

In the next month, Ieyasu returned to Edo Castle and Adams began a new routine. Every other day, at eight o'clock, he left home by horse and at nine o'clock began to teach Ieyasu every branch of western knowledge that he knew. Ieyasu was particularly interested in mathematics. First of all, Adams taught him arithmetic using the Arabic numerals. Ieyasu was impressed at how the correct answer was reached without an abacus. He also learnt the Roman numbers and then practiced arithmetic, even to three or four figures. When he found a correct answer, his joy was like that of a child. In turn, Adams was impressed at the Japanese abacus, a rectangular box formed with wood and crammed with wooden beads on bars. Calculations were done by flipping the beads. Adams was told that the abacus was introduced from China in the fourteenth century and he realized that Japanese culture had reached quite an advanced level.

However, their lessons were often disturbed by Ieyasu's close retainers, who needed decisions on various matters. Several retainers signalled Adams to leave the room, but Ieyasu ignored them and allowed Adams to stay and listen. In this way, Adams learnt who the Shogun's regular visitors were and who were his most important retainers.

Ieyasu's first priority was to deal with his government, the economy and negotiations with the Toyotomi family. He had support from his close *Fudai*, the highest-ranking retainers, Lord Honda, Lord Matsudaira, Lord Andō and others. The second was to deal with the temples and shrines, where philosophy, literature and other subjects were being taught. The third was to deal with finance and commerce, with support from Suminokura, Chaya Shirojirō and other merchants. The fourth was to familiarize himself with international affairs and obtain Western knowledge so he could deal with diplomacy, trade and Christianity in Japan; which is why Adams quickly became one of his closest advisers.

At first, Adams felt honoured to be accepted into a position of privilege that he would never have gained in his own country. However, he noticed that Ieyasu's other close retainers began to show some kind of jealousy towards him. Even when Ieyasu refused audiences to people because of ill health or a bad mood, Adams was allowed to meet him. Adams had often wondered what had happened between Ieyasu and his son Hidetada and one day, Hidetada suddenly expressed unmistakable bitterness towards Adams. Later, Lord Honda told Adams that Ieyasu had refused to meet his son on a day he had allowed Adams to come to his private room. So Lord Honda advised Adams not to be too forward. Adams regretted appearing to be ubiquitous. Did they think he was taking advantage of the fact that he enjoyed Ieyasu's favour? He might have recalled the sailor's proverb that the wind hates the highest mast. West or East, the proverb was true. Adams decided not to visit Ieyasu for a while.

A short while later, however, Ieyasu summoned Adams, rebuking him for not having come to see him for so long. Although Adams pretended that he had been ill, Ieyasu was not fooled. So Adams had to tell him the truth. Ieyasu laughed it away. He told Adams that it was not like him to be influenced by others; he could replace his Japanese retainers with others, but Adams was irreplaceable, so he must take no notice of anything others might say. Adams was relieved and honoured and resumed his regular visits.

One day, Ieyasu casually asked whether Adams liked Magome's daughter, Yuki?[127] Adams enquired why. Ieyasu asked, 'Is she called

---

[127] Author's words.

Yuki?,'[128] then said, 'I heard she is a nice girl.'[129] Adams was non-committal. He knew her only as the person who came to check what he needed twice a month and occasionally had a chat with him. She had told him she was named Yuki because she was born on a snowy day in spring. Her skin was certainly snowy white and she had big eyes and lovely small lips above a slightly protruding chin. Her smile was natural and wide, as the Japanese say, 'to the first double tooth'. Adams loved to catch the faint scent of her perfume. She was a lively, charming eighteen-year-old girl, who would have reminded Adams of the daughter he had left in England. That was all he thought of Yuki, so he replied to Ieyasu that she seemed a good-natured girl. Then Ieyasu asked Adams his age. He was forty-years old. After Adams replied, his pupil began to do some arithmetic. '40 minus 18 is 22, isn't it?' Ieyasu said, and then gave a meaningful smile.

On one of Adams' off-duty days, he was preparing to go fishing with friends when he was unexpectedly summoned by Ieyasu. Adams was mounted on a horse led by Matsuzo with Sukeji following on foot as his attendant. When Adams arrived at the Edo Castle, by chance he met Lord Honda Masanobu. The lord whispered in Adams' ear, 'The Shogun is waiting for you.'[130] Adams asked him, 'What does he want from me?' The lord answered: 'Jeronimo de Jesus, a Portuguese Jesuit , has an audience now, but he has made the Shogun angry with his unhelpful reply.'[131]

Jeronimo had originally travelled to Japan from the Philippines in 1594, carrying gifts and a message from Luzon's governor-general to governor-general Hideyoshi. On 5 February 1597, Hideyoshi had come to the conclusion that conversion of so many Japanese to Christianity through the efforts of the Spanish and Portuguese was a prelude to an invasion by these two countries. Adams was well aware of the fact that six Spanish and Portuguese

---

[128] Ibid.
[129] Ibid.
[130] Translated by the author from Oshima Masahiro.
[131] Ibid.

Jesuits and twenty Japanese Christians had been crucified in Naga-saki. Although Jeronimo was believed to have been sent into exile before this mass martyrdom, he had actually changed his name and hidden himself in Kyoto. After Hideyoshi's death in 1598, he had asked to see Ieyasu. Since the martyrdom, the Spanish had ceased trade with Japan and Ieyasu had ordered Jeronimo to endeavour to persuade Spanish merchants in the Philippines to resume trade. Jeronimo succeeded in negotiating the return of Spanish merchants to Nagasaki. Ieyasu greatly appreciated Jeronimo's efforts and rewarded the Jesuits with permission to establish a Christian church in Edo.

Ieyasu was now asking Jeronimo to negotiate with the Spanish merchants again. This time, he wanted them to send their ships from the Philippines to Edo directly, not stopping at Nagasaki. Jeronimo tried to drive a hard bargain, which angered Ieyasu. He was still angry when Adams entered the audience chamber.

Before he bowed low, he noticed Ieyasu's bad mood. Jeronimo realized he had gone too far and was embarrassed for Adams to see that he had made the Shogun angry. So that Adams could hear what Jeronimo had said, the Shogun asked, 'Well, is it true that there is no port at all in Edo suitable for the Spanish ships, as you said?' 'Yes sir,' Jeronimo answered, 'but according to a Spanish captain it could be possible if the ship is pulled in with ropes by several other boats, so you must provide us with these boats please.'[132] Ieyasu looked at Adams and asked: 'What do you think, Adams? You have sailed from Osaka to Edo. You must know whether or not the Spanish ships would be able to sail safely into Edo.'[133] Adams realized that Jeronimo and the Spanish merchants and captain were manipulating Ieyasu for their own benefit. Edo was a new city. They were not sure that their business would be successful. Although Adams felt sorry for Jeronimo, he decided to tell Ieyasu the truth. He said, 'I am sure I can prove that Spanish ships can come into port in the Edo Bay. When one of the ships arrives outside the bay, I will

---

[132] Translated by the author from Nishiyama Toshio.
[133] Ibid.

come on board and then pilot the ship into the Nihonbashi jetty.'[134] Jeronimo was visibly shocked and dismayed at Adams' intervention. Ieyasu triumphantly said to Jeronimo: 'This English captain has convinced me. I order you to do as he suggested.'[135]

In Japanese navigation, they did not make use of either charts or astrolabes. They had what they called *Fushin-jutsu*, 'the science of the winds', and they used the magnet and the iron in a European compass differently. They placed the magnet in an earthenware bowl full of salt water, which they often changed. Then they put the bowl into a round wooden box, on the top of which certain characters were written in a circle denoting all the principal winds. In the bowl full of water they placed a very thin leaf of iron just about the size of a fly's wing, sharp at one side and blunt at the other. As the floating leaf touched the magnet stone, it turned about and faced toward that part which, whether by the laws of Nature or of God, would be the north.

In the autumn of 1603, a large Spanish merchant ship with three masts sailed into Edo Bay and lay at anchor off the Misaki shore. Adams, Jeronimo, several retainers of Lord Mukai and Sukeji, who had been waiting in a small boat for her, came on board. They were met by an experienced and suntanned Spanish captain and his crew. Sukeji records his own surprise when he noticed the captain's ear-ring!

The anchor was weighed and Adams took the ship out to sea, with a view of green hills and Mt Fuji opening up behind. Jeronimo and Sukeji were standing under one of the masts, watching Adams instructing the Spanish crew. Suddenly, her bow was turned back towards the Edo Bay and she sailed full ahead with the spray flying. With a southerly wind, she moved rapidly and arrived at the Nihonbashi jetty safely and much earlier than expected. Ieyasu had been watching the process from the shore. He was now hugely impressed at Adams' skill. He exclaimed: 'What an excellent pilot Adams is!' In Japanese, a pilot was known as *Anjin*. Since that event, Ieyasu

---

[134] Ibid.
[135] Ibid.

started calling Adams Anjin, the name by which he is recalled in Japan today.

Once Adams had proved that Spanish ships could enter Edo Bay safely, Spanish merchants in the Philippines agreed to ply their trade directly and regularly with Edo, much to Ieyasu's great satisfaction.

Meanwhile, in a harbour nearby, *De Liefde* was afloat but deteriorating fast. After more than two years without repairs, she was barely seaworthy. Her timbers were rotten and her mullioned windows were falling apart. Her existence gave Adams and his crew some hope of escaping and returning home, but they knew their chances of survival in the East China Sea in such a wreck were poor. Her decline was a great distress to the seamen, who knew now that until another English or Dutch vessel arrived, they were marooned, about as far from home as it was possible to be.

De Liefde's poor state of repair was also a shock to Ieyasu, who had been so impressed at her passage through the Strait of Magellan and across the Pacific. He was aware that Adams and his crew must possess many skills to keep a vessel afloat in such severe conditions for nearly two years. He recalled how Adams had told him, in an audience three years earlier, that he had been an apprentice shipbuilder for twelve years in London. Ieyasu made a decision. He would employ Adams and his crew to build a replica of *De Liefde*.

The decision sent Adams into something of a panic. He had been taught the basic principles of shipbuilding by Nicholas Diggins, but he had never built a ship. Preparing timber for a ship's frame called for special skills. If it was not put together correctly, the vessel might capsize in rough seas. He would not want to be responsible for such a disaster. This time, it was Adams' turn to face the Shogun's frown, followed by a simple command to build the ship. 'Do your best. If it is not good, it does not matter.'[136]

At the back of the audience chamber, Sukeji whispered to Orito: 'Why does the Shogun trust Adams so much more than

---

[136] Ibid.

any other foreigner?'[137] Orito answered: 'I think it is because Adams is always honest, rational, realistic and modest. He talks little about himself, but achieves much. Our Shogun often feels manipulated by the Portuguese and Spanish Jesuits who maintain that the natural and human world is controlled at their God's will or according to ancient lore. He is personally more inclined to the explanations which Adams bases on science and self-determination.'[138]

After taking his leave of Ieyasu, Adams realized that the task ahead presented him with another opportunity to demonstrate what great value he and his men could be to the Shogun. Before starting, he decided to go to the Uraga Port with Captain Quaeckernaeck to check out *De Liefde*. Adams mounted his own horse and the captain and Sukeji followed him. That same night, they arrived at Mukai's mansion in Uraga. In the early morning, they went to the port and found *De Liefde* in a pitiful state. A fishing boat provided by Mukai, with a boatman and five retainers, took them alongside *De Liefde*. Once on board, Captain Quaeckernaeck said: 'It's been a long time. We sailed this old lady for two years. I feel as if I have come back home.'[139] He walked around the ship and Adams followed, checking all corners of her and sometimes asking the captain questions. Then he jumped aboard the fishing boat again and started inspecting *De Liefde*'s hull. He decided to remove the figurehead of Erasmus on *De Liefde*'s stern. It would be ruined if it was left as it was. Sukeji went back to Mukai and borrowed some carpentry tools. Adams took the tools, clambered over the stern and removed Erasmus. It would be the only keepsake that they would have of their old lady and her epic journey.

□

---

[137] Ibid.
[138] Ibid.
[139] Ibid.

Erasmus was the Dutch scholar who established some principles of Protestantism, a hundred years before Adams was born. It was said he laid the egg that Martin Luther hatched. His books were later burned by the Inquisition. Adams told Sukeji that Erasmus taught that every individual has value in the eyes of God and a responsibility to develop himself.

There is a curious sequel to this story which might have amused Erasmus. The figurehead found its way into the Ryūkō-In Temple in Sano, today's Tochigi Prefecture, where it was worshipped as one of the *Kateki-Sama* or guardian angels. One can imagine successive generations of worshippers wondering who this austere figure with his long high nose could be and deciding that, since it was in the temple, they had better show it some respect.[140] According to a descendant of Lord Makino Shigezumi, Ieyasu originally gave the figurehead to the lord of the Usuki Castle as a reward for his achievements. The lord and his descendants preserved it as a family treasure for more than thirty years.

In 1637, in what came to be called *Shimabara-no-ran*, some Christians rioted in Shimabara, today's Nagasaki Prefecture, at moves to suppress Christianity. Lord Makino, who had served the Tokugawa government with great loyalty, took responsibility for failing to quell the riot and resigned. The then lord of the Usuki Castle sympathized with Lord Makino and gave Erasmus to him. Although both lords had no idea who the figurehead was, they honoured it as a present from the Shogun. After Lord Makino took possession, he preserved it in the Ryūkō-In, his family temple. In 1920, the figurehead's identity was discovered and it is now preserved as a national treasure in the same temple under the control of the Tokyo National Museum. The Dutch government did ask the museum to sell the figurehead in 2009, but the museum decided to keep it in Japan.

□

---

[140] According to Chief Priest Ōsawa Yuhō at the Ryūkō-In Temple, the figurehead was originally named *Azuki baba'a* and parents used to threaten naughty children with a visit from *Azuki baba'a*.

Adams continued to inspect *De Liefde* for the next few days. On the last day before *De Liefde* was due to be broken apart and sunk, Adams suggested, 'Shall we take a picnic to Jōgashima Island to cheer us up?'[141] Captain Quaeckernaeck and Sukeji quickly agreed.

When Adams came back to his house in Edo, he immediately started on a design for the ship. He threw himself into the work. All his servants noticed that for many nights the lamp burned very late in Adams' study. One night, Matsuzo's wife became concerned about Adams and told Sukeji to take him the cup of tea that she had made. Sukeji put the tea cup outside Adams' room and, made bold[142] by Matsuzo's instruction, said quietly, 'Would you like to take a little rest, sir?' 'Come in, Sukeji,' came Adams' lively voice, 'I have just finished my work.' When Sukeji entered, he saw Adams relaxing with a broad smile, surrounded by many draft papers, scattered all over the desk and floor. Adams showed Sukeji the plans and started explaining all the details of the ship he planned to build, but the only detail this tired teenager remembers is where the cannon would be installed!

The skills of the Japanese shipwright were not too bad. The Portuguese had introduced Western technology fifty years before Adams' arrival. Many Japanese shipwrights had built miniature ships, which had sailed to Indonesia and the Philippines. However, Ieyasu now wanted a Western-style vessel for longer voyages and also for military action.

One evening, Captain Quaeckernaeck and Santvoort came back to Adams' house to look at his draft. The captain, with all his expertise, was enthusiastic. 'What a great ship! It is in the English-style isn't it? It's smaller than I expected but well stabilized.' Santvoort joked, 'Why didn't you design a much bigger victual store?' He was remembering the shortages on their voyage when *De Liefde* crew had resorted to eating leather ropes.

---

[141] Translated by the author from Nishiyama Toshio.
[142] Servants were not normally allowed to disturb their master when he was at work.

Next day, Adams got into his formal dress to visit Ieyasu and mounted his horse. As always, Sukeji followed, clutching the precious draft design. Ieyasu was pleased to see the plans and listened to Adams' explanation. Shortly afterwards, Ieyasu summoned Mukai and ordered him to discuss with Adams the most appropriate place to build the ship. After a long discussion, they decided to choose the area called Itoh Beach, Izu, in today's Shizuoka Prefecture, to the south of the mainland. This was one of the areas directly controlled by Ieyasu[143] and had a deep river flowing to the sea from Mt Amagi (see Plate 12).

Adams gathered together twenty skilled shipwrights, acquired timber from the Japanese Kusunoki or camphor tree and Hinoki or chamae-cyparis obtusa from Mt Amagi, bought tar from Portuguese merchants, had blacksmiths make iron implements and ordered his men to start working. He was helped by Pieter Janszoon, *De Liefde's* carpenter, who had many of the required tools and most of the skills. The men used the now-lost *De Liefde* as their template, building the new ship's frame in much the same manner.

For month after month, more than fifty workers cut timbers and planking and slowly assembled the ship. Finally, in three-and-a-half months, she was built. The men stood back to review their work and were satisfied. The ship was a third-size replica of *De Liefde*, accommodating thirty to forty crew compared with 110 on *De Liefde*. Adams wrote: '(We) made in all respects as our manners is and had a displacement of some eighty tones.'[144]

While building the ship, Adams had an eye-opening experience. Each day after work, all the workers took an outdoor hotspring bath. Ito is famous for these baths. His first view caught Adams totally by surprise. He saw hundreds of naked men and women mixed together in the bath, quite unashamed. Although he had got accustomed to a Japanese bath with other men, he was embarrassed to share with women. He was rescued by Mukai, who told him it was good Japanese etiquette for men to cover their

---

[143] Ieyasu was in direct control of a quarter of Japan.
[144] Adams, William.

crotch with a washing towel, at least until they reached the safety of the cloudy water. Clean new loincloths were also available, and they put them on when they washed and bathed themselves in order not to wet their silk ones, which they wore instead of underpants. For the most privileged men, there were even perfumed pants which gave off a sweet scent for hours after the bath.

The Portuguese did not hide their disgust at the 'shameless' Japanese women, who took these mixed baths or who lay topless or completely naked in their open-gardens in summer. Adams tried to understand rather than criticize and, once he was accustomed to mixed bathing, he came to enjoy the warmth, the relief from aches and pains and that warm glow in the body that lasts for hours. Later, he would seek out more private and tranquil spring baths among the mountain rocks.

The ship was built on a platform supported by pillars. As the work neared completion, the beach sand in front of her was trenched and the pillars lowered little by little until she eventually settled into the trench. Then a ditch was dug between the trench and the sea. Adams planned to divert and retain water from the higher part of the river and then run the water into the trench so that, as the trench filled, the ship would float. With the force of more river water, she would be pushed out through the ditch. Pebbles packed in hemp bags were then placed in the bottom of the ship to stabilize her. Adams, Captain Quaeckernaeck, Santvoort, several of their crew and ten of Mukai's naval officers came aboard. The rest of the workers stood along each side of her with long poles, to protect her from being bumped against the bank of the ditch. Sukeji stood above the bank and waited for the signal from Adams to release more water from the river. When Adams signalled, the water streamed into the trench. The vast crowd would have been mainly fishermen, farmers, their wives and children. The men, who were usually shy to express their emotion, and the perpetually stooped women, who normally hid their teeth with their hands, now threw custom to the winds and burst into cheers and excited clapping. For a moment, these reserved Japanese in their humble sober-coloured cotton kimonos were transformed. Bells were rung in celebration and to alert others to this great event. As the sails were hoisted up the two masts and caught the wind, the ship changed direction to sail ahead alongside the beach. She was absolutely sparkling under the morning sun. Sukeji had never seen such a wonderful sight.

After the launch, Adams examined the body of the ship carefully. He brought the spare sail and rope and placed them inside the ship. Before sailing to Edo, he prepared as for a long voyage. When he was ready, the new vessel set sail from Itō Beach and sailed confidently across the Sagami Open Sea. In just a few hours, she entered Edo Bay and dropped anchor in the mouth of the Sumida estuary.

When Ieyasu was invited to view the majestic vessel and to make the first cruise, he came dressed informally, in *kimono* with *haori*, a Japanese half-length coat with no sleeves, and casual sandals – a simple gesture of friendship to Adams. He was accompanied by Honda Masazumi, several other retainers, a Buddhist monk and a merchant. Adams and Mukai met them all at the temporary pier, constructed just for this purpose. Ieyasu looked over the ship very thoroughly. He was even interested in the ship's store, where victuals, drinks and gunpowder were kept. When he saw a solid plank on the deck of the after-cabin, he nodded and said, 'A cannon should be installed here, shouldn't it?'[145] The naval officers who had been trained by Adams mustered to their stations. The stern anchor was weighed. The sails were lowered. The last rope was drawn to the full. When the wind caught the sails, a group of gulls flew up in the sky and skimmed the waves ahead of the ship. Ieyasu sat on a fur-covered seat placed between the main mast and the deck of the after-cabin. He was looking back at the receding landscape and the townspeople at their daily work. Adams steered the vessel across Edo Bay towards the Haneda Offing and into the Kisarazu Offing, then turned her around and sailed back the same way.

Ieyasu was delighted with the cruise and with the ship and particularly praised Adams' mathematical talent. He told Adams, 'Henceforth, you will be welcome to visit my court whenever you

---

[145] Author's words.

wish and always seek my presence.'[146] He is believed to have given orders for a monument to be erected on the Itō Beach, to the first Western-style vessel built in Japan by William Adams at the beginning of 1604. The local district council erected a monument in modern times on the same site. Ieyasu also named the town where Adams lived in Nihon Bashi, Anjin-*Chō* (Anjin/Adams Town). The monument still stands on the beach and the name of the town remained for a further 380 years.

Ieyasu reflected on how wise he had been not to execute Adams and regularly summoned him to meetings, where he always treated his comments with great respect. From time to time, he gave Adams presents and then an annual salary of seventy ducats (£31.50) and a daily allowance of more than two pounds of rice. Adams continued to tutor Ieyasu in geometry, geography and mathematics and to act as his interpreter and diplomatic adviser.

The Portuguese and Spanish Jesuits were very concerned at the rise of Adams and his influence at court. They realized that with his new command of the Japanese language and access to Ieyasu and the palace at any time, he might, as a heretic, 'discredit the Catholic church as well as its ministers'.[147] So they looked for ways of weakening his position.

In the spring of 1604, Adams was informed that silk prices had fallen sharply and Japanese merchants were suffering. Portuguese traders had imported silk from Canton and Macao in considerably larger amounts than usual and oversupplied the market. Adams sensed that it was in revenge and in protest against the *Shuin-sen* [Red-seal ships], the Government Official Trader system, planned in 1601 and which was now developing well.

Ieyasu, too, was concerned about the sudden decline in silk prices and summoned Adams for advice. Adams emphasized that the situation presented a good opportunity to eliminate the Portuguese monopoly. He advised the Shogun to issue new restrictive legislation. He should decree that all the silk Portuguese traders

---

[146] Translated by the author from Miura Joshin.
[147] Author's words.

imported would have to be sold only to those leading Japanese merchants appointed to the Shogun. No other merchants would be allowed to buy the silk. In this way, silk prices would be commanded by the buyer not the seller and the arbitrary pricing by the Portuguese would end. As the *Shuin-sen* prospered, Adams hoped that Portuguese Jesuits and traders would leave Japan. He did not hide his antagonism towards the Portuguese, saying that the legislation would help to weaken the power of the Jesuits and thus limit the number of Japanese Buddhists converting to Catholicism.

Although Ieyasu was not as antagonistic to Catholics as Adams, he eventually took his advice. He invited leading Japanese merchants from Kyoto, Osaka and Nagasaki to persuade them to accept the legislation Adams had suggested. One of the merchants said that the Portuguese would surely resent the legislation and stop importing silk from China. He asked: 'What can we do then?.'[148] Adams replied that the Portuguese traders would still be granted permission to trade between Japan and China and they would still make profits, because they were able to buy silk so cheaply in China. They would lose only excess profit. If they did withdraw from trading with Japan, the Shogun could increase the number of the *Shuin-sen* and open trading with more foreign countries, including England. Adams looked to Ieyasu for confirmation. 'As Anjin said, silk is made in China and it can be imported by many other foreign traders, so we don't need to worry about the Portuguese.'[149] With that, all the merchants backed the legislation. This is the origin of the well-known legislation of *Ito-Wappu*, or silk yarn-allotment, which was extended to the whole of Japan.

According to the Portuguese record in *Great Ship from Amacon*, certain varieties of the best woven and patterned silks were to be reserved for purchase by Shogun Ieyasu at his local representatives' valuation; but as Padre João Rodrigues was nominated by Ieyasu as his agent in this business, it goes without saying that the Portuguese got a good price for their goods. With the exception of the

---

[148] Ibid.
[149] Translated by the author from Oshima Masahiro.

super-fine fabric reserved for the Shogun, the silk import trade now became the monopoly of the mercantile group or ring, operated by the leading silk merchants from the four Shogun-licenced cities of Edo, Kyoto, Osaka and Nagasaki.

The Portuguese and Spanish Jesuit fathers now needed a new plan to counter Adams' power. They were aware that it would be unwise to murder Adams, so they decided to approach him in a different way. They would try to convert him and his men to Catholicism. However, there was a good chance this would fail, so they would also offer to arrange secret and safe conduct for Adams and his men out of Japan.

One of the Jesuit priests then began visiting Adams at his house and, with the false hand of friendship, attempted to convert him to Catholicism. For days, they argued over many questions from the Holy Bible. Adams was scornful and defended his Protestant faith fiercely. When the priest realized his mission was a failure, he suggested that he could arrange safe transport for Adams and his men on the next Portuguese vessel to depart from Nagasaki to the Philippines. Adams was desperate to leave Japan, but he was not going to accept any help from his enemies. He angrily refused the offer and later warned his men not to swallow this bait, this 'evil invitation'.[150] He warned that any of them who attempted to reach the Portuguese vessels would be soon caught by Ieyasu's guards.

One friar, called Juan, had another idea. He would prove that the Jesuits had the only true faith by walking on water, as Jesus had done. When Adams and his men poured scorn on this, he summoned them to the Uraga Bay to see the miracle for themselves. They went and joined a large crowd, hoping to see him look foolish. The friar prepared himself zealously. When he seemed to be moving slowly over the surface of the sea, Adams' men became alarmed, until they realized he was supported by a large piece of wood. The wood soon slipped from under him and Friar Juan was ploughing through the water until only his head

---

[150] Adams, William

was visible. Shortly afterwards, he disappeared under the waves. Now, *De Liefde's* men felt sorry for him. Santvoort found a small boat on the beach and set off on a rescue mission. The next day, Adams went to visit Friar Juan to ask whether they had perhaps missed his miracle, but the friar was sick in bed. However, he still was well enough to try again to convert Adams by telling him about his other miraculous powers. Adams could not resist some more teasing, saying, 'I told you before that I did not believe you could do it, and now I have a better occasion to be of the same opinion still.'[151] The friar accepted defeat. Later he packed his bags and escaped to Manila.

□

By the end of 1604, Adams had still received no news of his wife and daughter and his desperation to return home resurfaced. He made an emotional appeal to Ieyasu for sympathy, 'desiring',[152] he wrote, 'to see my poor wife and daughter according to conscience and nature'.[153] Ieyasu was not pleased at this request. 'I will not let you go away. Settle in my country permanently,'[154] was his blunt response.

Ieyasu was concerned at Adams' constant requests to return home. The Englishman had many useful skills and knowledge and must be persuaded to settle in Japan. He announced that he would reward Adams further for all the services he had provided. Adams had already been given use of the mansion in Nihon Bashi. Now he was rewarded with something much larger, a 250-koku or 61-acre estate that made an annual income of 88 ryō (around £70,000 in today's money) from its rice harvest. It was situated at Hemi on the Miura Peninsula, in today's Kanagawa Prefecture, south of Edo. The estate was also granted to Adams' descendants for a further 200

---

[151] Ibid.
[152] Ibid.
[153] Ibid.
[154] Ibid.

years. Adams wrote, 'this living was a rambling country estate'.[155] Like most Japanese manor houses, it was built from cedar, pine, Chamaecyparis obtusa and Zelkova serrata, which wafted beautiful natural scents all over the house. It was raised above the ground on wooden stilts. Doors, shutters and windows were all sliding. Outside doors and shutters were made with bamboo crafted in lattice form or stripes and the inside doors and windows were made with latticed wood backed with paper. Because the house was built on a hill, from the veranda there was a magnificent view of snow-capped Mt Fuji. The house was surrounded with a vast number of grapevines, so it was also called the Grape Manor House. There were many fig and pear trees, too.

For Adams, the sailor's son who had experienced poverty in Gillingham and in Limehouse, this majestic country estate was another incredible high point in the graph of his extraordinary life. He was now one of the Japanese landowner lords, who commanded absolute allegiance from his retainers. He was served by over ninety 'husbandmen'[156] or serfs who saw themselves as his slaves. These servants lived in several villages within the estate's boundary. Some descendants of them still live in the same area today. Whenever Adams returned to his estate, these servants lined up on the road to greet him and his guests. In greeting them, Adams said in fluent Japanese, 'I am Miura Anjin. I leave any trouble entirely to you all,'[157] exactly as he had been taught by Lord Honda. Along with other feudal lords at that time, he could have been brutal to his retainers and servants and it would never have been reported. All these servants lived in fear of punishment, so Adams was treated with the highest respect by them. Adams wrote: 'They run alongside my horse whenever I return to Hemi and made extravagant displays of obeisance.'[158]

---

[155] Ibid.
[156] Ibid.
[157] Translated by the author from Miura Joshin and Katō Sango
[158] Adams, William

In 1605, and to everyone's surprise, Ieyasu presented Adams with further reward. In gratitude for his services to his court and as a mark of his respect for the Englishman, he took the startling decision to bestow upon him a lordship. Adams was honoured with the title, *hatamoto* or bannerman, a prestigious position that made him a direct retainer of the Shogun's court. This linked him to the great warrior class that dominated the early Edo period in the seventeenth century. *Hatamoto* were all elite samurai, battle hardened, who were like a military bureaucracy* (see overleaf). There is no other example in Japanese history of this great privilege being given to a foreigner. With this honour, Adams was called Miura Anjin-sama. *Miura* was after the Miura Peninsula, his Shogun-granted domain; Anjin means pilot and *sama* is an honorific suffix. It was an ancient royal title. The family of Lord Miura were part of the thirteenth-century Kan'mu-heishi royal family. Battling through the constant civil wars, the last lord was defeated by the Hōjō family in 1516. Since that time, no-one had inherited the lordship of Miura.

Although Adams' samurai status was high-ranking, he was not required to engage in battle-fighting for Ieyasu, nor in the martial arts. His role was as adviser, tutor and interpreter, who provided Ieyasu with news, information and knowledge from a world of which he had been completely ignorant.

The new *hatamoto* had set sail from Rotterdam as just another pilot. He was not permitted to join senior members of his vessel at their council meetings and was not very popular among his fellows, because of his self-absorbed, arrogant and aloof personality. On the deadly voyage, his rise to prominence had come about through his mental and physical strength and extraordinary powers of survival. At each stage these had been tested to the limit. His captain, Quaeckernaeck, was a lesser man; if he had been physically capable of going to the audience with Ieyasu after they landed in Japan, Adams' story and a part of Japanese history would have been very different.

The new test that Adams had had to face was quite simply, at the age of forty-one, to transform his personality. In his new role he had had to become a charming, empathetic and agreeable man,

who was carefully aware of Ieyasu's needs, able to handle his enemies and adapt quickly to the strange country in which he had set
foot. As a prisoner he had had to survive when his captors called
all the shots. He now acquired new talents and was admired for his
honesty, wisdom, braveness, confidence, patience, empathy, and a
flexible and steady personality. All these qualities eventually convinced Ieyasu to award his foreign prisoner this exceptional honour
for the first and last time in Japanese history.

*In the Edo period there were two types of lordships. One was for hereditary
lords or Daimyo and another for elite samurai. Under the feudal government,
no matter whether a samurai was Daimyo or Hatamoto, when the Shogun gave
him a large estate or domain with a significant number of servants, he was always
given the title of Lord. Adams' Shogun-granted domain was registered as Sou-
shu, Miura-gun, Hemi-mura at 250 *koku* and his servants and retainers numbered over ninety. Unusually, his family was permitted to own the domain for
a further 200 years. According to a local historian in Hemi, Adams would have
been entitled to forty per cent of the tax raised locally. There is a document to this
effect in the district council records.

In general terms, Hatamoto or bannerman means an army commander. There
were three different ranks: high, middle and low. High-ranking Hatamoto owned
between 200 and 600 *koku*. Exceptionally high-ranking Hatamoto, like Adams,
the aristocratic Kira family or top officials such as the Chief Justice of the High
Court, were selected to become the Shogun's personal adviser. These Hatamoto
were more powerful and influential than even middle-ranking Daimyo.

The Edo period lasted for 265 years, from 1603 to 1868. In the early years,
there were civil wars and frequent regional battles, to which Hatamoto were sent
to fight. So they were both needed and respected. Later, in more peaceful times,
but without employment, they drifted downhill and their traditional culture
started to unravel. According to the diary *Mandan Meiji Shonen*, written between
1854 and 1859 by Nagamine Hideki, when Shogun Iemochi ordered Hatamoto
to fight against the opposition Chō-shū Party, many wasted days en route drinking, feasting, painting and enjoying female company. Their corruption was symp-
tomatic of the decline of the Edo Bakufu or government and contributed to the
damaged image of Hatamoto today.

CHAPTER 8

SAMURAI LIFE AND NUPTIALS

આ

In this new life of comfort and privilege, Adams' thoughts turned more often to his wife and daughter. It seemed unnatural to be enjoying it alone. He had expected news of his family or friends by the end of 1604, but he had still received nothing. He wondered why and could only assume that it was all taking longer than he thought, depending on the Dutch vessels to and from Japan. He still hoped that he would return home and be reunited with his loved ones in England.

However, Lord Miura Anjin was also adapting well to the life-style of the elite in Japan. He had exchanged his English clothes for the samurai courtly kimono with what Adams described as two great scimitars.[159] Kimono were made of fine fabrics such as silk or satin and were dyed, decorated and embroidered. They had deep sleeves and their hems reached to the ground. They were lined with material of only one colour called *katairo*. Underneath, the Japanese wore other white garments, or *katabira*, of thin cotton or fine linen. In cold weather, they could put on two, three or four layers. Foreigners found it extremely hard to put on such large unwieldy garments. It took immense time and patience to master putting on the kimono in the correct way. They had to fold the right-hand side over the body, then wrap the left-hand side over this. A man's kimono is held with a

---

[159] *Katana* (60-80 cm) and *Wakizashi* (30-60 cm)

silk, satin or cotton sash, which has to be just tight enough around the belly and be tied in a knot at the hips. As the sash is the main fastener, if it is wrongly or loosely tied, the whole kimono would not hang well or even collapse into an unseemly, embarrassing heap on the floor.

In time, Adams succeeded in dressing in the kimono beautifully, as well as speaking the tremendously complicated Japanese language fluently and writing in calligraphy with a brush. He also adopted the Japanese lunar calendar in his diary. He was trusted to work with Japanese spies or *ninja,* who often came on board his ships. On one trip, Sukeji reports that Adams recognized several ninja spies in the vessel; they were there to monitor some descendants of the Shogun's former enemies who were suspected of planning to attack the Shogun. Adams also seems to have enjoyed Japanese cultural and social activities in the company of Captain Quaecker-naeck and Santvoort. They watched the Japanese shamanistic the-atre drama called *Okuni Kabuki* and developed friendships with actresses and members of the audience.

Created by a dancer called Okuni, *Okuni Kabuki* was a seven-teenth-century sensation. It is recorded that Okuni was neither beautiful nor elegant, but her dancing was certainly sexy. She and her all-female dance troupe wore the *kimono* as it had never been worn before, opening up the neck and shoulders to reveal the fresh white skin that is such a turn-on for the Japanese male. As the colourful kimono swirled and rippled a glimpse of pure white breast was revealed and the pose held for maximum effect. They would also lift the heavy hem of the kimono to display a shapely ankle. It was all so different from the chaste costume and almost imperceptible movement of traditional Noh theatre.[160]

---

[160] Okuni's dance troupe scored immediate success with their first performances at a Shinto shrine in Kyoto in 1603. However, when they went on tour, one of their performances was disrupted by male members of the audience jumping on the stage to accept what they saw as an invitation to have sex. Class made no differ-ence. Samurai and fishermen, farmers and carpenters, all fought each other for sex. The riotous scenes were repeated all over Japan. The government's response was to give the *Kabuki* theatre one of its most distinctive features, still true today. Female dancers and actors were banned and men were instructed to perform all the roles.

As the young Sukeji watched, untutored in Japanese poetic songs and dialogue, he wondered why his three foreign companions were not as bored as he. Their eyes seemed fixed on the stage from beginning to end. Santvoort, in particular, seemed very taken by one of the dancers, whom he was later to court and, in 1609, to marry.

Adams gained a reputation for being generally kind to people in need, giving complete strangers, who had lost their way, guidance or a ride on his way to his vessel. Adams was now happy to be called Anjin-sama, his Japanese name. The assimilation into his new homeland had been remarkably quick and smooth.

For years, Adams had petitioned regularly to leave Japan, but now the lordship and the gift of land convinced him that his fortunes were more assured than in England. In his log book he wrote: 'Good for evil ... God hath blessed my labours.'[161]

After Ieyasu's money was distributed to *De Liefde*'s survivors, they had split into groups or gone their separate ways. Five of them had led a low life and fallen into a drunken decline. However, a few prospered in their new country. Jan Joosten van Loodesteijn gained Ieyasu's favour and was granted a stipend, like Adams. The *Yaesu* or *Jajoos* Entrance, one of the current entrances to Tokyo Station, is named after him. Originally his name was given to a commercial area in central Tokyo, on which the station was built. Melchior van Santvoort, *De Liefde*'s enterprising purser, was even more successful. He established his own business with rented junks, trading between Japan and Indo-China.

Adams' achievements were of a different order. As the Shogun's close liege-man, he now took over the power the Jesuits had monopolized. For many years, Ieyasu had depended on Padre Rodrigues for learning about the world outside Japan and had used his services as interpreter, so his relegation was a nasty shock to the Jesuits. Adams' former enemies now had to beg for his intercession. They were the same Jesuits who had tried to have *De Liefde*'s crew crucified, so he was at first unwilling to help them and pass on their messages to Ieyasu. Later he changed his mind. It was better to know

---

[161] Adams, William.

what was in their minds. The heretic and sea-dog was learning a new trick, to act politically.

Early in January 1605, a Portuguese Jesuit visited Adams. Adams assumed that the Jesuit had come to attempt another conversion. He did try, but after Adams refused, the Jesuit abruptly smiled and said to Adams: 'I am authorized to tell you that a Dutch fleet has now arrived in Siam (today's Thailand) and docked at Pattani on the Malay Peninsula. If you would like to join our missionary ship sailing to Pattani soon, we could arrange it for you.'[162] Adams was tempted. He had waited for a good opportunity to petition Ieyasu again. This could be it.

In March 1605, Ieyasu completed copying out the last volume of the set of *Azuma Kagami*, the diary-styled history books about Minamoto Shogun and his government, written by the Minamoto family between 1180 and 1266. The total number of the original volumes is uncertain. Ieyasu eventually collected fifty-one volumes with the help of Lord Kuroda. The collection was always close by his desk and it was well known among his retainers and lieges that Ieyasu was devoted to his books. In April, following the example of Minamoto Shogun, Ieyasu announced that he would resign the position of Shogun in favour of his third son, Hidetada. He himself would retire to the Sumpu Castle in today's Shizuoka Prefecture in the south-east. It was now clear to all that Ieyasu never intended to yield the position of Shogun to the Toyotomi family.

Soon after the announcement, Ieyasu and Hidetada went up to Kyoto with many powerful feudal lords such as Uesugi Kagekatsu, Fukushima Masanori, Date Masamune, Mouri Hidemoto and others, accompanied by over 10,000 troops. On 16 April 1605, and in similar fashion to how Ieyasu came to the throne two years earlier, a representative of the Emperor solemnly declared that Hidetada could mount the throne as Shogun. The ceremony and the sight of the de jure capital Kyoto swarming with troops was designed to demonstrate Ieyasu's great power. The Toyotomi family, residing in the Osaka Castle, were powerless to intervene.

---

[162] Translated by the author from Miura Joshin.

When Ieyasu moved to the Sumpu Castle, he gave Adams a third property in this area, so he could be close to him and regularly take his tutorials. One day, in his mathematics lesson, Adams found Ieyasu particularly cheerful. Seizing his chance, he opened a map of the world and said to Ieyasu: 'Here is Pattani and I have heard that a Dutch fleet may call there soon. If you grant me permission to return to England, I shall willingly be your negotiator to develop trade for Japan with both the Dutch and English.' Ieyasu's answer was unequivocal: 'I would be grateful if Dutch and English traders came to my country, but my first priority is not to allow you to go away.'[163] He now ordered Adams to sign a deed that he would never leave Japan. Adams was deeply disappointed, but Ieyasu's intransigence and his great favours convinced him to give up further appeals. However, when he sought Ieyasu's permission for his two Dutch colleagues, Captain Quaeckernaeck and Melchior van Santvoort, to leave for Pattani, it was immediately granted.

There had been some sulking among *De Liefde*'s crew when Adams was honoured so exceptionally and, for some, when they heard rumours that he had been offered an eighteen- year-old Japanese wife. No-one doubted his great achievements, but, naturally, jealousy made some of the congratulations rather forced when he came to see them. However, Adams' news is unexpected. Two men are to be allowed to return home and Ieyasu has left Adams to choose the two. All the men's cloudy faces turn sunny. Everyone points to themselves and surge towards Adams, 'Choose me, let me go back.'[164] It is like a school playground. Adams keeps silent until they calm down. Then he announces that the men he has chosen are Captain Quaeckernaeck and Van Santvoort. Jan Joosten and many other disappointed men bite their lips. In contrast, the two hardened mariners hug each other and start jumping, skipping and dancing like young boys with a joy that cannot be contained.

---

[163] Translated by the author from Miura Joshin.
[164] Author's words.

Shortly afterwards, Adams mentions the Shogun's conditions. One is that the two men will have to pass to the King of Holland the certified document from the Shogun that invites trading ships from Holland to Japan, together with Adams' translation of the document into Dutch. After their audience with the King, one of the two men will have to return to Japan to carry the King's response. If they disobey the Shogun's orders, all the remaining men in Japan will be executed. Adams repeats the words 'be executed' to make it clear that the two men are to be given great responsibility. He then opens a black lacquer box, takes out the two important documents and hands them to Captain Quaeckernaeck. He also gives him another document, a few handwritten lines, ratified with the Shogun's red seal of state. It was the passport which will allow their vessel to stop at any harbour and port throughout Japan. The captain places all three papers carefully in his breast pocket.

An uncomfortable silence is broken by Jan Joosten. 'Can I suggest something?'[165] he says suddenly. Everybody pays attention. He suggests that since the gaps in their respective fortunes are widening, it will be hard for them to stay in a group peacefully, so everyone should be free to go their separate ways. He intends to remain in Edo. Adams says he has no objection. If he was in Joosten's position, he might suggest the same thing. Two men decide to follow Joosten, twelve men will move to Hirado Port and four will stay with Adams in Hemi. Their farewells are awkward and off-hand.

However, they all started writing letters to their family and friends in their homeland to be carried by the two lucky fellows. Adams wrote a fourteen-page letter to his wife, this time care of the English East India Company instead of the Dutch company. It began: 'My loving wife, I feel that I must tell you of all the things that have happened to me since the day we parted.'[166] This he did, including: 'On April 11, 1600, we spotted the land near Bungo that was part of Japan, but by this point we only had five men who were able to walk .... Nine days after our arrival the great King of

---

[165] Ibid.
[166] Adams, William.

all this land called for us to appear before him. .... I answered every one of his (King's) inquiries and he seemed to be very satisfied. Despite this I was ordered to go to prison again, but this time it was in a different location and the conditions were much better.'[167] In his conclusion, Adams hoped that 'by one means or other, in process of time, I shall have news from one good friend or other of my good acquaintance such as Nicholas Diggines, Thomas Best, William Isac, William Jones or Becket, (his) wife and daughter, the which with patience I do wait the pleasure of Almighty God'.[168]

Unknown to *De Liefde*'s crew, the first news of their arrival in Japan in 1600 had reached the Netherlands, through Admiral Oliver van Noort in 1601. One of van Noort's men reported what he had heard from some survivors of Admiral Mahu's expedition. And also on 3 January 1602, when van Noort's ship arrived off the coast of Borneo, they encountered an elderly Portuguese captain, who had come from Nagasaki in a Japanese junk. The Portuguese captain told van Noort's crew that he had learned from the crew of a large Dutch ship that they had sailed across from Chile with two ships, one of which had been lost. After a 'very miserable'[169] passage, they had drifted into a place called Bungo. On their arrival the survivors numbered only twenty-five. 'Since then eleven more had died, but the fourteen of them who had remained alive were free to go wherever they pleased and had been allowed to build a small ship to sail where they pleased.'[170]

At this point, however, Adams and his men realized that the only vessel large enough to take their two fellows directly to Europe or to join the Dutch fleet would be Spanish or Portuguese. In spite of his disagreements over religion, Adams held no prejudice towards Portuguese and Spanish merchants. He suggested that they should use a Portuguese trader, but Captain Quaeckernaeck was uncompromising; he would never forgive the Portuguese Jesuits for trying

---

[167] Ibid.
[168] Ibid.
[169] Ibid.
[170] Ibid.

to crucify his crew. Adams went to discuss the problem with the ever-helpful Mukai Shōgen.

In the spring of 1605, Lord Matsura Shigenobu learned from his Dutch instructors that the Shogun had allowed two Dutchmen to sail for Pattani in order to attract Dutch trade to Japan. Shigenobu had succeeded Matsura Takanobu in 1584. Takanobu had expelled the Jesuits from his fiefdom in 1559. They had destroyed numberless statues and idols in the local landscape, which had caused reprisals from the Japanese Buddhist monks, who set fire to a cross in Hirado's Christian cemetery. Serious riots ensued. A Buddhist temple was burned down and many people were injured. In 1565, the Portuguese were allowed to build a new church. During the following year, the execution of four Christians suspected of spying for Ōmura Sumitada, a neighbouring Christian lord, had caused another riot and a complete halt to Portuguese trade. This time, Lord Matsura was not able to restore trade relations because the merchants who had been scared away had found a new port in which to sell their wares. This was the nearby port of Nagasaki, which was opened to the Portuguese in 1568 by the same Ōmura Sumitada.

Exasperated by these events, Shigenobu was impatient to restore his Hirado Port to the prosperity it had enjoyed in his father's reign. He decided he would provide the two Dutchmen with a Japanese vessel at his own expense. It would be a reasonable investment in future Dutch trade. In April of 1605, the Shogun gave Shigenobu official permission and immediately work commenced to build a new ocean-going ship at a cost of 250 Japanese Ryō, approximately £190,000 in today's money. She was built by the autumn of 1605. Some of the remaining *De Liefde* survivors, who had for so long dreamed of returning home themselves, found their way to Hirado from different parts of Japan to see off their more fortunate countrymen. After a joyful reunion, tinged with sadness at those who had not made it to Hirado and perhaps with sailors' tales of the Japanese women they had left behind, the vessel set sail in the autumn of 1605. As the monsoon rain fell, Adams waved them off and kept quiet. Sukeji found him very sad after the farewell.

Adams tried to keep busy to distract his painful thoughts. He decided to build an observation tower on the top of a hill on his estate, from where there was a spectacular view of Edo Bay.

When Captain Quaeckernaeck and Van Santvoort arrived in Pattani on 2 December 1605, they met Ferdinand Michielszoon, the head of the Dutch factory and chief merchant on the largest of the Dutch fleets. The fleet of fourteen ships had sailed for the Far East from the Texel on 17 June 1602, under the command of Admiral Wijbrand van Warwijck. Two of these ships called *the Erasmus* and *the Nassau*, under the command of Claes Jansz van Dijck, had reached Bantam in Java on 29 April 1603. They had sailed on for the Chinese coast and arrived off Macao on 31 July 1603. There, quite by chance, they met the great ship from Goa, which was getting ready to sail for the Japanese port of Nagasaki, the last leg of its voyage. Surprisingly, the Portuguese captain and his crew seemed to have taken one look at the heavily-armoured Dutch vessels and abandoned ship. Inside the ship, the Dutch raiders found her cargo of silk valued at fl.1.4 million and a large quantity of gold. Word of this fabulous wealth soon spread. The following year, van Warwijck himself sailed for Macao in order to force the opening of trade with the Chinese, but his ship was blown off course by strong winds. He did attempt to negotiate with Chinese settlers on the Pescadores Island, but failed there too. It had been on his return voyage to Bantam that van Warwijck had called at Pattani and had appointed Michielszoon to take charge of the Dutch factory.

As the head of the factory, Michielszoon informed his guests that the Dutch toe-hold in Asia remained precarious. The Portuguese continued to dominate the South China Sea and all the Dutch energy and endeavour had been spent on driving them out of the East Indian archipelago. As a result, he had no intention of sending any ships to trade with Japan. Nor did he expect the arrival soon of any Dutch ship on which Quaeckernaeck and Van Santvoort could sail for the Netherlands, in order to deliver the Shogun's trade certificate to Prince Maurits. He could not even offer the two men employment, since the factory had already overspent on its expansion. He could only offer his guests shelter, until they could find a chance to sail.

Early in 1606, Adams still yearned for his English wife and showed only passing interest in Japanese women. He had to decide on the arranged marriage to Yuki, that the Shogun had offered him the previous year. Bigamy was of course forbidden to both Protestants and Catholics, although where seamen had been out of contact with their wife for more than three years, their wives were allowed to remarry. Adams had heard that some devoted wives had waited for their mariner-husband for more than three years and he hoped that Mary would be one of them. He had no idea and no way of finding out. Now that Quaeckernaeck had been permitted to leave Japan, his hope was that he would be able to return home this year or next. Also, if he accepted an arranged marriage to Yuki, would it be assumed his intention to return home had been abandoned? Adams was concerned too about Yuki's feelings. Would the eighteen-year-old girl be happy to marry a man old enough to be her father and a foreigner to boot? Adams assumed that Yuki had no choice but to obey her Shogun, so she would be marrying him in tears, and he would be embarrassed. He could accept the offer from the Shogun if Mary had remarried and if Yuki were happy to marry him.

Adams took his troubles to the Buddhist priest, Joshin, the Shogun's close retainer. Joshin smiled and opined that Anjin's English wife had probably already remarried. In Japanese law, marriage with seamen was the same as in England. Their wives normally remarried in three years, if they had heard nothing from their husband. If her first husband came back after her remarriage, the three spouses must discuss the matter with each other, and eventually the wife was given the choice. Mostly, these wives chose the first husband. Then, if she had children by the second husband, she and her first husband would be responsible for looking after the children. The impulse to protect women with children seemed universal.

When Joshin noticed that Adams was still in a muddle, he advised him that in samurai society it was legitimate for lords to have several concubines or mistresses so as to produce as many children, and thus successors, as possible. William Adams was now

Lord Miura Anjin and should follow this custom. Even though there would be a wedding ceremony, he could treat Yuki not as his wife but his Japanese concubine. Adams answered that his God would not allow him to do this. Joshin was losing patience, 'What an inconvenient religion you have! Your God is not very flexible, is he?'[171] He emphasized that Shogun Ieyasu was a serious Buddhist, but had had many concubines since he was young, and Joshin himself, as a priest, had several mistresses, but that had never caused difficulties so far. Joshin reminded Adams that in the future the Shogun would summon him as often as now, so sometimes he would have to stay at his mansion in Nihonbashi, Edo, for a long time. At such times, his estate in Hemi would need to be well maintained by his 'wife'. His ninety-plus servants would also find it easier to communicate with Yuki rather than their foreign lord. Since Yuki's father was not a lord, the Shogun would arrange for Mukai to have ultimate authority over the servants.

Unbidden, Joshin volunteered to find out how Yuki was feeling about marrying Adams. In ten days, he came back to report that the most willing person was Yuki's father, Magome Kageyū. Magome was a highway official, who was in charge of a *Tenma-yaku* or packhorse exchange on one of the great imperial roads that led out of Edo. Although Magome's position was important, he was not of noble birth, nor did he have high social standing. Ieyasu understood that Japanese nobles or higher-ranking samurai lords would not want their daughter to marry the fair-haired foreigner and to produce children of mixed parentage, even though Adams was now *hatamoto*. Adams certainly would gain no political, social or financial advantage from Magome, but Magome would subsequently receive many benefits. Because Magome had his eye on some profitable trade with the Dutch, he was eager to become the stepfather of Lord Miura[172] Anjin. All his family members, includ-

---

[171] Translated by the author from Oshima Masahiro.
[172] There is no official record of Magome having a daughter, so Nishiyama Toshio (*Aoime no Sōdanyaku*) opens up the intriguing possibility that he adopted Yuki with a profitable marriage in mind.

ing Yuki, agreed with this ambition. Although Yuki was already engaged to a Japanese man, she was inclined to accept this new offer. She would feel honoured if her family status rose and she had found Adams much kinder than her Japanese fiancé and indeed than most Japanese men. She did not mind Adams' age, because there was a fifteen-year age gap between her parents. Regarding Adams' English wife, Yuki felt sorry for both Adams and his wife, so if Shogun permitted him to return to England, she would let him go.

Joshin's report to Adams left out one thing. Lord Honda had told Yuki and her parents that the Shogun would never permit Adams to leave Japan. Joshin strictly warned the parents and daughter never to mention this to Adams. He did tell Adams that, in his own view, and 'under these extraordinary circumstances, you might be forgiven by your God even if you have another mistress at your mansion in Edo'.[173] Adams kept silent for a while, before reaching a decision. As the Shogun's 'falcon', he suspected he would not be allowed to refuse to live with Yuki. Although Ieyasu had yielded the title to Hidetada, it was for political reasons, to establish his dynasty. Adams knew that the retired Ieyasu would maintain total power and control of his country. As he had several trading and political matters to suggest to Ieyasu, he did not want to be out of favour. Mary must have been remarried by now and Deliverance must be living a contented life. Lord Miura Anjin persuaded William Adams to believe that.

In May 1606, with Joshin as a go-between, Adams and Yuki exchanged traditional betrothal gifts such as money, yards of silk-made goods, fishes, fruits and bottles of rice wine. In the middle of June in the Hemi estate, with Mukai Shōgen officiating as *nakōdo* [matchmaker], Adams' and Yuki's wedding ceremony was held with the local village people. Curiously, there is no record of a certificate of Adams' marriage with Yuki or any other Japanese woman, which suggests he did not want one. However, there are records that Adams had several mistresses officially accepted in Court.

---

[173] Translated by the author from Miura Joshin.

Sukeji records that Adams often told Yuki that when he had an opportunity to return to England, he would leave her. This Yuki accepted.[174]

Adams remembered very little of his wedding ceremony. He recalled Yuki's body was completely enclosed with a pure white, heavily padded wedding costume and a bride's hood so enormous that he was unable to see her face at all. According to Japanese nuptial custom, rice wine or *shinshu* (God's spirit) should be either sipped from a red lacquered cup three times by both the bride and bridegroom or they can just touch their lips to the cup three times. When Yuki dipped her lips to the wine, Adams was still unable to see any part of her face behind the monster hood. Soon afterwards, Mukai started singing Noh or Japanese lyric songs, which would have been loudly appreciated whatever the quality of the performance. The village people then filed past to pour rice wine for Adams and, assuming this to be the Japanese custom, he drained the cup each time. It is impolite for a cup to be empty, so the village people would have continued to pour. Joshin did not help by repeating his congratulations and pushing Adams to drink more. Soon Lord Anjin had drunk himself insensible.

How much time has passed? Adams wakes up feeling thirsty in a dark room, where a candle is twinkling in a corner and a white face looking down at him. Adams blinks a few times. 'Are you awake?' and with this whisper he also hears the sound of water pouring into a cup. Yuki, wearing white nightclothes, extends her hand to give Adams the cup. When the fresh cold water goes down his throat, Adams regains his senses. He realizes to his shame that he was dead drunk in his own solemn wedding ceremony. He does not remember when the ceremony ended and how he went to bed. Yuki probably says, with a smile, that he did not have to drink all the rice

---

[174] The inconvenient truth is that there was no 'love story' of the kind described in the film *Shogun* and other books. In those days, the samurai class expected to have a marriage arranged by family or by the authorities. Under the samurai code, Yuki would be sacrificing her body not just to Adams, but in obedience to her Shogun and Adams realized this.

wine poured for him, just touch his lips to the cup. She would not have known whether he had finished the drinks out of duty or had genuinely enjoyed it. He asks her whether he did something wrong. Yuki answers 'not at all',[175] but mentions that he had sung a foreign song rather loudly. All the guests had beat on time with their hands and it had been a very cheerful moment. When Yuki remembers that time, she nearly laughs, but as her relationship with Adams is not yet equal,[176] she stifles her laughter behind a bowed head.

Sitting on the bed together in their nightclothes, Adams feels surprisingly relaxed. It is as if he has known Yuki for a long time. He says, 'Yuki, I am a married man and have a daughter in England. I might go back home soon. Are you sure you want to become a concubine of this foreigner?'[177] Yuki asks Adams coyly, 'Don't you like me?'[178] When Adams nods, Yuki suddenly hides her head and calls him 'Anjin sama' in a low voice. Even in the dark room, Adams notices that Yuki's snowy-white cheeks are turning to cherry-pink and she begins to breathe heavily. Adams holds out his hands to embrace her; beside the bed a candle dies. In the darkness Adams hears Yuki whimpering. She feels honoured that her marriage has helped raise her family's status, but she has given up her Japanese fiancé and her virginity will be taken by a barbarian. If Adams returns home or dies, she will still be responsible for his estate, as his concubine, and no decent Japanese man will marry her. Her marriage bed is also the deathbed of her personal life.

In the early morning, we can imagine Adams and Yuki taking a walk on the beach, alone except for the seagulls pecking in the sand. Yuki follows behind her husband in the traditional Japanese way. Adams spreads his arms wide and breathes in the fresh, salty air. When Yuki closes her eyes and breathes in too, Adams

---

[175] Author's words.
[176] Under the samurai code a wife could achieve spiritual equality with her husband through her support and devotion to him over time.
[177] Translated by the author from Oshima Masahiro.
[178] Ibid.

pulls her towards him and kisses her lips. She is very embarrassed because kissing and touching another's body in public are indecent in Japanese culture. Yuki pushes her master aside and rushes away, in so far as one can rush in a kimono and impractical shoes. Adams follows her at his normal pace. When he reaches her, he takes her hand. It still feels wrong, but this time she rather willingly holds on to her husband's hand. The newlyweds now walk side by side and, on the wet sand, their footprints tell the whole story.

□

In September, Ieyasu came back to Edo from Fushimi, Kyoto, refreshed after enjoying falconry on the way. Adams visited him in the Edo Castle and reported on his and Yuki's wedding ceremony. Ieyasu would have expressed his hope that Adams was satisfied with his young bride in their wedding bed and that they would soon produce a baby. When he was sixty-two-years old, Ieyasu had fathered his eleventh baby. It was well known that the Shogun's legendary vitality sprang partly from frequent sexual activity and for a moment Adams would have been distracted in recalling Yuki's fresh full body and silky smooth skin. He recovered in time to hear the Shogun offering something quite extraordinary, that he would like to stand as godfather to Adams' baby, if it was boy.

Then he ordered a servant to fill his pipe with tobacco and as he smoked he watched the fumes curling upwards. Tobacco was not particularly Ieyasu's favourite pastime, but when he felt relaxed he took a few puffs. Tobacco had been introduced by the Portuguese Jesuits ten years before and was now cultivated in Kyushu, southern Japan. Among all classes, the number of tobacco-smokers was increasing.

Adams did not particularly want Ieyasu and others to be involved in his private life, so he tried to change the subject by asking Ieyasu about his meeting with the Toyotomi family in Fushimi. 'What a conceited widow she is!'[179] Ieyasu said, puffing furiously on his pipe. She had declined Ieyasu's invitation for her son Hideyori to attend the inauguration of Ieyasu's third son, Hidetada, as Shogun, even though she was advised to attend by Kodai-in, the mother-in-law and the widow of former governor-general Hideyoshi. This time, Ieyasu had gone to try to reconcile with Yodo, but she had become hysterical and rather demanded Ieyasu to return the power and position of Shogun to the Toyotomi family, when Hideyori reached twenty years of age. 'Foolish woman!'[180] Ieyasu said, but Adams noticed he was not seriously angry. There was a calm confidence and Adams assumed that, whatever happened, Ieyasu had already resolved to find a pretext for completely destroying the Toyotomi family.

---

[179] Author's words.
[180] Ibid.

CHAPTER 9

THE BATTLE FOR NAVAL SUPREMACY

One day, Ieyasu again asked Adams where Pattani was. Adams pointed to a spot on a globe. He explained that Pattani was a small settlement located on the eastern coast of the Malay Peninsula and that it was well known as a port for ships trading with China and Siam. However, as Pattani was under Portuguese control, Dutch ships avoided it. 'That was in the past,'[181] said Ieyasu; 'Pattani is now fully under Dutch control.'[182] Ieyasu had learnt this from Lord Matsura Shigenobu, when they met at the inauguration ceremony for Hidetada. Lord Matsura had learnt it while researching the best route on which to send the two Dutchmen, Quaeckernaeck and Van Santvoort, in December 1605. Adams initially could not believe that the Dutch had removed such a well entrenched enemy. He realized much must have changed in the world while he was locked away in Japan. Imagining these changes inspired him with hope and excitement.

In September 1606, Ieyasu ordered Adams to build another ship, but larger than he had built before. Ieyasu intended to use the ship himself, as he would more often need to ply between Edo and

---

[181] Translated by the author from Miura Joshin.
[182] Ibid.

Sumpu. He also thought that he would need another open-sea vessel. This time Adams had no hesitation in obeying the order.

Adams decided to build a 120-ton vessel, half as large again as the first. He chose the same building site and the same local carpenters as before. The first inkling that boat men Karosuke and Onusuke with Sukezo, Yojuro and the other carpenters must have had of the ship's size was when Adams' order came to gather so much more wood from the Amagi Mountain. They and their community would have burst with pride at this vote of confidence and from the Shogun himself. The Itō beach is soon crowded, with double the number of sightseers from before. This time, several stalls are selling rice cakes and tea appears and there are queues at each. Every day a festive spirit fills the air and in the evening all the workers sink their tired bodies into hot spring baths.

At the beginning of 1606, Adams went back to Hemi. Forewarned, a kneeling Yuki welcomes her husband home. She is dressed for the New Year in a more brightly-coloured kimono than usual and her hair is decorated with a boxwood comb painted with flowers. With a shy smile, she whispers in Adams' ear that she is four months pregnant. Just as when he asked Captain Quaeckernaeck to pass on his letter to his English wife, his feelings swing between guilt and joy, but Lord Miura Anjin recovers to express his delight at having a successor. According to the custom of the day, Japanese feudal lords were expected to produce as many children as possible, whether by their wife or mistresses. Adams was no exception. He, too, had had several mistresses.

Meanwhile in Pattani, Captain Quaeckernaeck and Melchior van Santvoort had been waiting half a year for a chance to sail for the Netherlands. Towards the end of July, they heard that a Dutch fleet of nine ships had arrived on the other side of the peninsula, where it had laid siege to Malacca.

The best news Quaeckernaeck learned was that this fleet was under the command of his very own cousin, Cornelis Matelieff de Jonge. Quaeckernaeck, taking his shipmates' precious letters with him, immediately set out to join the fleet. He arrived in Johor, the southernmost point of the Malay Peninsula, in the middle of August.

Here he met Dasa Zabrang, the local raja and the rightful ruler of Malacca, who had been forced out by the Portuguese and had rushed to ally himself with the Dutch. Three months before, Zabrang had provided a large number of his men to help in the siege.

By 18 August, the battle seemed to have relocated to the sea, where the Dutch had been attacked by a large Portuguese fleet. Early the following morning, as the wind dropped, Zabrang and Quaeckernaeck set off with six of the raja's boats called *Kora-Kora* toward Matelieff's flagship, *the Oranje*, to learn how the battle was progressing.

After the cousins were reunited, Cornelis told how he had sailed from Holland in 1605 with instructions to occupy the strategic port of Malacca, the last Portuguese fort on the peninsula. He had been beseiging the port since the beginning of May, but had failed to drive the Portuguese out, despite Zabrang's reinforcements, the arrival of two more Dutch ships in July, and his vastly superior numbers. He admitted that his troops were mainly being thwarted by the genius of the fort's commander, the formidable André Furtado de Mendoça, and the bravery of his garrison of only 150 men, including a small contingent of Japanese warriors. Over 500,000 shots had been fired into the stronghold to little effect and almost 200 men had been lost. The flagging Dutch spirits had not been helped by the news, five days earlier, that sixteen Portuguese ships were off Cape Rachado, only some thirty miles away, to the north-west. Troops and cavalry had again gone on board in preparation for a sea battle and although a Dutch victory was not in sight, they had done better at sea than on land. Both the Portuguese and Dutch had lost two ships, but, with 150 dead, the Dutch casualties were only a third of their enemy's.

Matelieff's fleet was now getting ready for battle again, but one of his chief officers, the Captain of the *Erasmus*, was wounded so the admiral offered his cousin the ship's captaincy. Cornelis promised that the letters from *De Liefde*'s crew would be sent home at the earliest opportunity and he would take back the trade certificate from the Japanese Shogun to the Netherlands himself; after which, he would instruct his chief merchant, Victor Sprinckel, who had been tasked to establish a factory in Macao, to send a ship to Japan at the earliest opportunity. However, before that, there were fourteen Portuguese ships to deal with. Quaeckernaeck was quickly won over by his eminent cousin and that same day he took up his post on the ship which, coincidentally, bore the original name of his own ship *De Liefde*.

Over the next few days, the two fleets occasionally exchanged fire, but from a long distance. The stand-off continued until 23 August, when Matelieff was forced to divert his fleet to Johor, because of a shortage of gunpowder. The admiral of the Portuguese fleet, Don Martim Affonso, rode his luck and landed in Malacca in triumph to relieve its starving citizens. On 10 October, Matelieff, with his fleet repaired and restocked, departed from Johor having heard that his enemy had divided his fleet into two squadrons of seven ships each. One squadron, under the command of Dom Alvaro de Menezes, had sailed north, through the Strait of Malacca. The other, under the command of the admiral himself, had eased towards Cape Rachado [on Sumatra Island]. Matelieff saw his chance and immediately conducted his fleet back up the strait and reached the cape on 22 October.

The second battle started the same day and continued into the night. By morning, the Dutch had total victory. The Portuguese vice-admiral's ship, *the Sào Nicolau*, was surrounded by three ships and twelve of her crew were slaughtered to a man. The crew of another Portuguese ship, *the Todos os Sautos,* suffered the same fate. Captain André Pessoa, one of the courageous men in the defence of Malacca, who was in command of the stricken *São Simâo*, attacked and boarded the *Amsterdam,* but was rebuffed. The next morning, she was found drifting with only twelve men alive. The battle ended when the Portuguese admiral ran his remaining four ships ashore and into hiding.

Among the great number of both Portuguese and Dutch casualties was Captain Quaeckernaeck. His last moments were described by Jacques L'Hermite de Jonge, a young scribe on board the *Erasmus*. 'In the fury, our skipper, Jacob Quaeckernaeck was shot straight through the head with a musket bullet, upon which he fell over dead without uttering a word; so that it seems that this man has had to dwell in these countries for so long to die so senselessly here.' However, the captain's death was not in vain. Dutch interest in the profitable trade in silver and silk between China and Japan, was first fired by the account of Dirck Gerritszoon Pomp, Adams' old ship-mate on *De Hoop*, and rekindled in the summer of 1601 when the Dutch adventurer Oliver van Noort brought back the news from Japanese traders that one of the fleet of five ships commanded by Mahu had drifted to Japan and that her crew was employed by its 'king'. So in 1606, when the news reached the Netherlands from their factory in Pattani that the Japanese king had dispatched Captain Quaeckernaeck with a licence to trade, it encouraged the Dutch to renew their efforts to return to Japan.

Back in 1600, when his vessel returned to Holland, Jan Outgherszoon, the chief pilot on *Het Geloof*, had been instructed by De Cordes to draw the coastlines of the Magellan Strait, through which his vessel had sailed. However, he had originally trained as a carpenter and his sketching skills were not accurate enough. So, after he had improved those skills, he redrew the sketches 'with coastal profiles and natural charts of the passage in which are recorded various data such as sounding, distances, and the magnetic north'.[183] In 1606, the chart appeared in the first Amsterdam edition of an atlas by the Flemish cartographer Gerhardus Mercator, entitled *The New Complete Description of the Treacherous Strait Magellani*. The work charts the geographical characteristics of the strait in detailed rather than general descriptions, according to *Pars Japonica*, and was the first detailed chart of the Strait of Magellan to appear in print in the Netherlands. The sketches and descriptions on the chart were clearly made by Outgherszoon, although his name is not mentioned. He was ashamed of turning back for home and feared being thought a coward.

Between July and September 1607, during which Admiral Cornelis Matelieff's squadron in and around Macao prevented the Portuguese Great Ship from sailing from Goa, no official Japanese

---

[183] Wieder, F.C.

ships ventured into this maritime war zone. However, on 14 September, Matelieff's ships encountered the fearsome Japanese pirate-junks, *wakō-sen*, soon after they were driven away by the Portuguese fleet's commander, Captain-Major André Pessoa. Although they were obviously pirates, according to his own record, Matelieff treated them with courtesy, even inviting aboard their chieftain, who presented him with a Japanese sword and a suit of armour and expressed his desire that the Dutch regard them as friends. The admiral asked the Japanese chieftain to pass on his greetings to the lord of Hirado, as his junks were on the way to that port from Cambodia. Matelieff described the Japanese pirates in his journal:

> All these Japanese crews were robust men and had a marked appearance of being pirates, as in fact they were. They are a firm and resolute nature, for when they see that Chinese have the upper hand of them, they slit their own bellies in order to avoid falling alive into the hands of those pitiless enemies, who would make them endure unspeakable torments, even going as far as to slice up their limbs one after another. They said that they knew of Jaep Quaeck,[184] and that there were still in Japan eight or ten Dutchmen who were building ships for the Emperor, and that these were shortly expected to arrive in Pattani.

After Matelieff encountered the *wakō-sen*, he sailed for Bantam in Java, but acting on the chieftain's information, he sent a ship called the *Mauritius* to Pattani to instruct his chief merchant, Victor Sprinckel, to take charge of the Dutch factory and await the arrival of the Shogun's ship from Japan.

Meanwhile back in the Netherlands, the Dutch were persisting in their efforts to reach Japan. They succeeded in requesting Prince Maurits 'to write a letter to the King of Japan' and order that 'such persons will be sent (there) by his Excellency as are appointed by Admiral Paulus van Cearden'.[185] One of the men selected by Van

---

[184] Jacob Quaeckernaeck.
[185] Wieder, F.C. and Hakluyt Society.

Caerden was the sixty-two-year-old veteran of the ill- fated 1600 voyage, Dirck Gerritszoon Pomp, who had only returned from Spanish imprisonment the year before. Van Caerden sailed on 20 April 1606. Because his ships had laid siege to a Portuguese fort on the East African coast, he did not anchor in Bantam until 6 January 1608. Van Caerden sailed on towards the Spice Islands and arrived at Ternate in the middle of May. Over the following months, they spent a lot of the expedition's resources on the establishment of a stronghold on the nearby island of Makian. Then the fleet broke up, when first two of its ships were wrecked on the island's reefs, Van Caerden was captured by the Spanish and two other ships abandoned the mission and sailed back home. During the failed two-year voyage, Dirck Gerritszoon Pomp became blind. He was transferred to Matelieff's ship with six other crew members and sent back to the Netherlands, but died midway on the voyage home.

What the chieftain of the *wakō-sen* had told the Dutch was half true. On 8 November, when Sprinckel arrived in Pattani to take charge of the Dutch factory, he found a ship from Japan moored on the port's roadstead. However, it was a Japanese junk, not a decent ship built by *De Liefde's* survivors, nor was it the Shogun's ship and there was only one Dutchman on board, Melchior van Santvoort. When Quaeckernaeck departed for Johor, Van Santvoort had decided to return to Hirado on the south-westerly monsoon and to his wife and his shop in Osaka. Back in Japan, he obtained another red-seal passport, then he sailed for Pattani again, but this time it was entirely for commercial purposes. Lord Matsura of Hirado had arranged a junk loaded with cereals for the Dutch merchant to trade against the commodities on offer in Pattani.

Van Santvoort's return to Pattani gave the new head of the Dutch factory a great chance to take some action on some outstanding business to which he had given low priority. The lethargic Sprinckel was under instructions from Admiral Matelieff to respond to the trading proposal from the Japanese ruler as soon as the factory was established in Macao. Matelieff had failed to reach Macao and with no ships to spare, Sprinckel had neglected the matter and was the cause of serious delay in establishing Dutch trade with Japan. The arrival of the Japanese pirate junk was not much of a step forward, but at least, by Van Santvoort's arrival, he was able to make contact with the Japanese ruler. On 6 February 1608, just before Van Santvoort sailed for Japan, Victor Sprinckel wrote two long letters to the Japanese Shogun and William Adams, which he entrusted to Van Santvoort with a small collection of Dutch porcelain, crystal mugs, French wineglasses and some samples of Dutch cloth for the Shogun.

In the letter to Adams, he thanked him profusely for the services he had provided to the Dutch East India Company and also reported how Captain Quaeckernaeck had joined his cousin's fleet in Malacca, had explained to the Admiral about the Dutch sailors' distress in Japan and how he had been killed in the battle at Cape Rochado. The reasons for the delay in visiting Japan were mentioned in his second letter, addressed to the Shogun, but he asked Adams to study it several times to make sure that the content would be correctly understood. In the letter, Sprinckel confirmed that he had received the trade licence and, on behalf of Prince Maurits, expressed his deep gratitude and explained what the prince would give the Shogun in return for his generous gesture.

My dear honourable William Adams
Although I have never known you and you have never known me either, I have heard a lot about you from Melchor van Santvoort, who will deliver this letter to you.

We are honoured to be given the permission from the Shogun for the Dutch to trade with Japan. We would have had to spend a large sum of money, make great efforts and take a lot of trouble to obtain this permission if you did not help us. I hope the Dutch East India Company will express their appreciation to you for your great achievement. ....

.... I have something to ask you to do for me please. I made a letter and prepared some presents for the Shogun. Could you kindly give them to him, please. After you pass them on to him, I would like you to translate my letter into Japanese please. I enclose a copy of the letter, so you can read it several times and clearly understand what I have said before giving the letter to the Shogun. I would also like you to see what happened here in Pattani for the last few years. You will find reasons to explain to the Shogun why the Dutch have not been able to visit Japan and why we are unable to visit immediately, although it is our wish. ....

...... His Majesty shall be advised how in the twelfth month of the year 1605, eleven ships sailed from our fatherland for the East Indies under the command of Admiral Cornelis Matelieff de Jonge, amongst which were four, namely the flagship *Orange*, the *Middelburgh*, the *Mauritius* & *Erasmus*, which were destined to sail to the kingdom of China with great quantities of money and goods so as to seek trade as do the Portuguese and other nations; and that I myself was destined to stay there in case that trade might have been acquired; and from where for the first time a ship would have sailed for Japan with silk and goods according to my instructions. ......

Sprinckel then described how Matelieff had been forced to leave Macao because of the weather and interference by the Chinese, 'lawful and natural' causes, he stressed. However, in the separate letter to Adams, he blamed the Portuguese, maintaining that their ships had been peppered with shots by the Portuguese in the battle at Cape Rachado and had been forced to return home without delay. This version was perhaps to cover his own inactivity in promoting trade with China and Japan. At the end of his letter, Sprinckel apologized again for the delay and expressed his enthusiastic hope that

> His Majesty shall not slacken his love and affection toward us, even though we do not doubt that the Portuguese (our mortal enemies) will not rest to persuade His Majesty otherwise by every kind of cunning and deceit, yea the greatest of lies.

There might be no excuse for telling a lie, but in his expectation of future expeditions Sprinckel had been sincere enough. On 20 December 1607, another fleet of thirteen ships under the command of Admiral Pieter Willemsz Verhoeff and Vice Admiral Francois

Wittert departed for the Far East. It was the second-largest fleet ever to have sailed out of Holland. However, the official record says 'the Dutch East India Company attach the greatest importance to the Chinese silk-trade and the Moluccan spice-trade ....'.[186] Japan was not specifically mentioned yet.

While history was being made in the South China Sea, in May 1607 Yuki gave birth to a boy. Adams lifted the baby in his arms and named him Joseph, the name he is believed to have given to his short-lived son in England. The new Joseph had green-brown eyes, black hair and whiter skin than the average Japanese. For days after the birth, the boy's future prayed on Adams' mind. His son would inherit the Hemi estate, but he had seen the mixed-race children in the ports of Hirado and Nagasaki and how badly they were treated. Then came a remarkable honour, in the form of an official document called *Kokuin-Jō* from Ieyasu. The Shogun wished to name the child himself and with a name derived from the traditions of the Tokugawa Family. He was to be called *Sen Matsu* (the pine blessed for one thousand years).

On 2 July 1609, *De Griffioen*, one of the thirteen ships that had set sail from Holland eighteen months before, arrived off the port of Hirado, although only with the help of Japanese sailors as she had reached Japan four days earlier and had been drifting along the unfamiliar coast. She was joined by the *Roode Leeuw met Pylen*, with the assistance of a Japanese pilot who had climbed aboard near Nagasaki. Later in the day, as the tide came in, the two ships were met by a large fleet of boats, each manned with a dozen oarsmen, which pulled both ships into the narrow harbour. The next day the boats returned and were now escorting a canal boat, carrying three Japanese officials, who were invited on board *De Griffioen*. The officials informed the ships' council that they had come in haste to meet them on behalf of their lord, Matsura Shigenobu, as he had gone up to Edo for his annual visit to Shogun Hidetada, Ieyasu's successor. The officials explained that their lord should return within five or six weeks, but if the Dutch wanted to establish

---

[186] Wieder, F.C. and Hakluyt Society.

trade in Hirado, they were required first to visit Tokugawa Ieyasu, who currently resided in *Fuchū*, Tōkai-dō, on the Eastern highway to Edo. Although he was officially retired, the old Shogun still held the reins of power, particularly concerning Japan's foreign relations.

On 4 July 1609, the members of the ships' councils set foot in Japan for the first time. They were warmly welcomed by the same officials who had invited them the day before and were taken to Lord Matsura's residence, which stood on the top of a hill overlooking the Hirado harbour. The Dutch members received generous hospitality there. Their interpreter assured them that the lord of Hirado would be greatly pleased by their arrival at his harbour and that he would willingly provide them with whatever they needed. A message had already been sent to Lord Matsura, as well as to the governor in Nagasaki, that the Dutch had arrived. At noon, the Dutchmen were returned to their ships. The next two days were spent writing letters to the Shogun and *De Liefde*'s survivors. A couple of days later, Matsura's officials sailed a junk up the narrow bay and received the letters. One of the officials was Melchior van Santvoort. In 1608, after his departure from Pattani, he had first sailed to Siam to call on one of Sprinckel's agents. The diversion had forced him to spend the winter in Cambodia. He had arrived in Hirado on the same monsoon winds as they had, although several months earlier. On landing he had gone to see Adams to hand him Sprinckel's letters and the gifts.

□

At Adams' country estate in Hemi, the orange trees planted three years before are in full blossom for the first time. Adams is proudly showing their tiny white flowers to Sukeji, when Matsuzo shuffles up and announces 'Melchoir van Santvoort is visiting you now.'[187] Adams and Sukeji are happily surprised. Before they can run to greet him, Santvoort is standing behind Matsuzo smiling and sur-

---

[187] Translated by the author from Nishiyama Toshio.

rounded by his luggage. He is as cheerful as when he left them two years ago.

The three men move to the sitting-room. Santvoort makes himself comfortable. He tells Adams why he has not returned to the Netherlands but stayed in Pattani for half a year and all that has happened in that time, including their captain's death. Santvoort explains to Adams why the Dutch showed no interest in *De Liefde*'s arrival in Japan in 1600, although the news had reached them. Macao and then Pattani were the nearest Dutch outposts to Japan. The man in charge, the lethargic Victor Sprinckel, had had little enthusiasm for attempting to cross the East China Sea and even less for going to rescue his compatriots. When Santvoort and Captain Quaeckernaeck made contact with Sprinckel, he resisted their calls to open trading links with Japan, berating them instead for allowing William Adams, *De Liefde*'s sole surviving Englishman, to become the one most trusted by the Shogun.

Listening intently as always, Sukeji was learning how different and complex the world was beyond the shores of Japan. He understood that the Japanese warlords fought for power and control, but the Europeans seemed to fight for trade and religion. This wasn't just the ignorance of a teenager. It was an ignorance shared by most of the Japanese ruling class. Japan's isolation must have been a strong reason why, in later life, Sukeji became a teacher.

In three days, the three men visited Ieyasu with the letter and the gifts from Victor Sprinckel. Sukeji saw Adams accurately translating Sprinckel's letter and entreating Ieyasu for the Dutch trade privileges. All the Dutch gifts were laid out – luxurious plates, small mugs, bowls, goblets, cloth, velvet and guns. Ieyasu asked Adams, 'When the Dutch ships come, will they bring this kind of exotic and beautiful merchandise?'[188] Adams assured Ieyasu that this would be the case, 'promising that the vessels would bring many beautiful things'.[189] Ieyasu answered: 'Yes, yes, I can see that the Dutch are

---

[188] Translated by the author from Miura Joshin.
[189] Ibid.

Luis Teixeira map of Japan of 1595 which would probably have been amongst the maps and charts used by Adams as pilot of *De Liefde*. Courtesy: Sir Hugh and Lady Cortazzi Japanese Map Collection, SISJAC

The raid on Annobon, Gulf of Guinea, west Africa, in December 1598 by the Dutch trading fleet. Adams' ship *De Liefde* is far left, although he was on *De Hoope* at this point in the journey. From a collection entitled 'Voyages of the Dutch East India Company', published in Amsterdam in 1646. Courtesy: Archives of the Dutch East India Company (VOC)

Carving of Erasmus that was on the stern of the *De Liefde*. Preserved at the Ryuko-in temple, Tochigi prefecture. Courtesy: Tokyo National Museum

4

Anglo-Dutch sea battle of 20 April 1605. Painting by Hendrik Cornelisz Vroom.
Courtesy: National Maritime Museum, Amsterdam

5

Segment of another illustration showing the five ships of the Dutch trading fleet, including
De Liefde, piloted by Adams. From the collection entitled 'Voyages of the Dutch East India
Company', published in Amsterdam in 1646.
Courtesy: Archives of the Dutch East India Company (VOC)

Portrait of Tokugawa Ieyasu (1543-1616).
Courtesy: Wikimedia Commons

The Tokugawa family crest.
Courtesy: Wikimedia Commons

Dutch East India Company factory at Hirado. Engraving by Arnolds Montanus.
Courtesy: Bunka Kōryū ka (Department of Cultural Exchange), Hirado City Council, Nagasaki

9

'Arita' porcelain plate of the Dutch East India
Company (VOC), common throughout their
trading posts. From c.1660 great quantities of
such tableware were exported from Nabeshima,
Kyushu. Considered to be the first European-
style tableware found in Japan.
Courtesy: Archives of the Dutch East India
Company (VOC)

Portrait of Matsura Shigenobu (1549-1614).
Courtesy: Matsura Historical Museum, Hirado

Model of the *San Buena Ventura* built by Adams – the design being based on *De Liefde*.
Courtesy: Rotterdam Maritime Museum

Seventeenth-century painting showing Adams building his first ship at
Itō, Shizuoka Prefecture. Courtesy: Tsukuda Hiromi, Mayor of Itō City Council.

Public notice adjacent to the tombstone (pl.14) stating 'The Tombstone of Anjin Miura/ William Adams'. Courtesy: Author

14

Tombstone of William Adams, Hirado.
Courtesy: Author

Statue of William Adams in Hirado town centre. Courtesy: Author

Plaque in Hirado, stating: 'This plaque marks the site of the English Trading House (1613-1623)'. Courtesy: Author

William Adams' home in Hirado (currently a confectionary shop). Courtesy: Author

Site of the English Trading House, Hirado. Public notice recording its history. It states: 'This memorial was erected in 1927, here on the opposite shore of where the English Trading House is thought to have been located'. Courtesy: Author

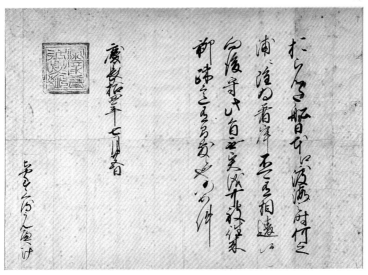

Trade pass (Dutch: *handelspas*) issued in the name of Tokugawa Ieyasu. The text commands: 'Dutch ships are allowed to travel to Japan, and they can disembark on any coast, without any reserve. From now on this regulation must be observed, and the Dutch left free to sail where they want throughout Japan. No offenses to them will be allowed, such as on previous occasions' – dated 24 August 1609 , bearing the the Shogun's official scarlet seal. Courtesy: Wikipedia Commons

Monuments believed to have been erected by Joseph Adams to honour his parents (William and Yuki) at Hemi, Yokosuka, following his mother's death in 1634. A memorial service is held annually in April by Yokosuka City Council. Courtesy: Author

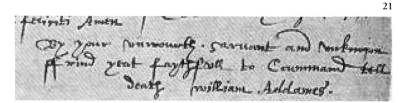

21

Handwriting of William Adams – from his letter dated December 1613 addressed to the East India Company. It reads: 'By your unworthy servant and unknown friend, yours faithfully to command till death. William Addames'. Preserved in the Bodleian Library. Courtesy: Wikipedia Commons

masters in the manufacturing trade as well as in the machinery of war.'[190]

With Adams' help, Sprinckel's approach was successful. Ieyasu wrote an enthusiastic letter to Prince Maurice to tell him of his delight at the prospect of Dutchmen visiting his land and asking what objection there might be to an annual visit.

Van Santvoort's presence among the junk's officials that day in Hirado stemmed from his business dealings with Hasegawa Fujihiro, the Nagasaki Port's new governor. When the governor learned that the Dutch ships had anchored in Hirado, he asked Santvoort to go and meet the Dutch ship's council with two of his deputies and invite them to his residence in Nagasaki. When the ship's council received the invitation from Santvoort, they decided to dispatch Jacques Specx, one of the junior merchants, who would in time succeed Sprinckel, to return with Santvoort and explain the purpose of their visit to the governor.

On 9 July, the two Dutchmen arrived in Nagasaki. An unwelcome sight greeted them. Moored in the expansive harbour was the Portuguese Great Ship, *Nossa Senhora da Graça [Our Lady of Grace]*, out of Goa. This was their richest ship and the one the Dutch most wanted to catch. When the Dutch learned that the Portuguese ship had been a regular visitor to Japan for many years, it would have been two anxious and apprehensive men who were met by palanquin carriers and taken to the Nagasaki governor's residence. However, a sumptuous feast and pretty waitresses cheered them up, as did what followed, bedding with the waitresses throughout the night.

According to Japanese sources, the governor found Specx a charming and impressive young man, in his mid-twenties, with ginger hair neatly combed and the chubby face and plump belly that suggested a successful merchant. He asked the Dutchman several questions, such as from where exactly the Dutch vessels came, what they were carrying, whether they were interested in the Nagasaki harbour and their purpose in visiting Japan. It was his duty to

---

[190] Ibid.

report all the answers to Ieyasu. After being warmly entertained by the waitresses, and with generous amounts of sake (rice wine) at the banquet, the two Dutchmen would have been in a very good mood and replied that they were satisfied with their harbour and that the purpose of their visit was to seek friendship with the Shogun and free-trade on behalf of their own king and country. They showed a sample of the goods which they sought to trade and said they had brought presents for Ieyasu, which were 'two cases of raw silk, one hundred and thirty bars of lead, and two golden decanters with a value of 240 florins'. In five days, the two men came back to Hirado and made a glowing report on their visit to Nagasaki, 'very great friendship and presentations received and offered in that place'.

In spite of this generosity, the Nagasaki governor was not particularly drawn to the Dutch, but he saw how he could use them to take his cut from government funds. Hasegawa was one of the old Shogun's trusted governors, who was also licensed to fix the price and procure the finest samples of raw silk for the Shogun. However, as the Jesuits who had resided in Nagasaki for many years knew very well, most of the commodities purchased in the name of the Shogun were sold locally and the profit ended up in the governor's pocket. With the growing importance of the Nagasaki Port, Hasegawa had become a mediator between Ieyasu and the Portuguese, cleverly administering to his Shogun's needs and regularly using his sister, O-Natsu, who was Ieyasu's favourite concubine. He did not want to lose a position that was proving so profitable. However, he was having some trouble with the Portuguese, who regularly refused to allow his officials to come aboard their ships and demanded wildly fluctuating and unreasonable prices for their commodities. The *Ito-wappu*, silk-yarn allotment system, suggested by William Adams back in 1604, was proving difficult to enforce.

For Governor Hasegawa, therefore, the Dutchmen's arrival was opportune. However, he knew from Santvoort that the Dutch were forced to obtain their silk in Pattani, so clearly were not yet in a strong position to take over the Portuguese monopoly of the silk trade. Also they had chosen to anchor in the Hirado Port rather than his Nagasaki Port. Furthermore, moored at his port at that moment was a certain Captain-Major André Pessoa, a former governor of Macau and captain of *Nossa Senhora da Graça* with 200 tons of Chinese white silk and a huge amount of silver bullion.

Before his ship's arrival, Pessoa had chased Matelieff's squadron down the Pearl River, but withdrawn when he realized the fleet was larger than his ship, which might also be in difficulties in the China Sea in winter. So he had decided to sail for Japan at the end of July to transport the two-year backlog of supplies for the Japanese market, since no Portuguese vessels had risked sailing to Japan for one year. His plan, however, had to be changed when he received a warning letter from Bantam that another Dutch fleet had orders to attack the Great Ship. Then, before he could escape from the Dutch raiders, a heaven-sent typhoon had suddenly swept his ship away to the south and through a blessed mist he had succeeded in leaving his enemy behind and reached Nagasaki. Now his hope was not only to receive the usual cooperation and security from the Nagasaki governor, but also a guarantee that he, not the Dutch, would be able to visit the old Shogun first and secure the Jesuit fathers, as middlemen, a position from which to reap rewards from the sale of the Portuguese cargo.

It was a mouth-watering prospect, so he was delighted when the governor accepted all his requests and promised to keep obstructing all the Dutch activities and do whatever he could to help him maintain his superiority. However, Hasegawa was now playing a double game. He proceeded to honour his promise, made during the lavish dinner of 9 July, to ferry the Dutch by one of his barges to Osaka, where they would see Ieyasu before their rivals.

In actual fact, the granting of an audience for the Dutch with Ieyasu was more likely to have been secured by William Adams. Jacques Specx, knowing nothing about Japan and fearing that Ieyasu might change his mind and rescind his permission for the Dutch to trade, had made contact with Adams and asked for help in meeting Ieyasu and obtaining an audience with the new Shogun.

CHAPTER 10

TRADE WITH THE DUTCH

❧

On 27 July 1609, the governor's barge carrying the first official Dutch emissaries, Jacob van den Broeck, Nicolaes Puyck and Melchoir van Santvoort, departed from Hirado to visit Ieyasu in Sumpu. Throughout the long journey Puyck recorded his view of Japan. He found the country 'very beautiful….high and mountainous….very populous and fertile' on the land and 'small sails everywhere' on the water.

Two days later, one of these small sails drew up alongside the governor's barge. It carried a messenger from Lord Matsura, who expressed his master's delight at the Dutch arrival and informed them that the lord, whose ship was on the water midway from Osaka, was awaiting them. Later in the day, another of his boats came to provide them with gifts of salted salmon and *sake*. In return, they presented the lord with two lengths of silk, and sailed on for the Strait of Shimonoseki, at the tip of Honshu, the main island. They passed through the strait at night and at noon they moored in the shelter of Mukō-jima, a small island off Honshu's southern shore, some sixty miles east of the strait. There they waited for the ideal wind that would speed their barge into the Inland Sea.

Before the end of the following day, the wind turned to the west and allowed the barge to curve up to Kaminoseki, Honshu's southeastern cape. From the cape, the direction was north-east, up the Inland Sea. At dusk they met another of Lord Matsura's boats, from which a messenger informed them that his master had anchored with three of his barges just off Yashiro Island, which was not so far from where they were. The Dutch emissaries anchored near one of the barges and embarked. On the barge, they were finally welcomed in person by Matsura Shigenobu (see Plate 10). His imposing figure, very young-looking for a sixty-five-year old, impressed Puyck. Puyck writes that the lord was 'gay in spirit' and 'very curious to hear or see all things foreign'.[191] They had a satisfactory exchange well into the night and were provided with a letter of recommendation to the Shogun by one of Matsura's retainers. The visitors returned to their own barge in high spirits.

On 4 August, the party sailed up the Yodo River, the estuary to the metropolis of Osaka. A few miles before their destination, they were caught up in a marine traffic jam, with, they estimated, some five hundred large and small vessels.

The Dutch visitors were amazed at the sprawling and commercially flourishing metropolis of Osaka. They had never seen this kind of city before. The only familiar sight was the canals of Osaka, as in Amsterdam, the commercial capital of their home country. Most houses were one-storey and all were constructed of wood, clay and paper. Their sliding doors were mostly left open, but protected from wind, rain and snow by *Noren*, a short curtain, so passers-by could see inside, where shop-owners and workmen plied their trades. The demarkation lines between the commercial areas and the Buddhist temples and shrines were remarkably informal, given the usual tensions between the two. It was well known that in the commercial areas a large number of hostels and inns served nightly pleasures for business travellers.

The emissaries were transferred to a small craft. When the craft approached the side of the canal, her passengers were warmly welcomed by two waving and smiling men. They were *De Liefde* survivors, Jan Joosten van Lodensteyn and Pieter Janszoon. As Jan Joosten and Pieter had to depart for Nagasaki on 5 August for business reasons, the fellow countrymen spent only one night and one

---

[191] De Lange, William.

day enjoying each other's company and exchanging experiences. Back on board, the emissaries continued their journey, heading for the castle town of Fushimi. The following evening, they arrived there and lodged for one night. Next day, they mounted horses and continued their journey on land.

It was now high summer in Japan. Typically, this is a terribly humid time of year and the heat would have been sweltering. On the road, the Dutch seamen came to miss the cool and fresh breeze when they were on the water. The only time they had cool comfort was in the early hours of the morning and in the shade of *Matsu-no-ki*, the pine trees. Although the two-hundred-mile journey was tiresome, it gave the Western visitors some unique experiences on the Tōkai-dō, the main eastern highway. They were fascinated at the magnificent scenery, mountains that ran down to the sea, lakes encircled by forests. Soldiers, merchants, peddlers, messengers, pilgrims and countrymen and women bustled endlessly up and down the road. With speed and efficiency the horses were changed at each post town, so that, despite the heat, the emissaries exceeded thirty-five miles a day and arrived in Sumpu on 13 August 1609.

When the Dutch party reached Sumpu, they were welcomed by two more of the *De Liefde* crew, Pieter Blancket and Thomas Corneliszoon. Soon after they departed from Osaka, they had met two other *De Liefde* survivors; so they had now met half of the remaining crew of the vessel without realizing that it was all arranged by William Adams. Some of these *De Liefde* crew members were living in Uraga, part of Adams' estate, and were married to Japanese women. Their spoken Japanese was good. They seemed very happy to become permanent residents there, even though they had permission from the Shogun to return home with their fellow countrymen's arrival. Puyck offered them free passage, but all of them replied that they would remain 'in that place of their own free will'.[192] Two of these men informed the Dutch envoys that the Portuguese party, which Specx and Van Santvoort had seen in Nagasaki, had arrived in Sumpu three days earlier. The commander had

---

[192] Ibid·

expected an immediate audience with the Shogun, but despite his insistent requests, he was ordered to wait his turn until the Dutch had been received.

On the same day of their arrival, the Dutch emissaries were informed that they should see Gotō Shōzaburō, Master of the Mint. He was, like William Adams, one of Ieyasu's talented retainers. Ieyasu had been closely protected by these selected and trusted retainers, since he yielded the formal affairs of state to his son Hidetada and moved to his retirement home. A long time before the Battle of Sekigahara, Gotō had pledged to support Ieyasu's armies and was now the best man to handle his finances.

The Dutch envoys remembered to give tangible expression to their respect, with a gift of three lengths of satin. After Gotō accepted the gift, he informed his guests that he would report their arrival and their request to Ieyasu. The Dutch visitors were then invited to the residency of Honda Masanobu, head of the Council of Regents. They found Lord Honda well-mannered, at ease with Westerners and clearly a close friend of Adams. He often worked as Ieyasu's foreign minister. He was also the officer who personally authorized all applications for a red-seal passport, including the one which was issued for Quaeckernaeck and Van Santvoort to sail for Pattani. Honda accepted the letter of recommendation from Lord Matsura, but would not accept any of their gifts. Instead he simply expressed his welcome to the Western guests and promised to arrange an audience with Ieyasu the next day.

Next day, in Ieyasu's residency, the Dutchmen behaved exactly as Adams had advised, exchanging many compliments in the Japanese manner. When the time came for the audience with Ieyasu, the door was opened by an elaborately dressed courtier. Puyck was called in and ordered to leave his gifts of raw silk and bars of lead on a little display table. He was then ushered before Ieyasu to pay his respects. He saluted Ieyasu. At that moment his doubts about the outcome of their mission evaporated. The well-built and gentle-looking ruler showed that he was 'very pleased' with all the gifts and genuinely so. He seemed to feel particular gratitude for the respectful letter from the Dutch Prince Maurits, the kind of respect that the King of Spain had never shown.

Ieyasu fired a volley of questions at Puyck, how many soldiers the Dutch fleet had on the Moluccas, if they were trading in Borneo, if it was true that they could find the best camphor. Next, Ieyasu quizzed him about the best products found in northern Europe and which other scented wood the Dutch had in their country and which one they valued most. After Puyck's answers were interpreted, matching what he had learnt from Adams before, Ieyasu was evidently pleased. In Puyck's own words, he 'offered free traffic, promised to reimburse our expenses and assisted us in case we were in need of money'.[193]

On 18 August, Pessoa at last received his audience with Ieyasu, but he failed to persuade him to exclude the Dutch. Two days later, the Dutch envoys were summoned by Ieyasu again. This time, the Shogun presented the Dutchmen 'with a beautifully ornamented Japanese sword',[194] and a written and translated reply to Prince Maurits sealed with the *shuin*, the red imprint of his great seal of state. The three other official documents were permissions for trading rights, to establish a trading house as large as they wished in Nagasaki, and to bring their goods and merchandise to sell there as best they could (see Plate 19). The Dutch record reveals their delight that the permission was 'in no way restricted as the Portuguese are, who have watchmen in their ships by night and day, whilst a fixed price is set upon their merchandise and they cannot sell it for a penny more, all of which they deeply regret'.[195] The Dutch envoys then travelled to Edo for the formality of their audience with Shogun Hidetada, which passed off successfully.

On 3 September, the Dutch emissaries set sail from Osaka for Hirado. The following day, as the governor's barge approached the eastern narrows between Honshu and the island of Shikoku, the Dutchmen met one of the Shogun's ships, piloted by William

Adams. In fact, the ship was one built by Adams, although they did not know that. What was becoming clear was how much they owed to this confident Englishman. On a calm Inland Sea, the meeting was brief. Adams was the first to greet them. He explained that he had come from Hirado, where he had been sent with letters from the Shogun. He was instructed by Lord Matsura to express his friendship to them and inform them that the lord had provided them with a large house and a plot of land to establish a factory in Hirado. As they parted, the Dutch emissaries urged Adams to continue his support for them with the Shogun and Lord Matsura. Adams promised to do so, as 'a friend of the Netherlands and to regard it as his fatherland'.

On 13 September, the Dutch envoys returned to Hirado, where they learnt that four weeks earlier Adams had visited their ships in the company of Governor Hasegawa on a courtesy call. Adams had advised the Dutchmen to obey absolutely the Japanese rules and regulations and to refrain from the arrogant and presumptuous behaviour that the Spanish and Portuguese had showed, which had caused them such trouble. After Hasegawa had left Hirado, Adams had stayed on to help negotiate a site for a Dutch factory with Lord Matsura.

On Adams' advice, the Dutch ship's council had prepared gifts for all the important people with whom they had to deal. Respecting the Japanese custom, each of the gifts was selected according to the recipient's status. They had sent Governor Hasegawa generous gifts, such as an exquisite ornamental Dutch harquebus, fifteen bars of lead, fifteen lengths of the highly-prized scarlet cloth, some large flasks filled with olive oil, Spanish wine and brandy; whilst his interpreter and senior servant had been given a length of damask each. Similar presents had been offered to Gotō Shōzaburō and Honda Masanobu. For Lord Matsura, who continued to show great interest in Western armaments and required all foreign vessels that entered Hirado to discharge at least one piece of ordnance, the Dutch had given both the lord and his son 'a small piece of artillery, complete with powder and accessories'.[196] His servants and the

---

[196] De Lange, William and Uni Book.

four guards who had been assigned to two of the Dutch vessels were also given rewards for their task. The total expenditure for all these gifts was the considerable sum of fl. (silver florin) 888.60, approximately £300 (in England in those times, £400 was an annual salary for knights of the realm). The expensive custom had surprised the Dutch ship's councillors, but they were convinced of it as an investment in their future prosperity.

On 20 September, the council met again. This time, they held a discussion on the organization of the factory. Unanimously they nominated Jacques Specx as the first Dutch factor, to be assisted by three merchants, Hans Verstrepen, Laurens Adriaenszoon, and Nicolaes Pieterszoon, and a young lad for errands, Crijn Corneliszoon. To help establish them in the Japanese market, they appointed Melchior van Santvoort to act as the East India Company's agent in Sakai. For this service, he would be paid the same as a captain's salary. One more man, Jan Cousynen, one of *De Liefde's* survivors, whom the envoys had met on the Tōkai-dō, was given a position as interpreter and would be paid almost half a captain's salary. Specx and his staff were to live in rooms above the factory, where they would be well looked after by a gentle and polite Japanese hostess and a small group of cooks and assistants. They could look forward to a reasonably comfortable life. The only disadvantage was the lack of European professional medical care. They had relied on the *Griffioen's* own physician, but soon after they arrived in Japan, he was stabbed during a brawl with one of his own crew members. With no medical care, both men had died of their wounds! So the factory's staff would have to treat themselves with limited medical supplies and a medical dictionary. They were not willing to try Japanese or Oriental herbal medicine, such as cauterization with moxa from dried *yomogi* (from the chrysanthemum family of plants).

However, what worried the Dutch more was how little merchandise was left from the token cargo, which had been brought from Pattani; '15,231 florins (£5163) worth of raw silk, 203 bars of lead, 12,000 pounds of paper, and some 300 Spanish *reals*',[197] was all

---

[197]   Blusse, L. and Uni Book.

they had to trade with until the next Dutch vessel arrived at Hirado, whenever that would be. As a contribution to the advancement of Dutch-Japanese commerce, these items were 'modest at best'.[198] They would certainly have to rely on favours from the Japanese authorities, but also on a good relationship with the English pilot, Lord Miura Anjin. So on the eve of their departure from Japan, on 2 October 1609, the Dutch ship's council carefully instructed Specx, in all matters to obey the requests from the lord of Hirado and the governor of Nagasaki. For William Adams, and to 'sustain him in his devotion', they decided Specx should regularly send him presents. When later at sea Puyck writes his report, he records it as of supreme importance that 'attention be paid to the pilot of the ship of Jacob Quaeckernaeck, who resides in Japan, for he is a man of standing and has great prestige and intimacy with the Emperor (Shogun)'.

Specx visited Adams to express his country's appreciation that 'everything had been done well through his help'.[199] Adams wrote with evident satisfaction: 'I have got them the trading privilege that the Spaniards and Portuguese could never get in their fifty or sixty years in Japan.'[200]

In front of the Dutch factory, a mud-walled warehouse on whose roof the company flag now flutters beside the Dutch national flag, Specx and Adams bid farewell to the *Griffioen* and the *Roode Leeuw met Pylen*. Adams mentions that his letters to his wife and friends must have reached England by now, so he hopes that the English East India Company will be established in Japan soon. When the Dutch captain nods in support and expresses the hope that Adams' dream will come true the following year, a look may have passed between him and Specx which Adams does not notice, because hope rises in his heart again.

It is a well-known milestone in Japanese history that the Dutch East India Company established itself in Japan in 1609 and since

---

[198] De Lange, William.
[199] Ibid.
[200] Ibid.

then the friendship between the Japanese and the Dutch has been close. What is less well known is that this would not have happened without the help of an Englishman, William Adams – help that he was later to regret.

One month passed and Adams received a letter from Van Santvoort in Sakai. In the letter, he expressed his thanks for Adams' help to establish the Dutch East India Company in Hirado, which was now developing well. He reported that he had been appointed an agent for the company, but as he was settled with his Japanese wife in Osaka, he had agreed to help only during the preparation phase. When Santvoort mentioned his wife and that Adams, Sukeji and Captain Quaeckernaeck had met her before, Adams and Sukeji guessed she was the *Kabuki* dancer, with whom he had exchanged presents outside the theatre in Osaka.

A few days later, Adams was summoned urgently by Lord Matsura Shigenobu. In a chamber of his Hirado Castle, the lord asked Adams anxiously how he would explain a letter from the Shogun, which had just arrived from Edo. In the letter, the Shogun ordered that all the vessels shipping over 500 *koku* or 90,000 litres, belonging to lords in the entire western region, should be seized and no new vessel built. All such vessels in the lords' possession should be sent to Ura Port immediately. The official reason given was that no lord should have a vessel large enough to carry an army. Adams had no inside information as to why the order was issued, but when he considered which vessels carried over 500 koku cargo, he realized it must be the *shuin-sen*, Red-seal ships. After the government permitted the Dutch East India Company to open up trade, it was likely that lords in the Western region would increase the number of Red-seal ships for trade that would help them build up armaments. Adams wondered whether the Shogun intended to impose a government monopoly on the Red-seal ships, because Ieyasu was cautious of attacks from these wealthy lords, some of whom were already much richer than the Shogun himself.

Adams explained these possible reasons, but Shigenobu looked sceptical. After a while, Shigenobu said bluntly that Ieyasu must be angry that the Dutch East India Company had chosen the Hirado

Port when he had wanted them to set up in Uraga Port near Edo. However, that was not his fault; he had never been involved in the company's decision. The merchant director Specx had decided. Adams must have strangled a wry smile, thinking what an old fox Shigenobu was! It was now clear to Adams that Shigenobu and Specx had found they shared the same goals and had made the decision together on the Hirado Port. Adams was not offended, because he hoped the Dutch East India Company would build a smooth-running business with the right partner. Adams promised Shigenobu to pass on a respectful response to Ieyasu's letter.

Many Japanese merchants in Nagasaki, Sakai and other prefectures now gathered in Hirado to buy raw silk from the Dutch merchants. Although, after a warning from Lord Matsura, they made light of the matter, they were, in fact, dissatisfied with the higher than expected prices. They accepted them because, on Adams' advice, the Dutch offered the other commodities at prices ten to twenty per cent below those of the Portuguese. After a long and risky voyage, it was common for all the merchandise to be traded at several times base costs, but Adams had persuaded Specx that the priority was to undermine the Portuguese monopoly. The Japanese merchants were in fact able to sell the raw silk to wealthy lords and upper-class customers at several times higher prices and the government was able to benefit from a higher tax take or *zatsu-zei*. The low prices from the Dutch merchants on other commodities created higher profits and a stronger economy.

Although Specx had agreed to sell all goods in his factory, he had actually hidden half. Adams found Specx another old fox, but he was tolerant because he understood that the situation was precarious until the next ship came.

Before leaving Hirado for Uraga, Adams satisfied himself that the new business for the Dutch East India Company was off to a reasonable start. He was dissatisfied that Specx had given him only a trifling amount of merchandise for Ieyasu, such as woollen cloth, cotton and deer skin. Specx explained it was because the prices he was able to charge were low, so he wanted to hold most of the goods in their warehouse until the market was better. Reluctantly,

Adams agreed to make the excuse that the company had received only a modest amount of merchandise from Pattani and, as they were cautious about first-time trade at Uraga, they were shipping samples this time.

On the way to Uraga, Adams' ship anchored at the Shimizu Port in Sumpu, where Ieyasu resided. Adams gives Ieyasu some presents from Specx and informs him that the early trade between the Dutch and Japanese merchants in Hirado has been very successful, a sell-out of almost all the goods. As a result, he is unable to bring many goods to Uraga this time, but he will bring more next time. Ieyasu is probably only partly convinced. He is more interested in asking about Matsura Shigenobu. He imagines that Shigenobu is delighted to be the first to make a big profit. Adams senses it might be wise to pretend not to know anything about Shigenobu's business. He changes the subject to report that Shigenobu is ready to comply with the decree forbidding large vessels, but has expressed reservations. Ieyasu says knowingly, 'I think so'[201] and then turns away. When Lord Honda Masanobu realizes that Adams might be about to object to the decree, he moistens his thin lips and informs Adams that the number of lords granted the Red-seal licence has increased to seventy-five and the number of licensed ships, which have sailed from Japan to Luzon, Annan and Siam so far, has increased to 169. If these ships are developed into military vessels, very large numbers of soldiers could be conveyed. To protect the government, the Shogun has to issue the decree. Ieyasu breaks his silence, saying, 'nothing is better than precaution'. Lord Honda gives Adams a sign not to mention this subject any more.

Ieyasu had good reasons to be suspicious. An ancestor of Lord Matsura Shigenobu had prospered in private trade with the Chinese, including with its smugglers in the Ryukyu Archipelago (then part of China and today's Okinawa in Japan). This was after he discovered that it would take only six or seven days to reach the archipelago from Hirado, helped by the Tsushima Current. Later his sea troops came into conflict with Korean troops from Tsu-

---

[201] Author's words.

shima Island, who obstructed trade between the north-west part of Nagasaki and the Chŏsen (Korean) Peninsula. In reprisal, Matsura's sea troops took up pirating along the Korean coast. As we learned earlier, they were called *wakō*; *wa* means Japanese and *kō* means pirate in Chinese and Korean. In the Kamakura era (1185–1333) the *wakō* had been banned, but after the Mongolians raided Japan in 1274 and 1281, *wakō* activity increased. Korean envoys visited the Japanese ruler to request him to issue a decree forbidding *wakō*, but Korean products fetched a high price in Japan and so the *wako* numbers did not decline at all.

Towards the end of the Muromachi era (1336–1573), the twenty-fifth Lord Matsura Takanobu, father of Shigenobu, was the one most blessed with business acumen. He had not only supported the *wakō* in the Tung Hai, part of the East-China Sea, but also, in 1542, warmly welcomed to Hirado the great Chinese pirate Ōchoku (Wang Zhi in Chinese) from the Kingdom of Min. Ōchoku was admiral of a fleet of three hundred ships with several thousand retainers. He had made an enormous profit from smuggling prohibited commodities from the Satsuma and Itsu-shima Islands in Japan to Luzon (Philippines), Annam (Vietnam), Siam (Thailand), Malacca and other Asian countries. The authorities of the Kingdom of Min had put a price on his head and spread a nationwide dragnet to catch him. In the full knowledge that Ōchoku was a notorious pirate, Takanobu still treated him handsomely, opening his Hirado Port for him and handing over his own Byakko-san Castle, after he had himself moved to the Kotachi Castle, newly built in Sakikata.

Ōchoku built a Chinese-style mansion beside his castle and titled himself the '*Ki-O*' [Little Graceful King]. The 'king' gave Takanobu frequent gifts, pirated from many foreign countries. He became a middle-man between smugglers. Hirado flourished as the main city in western Japan where wealthy merchants from Osaka and Kyoto came to buy jewels, ivory, skins, sweets, satin, etc., all at high prices. Takanobu then requested Ōchoku to persuade the Portuguese ships to use the Hirado port. He knew that Ōchoku had a close business partnership with a Portuguese trader and, in 1543, had been on board the Portuguese ship which arrived at Tanega-shima Island in Kagoshima Prefecture, southern Japan, when the Portuguese first introduced Western muskets. The Portuguese had selected this island port because it was where the Spanish missionary Francisco Xavier had arrived and settled in July 1549.

In 1555, Takanobu realized his ambition and with it a large quantity of the new Western-style weapons such as muskets and *harakan* or small cannon. Those weapons would be useful in feuds with the neighbouring lords, Ōmura Sumitada, Ryuzoji Takanobu and Arima Harunobu. However, when Takanobu asked the Portuguese how to use the *harakan* cannon, the Portuguese would only agree if he converted to Christianity. This was a problem to a faithful Buddhist. Eventually, he explained to the Portuguese why he must decline, but that he had three of his senior retinue, Koteda Sadatsune and the Kageyū brothers, who were willing to convert to Christianity. As a result of this strategy, Takanobu learned how to use the cannon and also how to make gunpowder. After obtaining all he wanted, Takanobu ordered the three converts to desert their religion. His craftiness and that of his son Shigenobu was notorious.[202] The Portuguese were understandably resentful and seemed to have given up on the Matsura clan. So in 1611, Shigenobu was delighted at the prospect of a close partnership with the Dutch, and potentially with the Spanish, too.

After leaving Ieyasu's residence on the way to his own, Adams pondered Ieyasu's disquiet, rather greater than he had expected, that the Dutch had chosen to locate their company at Hirado on generous terms from Shigenobu. He just wondered whether such negative feelings had prompted Ieyasu to issue the decree forbidding large vessels in the western regions. Adams was not surprised that, with such huge profits available from trade, Ieyasu's and Shigenobu's ambitions might be on a collision course. If so, the winner

---

[202] A later member of the Matsura clan was more respected. Lord Matsura Seizan [1760-1841] was not only a good swordsman but a noted scholar, artist and poet. He wrote a total of 178 books on politics, diplomacy and military affairs, many of which are still studied today.

was obvious. Although Adams had no obligation to Shigenobu, he had sympathies for the terrible price he might have to pay later. Adams was thinking that when he returned to Hirado, he would advise Specx to move the Dutch East India Company to Uraga or Sakai.

On the way to Uraga, Adams called at Itō. Whenever he could and spontaneously, it had become his habit at night to relax in a hot spring bath in the valley there. As he valued his privacy and preferred not to bother with the modesty towel, he asked his men to leave him alone. The men, who already knew Adams' preference, had gone to separate spring baths. The bitterly cold winter wind would have cut him to the bone. Naked now, Adams hangs a lantern on a branch of a tree and hurries to sink into the hot water. When he looks up at the sky, he feels as if the countless twinkling stars are gliding down towards him. As his body, numb with cold, warms up, he has that familiar tingling sensation all over his body, like the tips of a thousand massaging fingers.

Suddenly, there is a sharp sound and something glances off Adams' ear. Adams thinks that an owl has flown past, but there has been no flapping sound. Then through the darkness, he glimpses above him a figure leaping from one tree to another. Adams notices a human form, clothed completely in black. Could it be a *Ninja*? He immediately dives into the spring water and edges closer to the rock where he has left his sword. As soon as Adams draws the sword, the *Ninja* springs closer, undeterred. Adams jumps away, and then hacks down the hanging lantern with his sword. Everything vanishes in the ebony blackness. 'Villain! Villain! Is there anyone to help me',[203] shouts Adams. Then he hurls a stone at where the villain has been. There is the sound of bushes being brushed aside as someone runs away, then loud voices from many people, 'Anjin-sama, Anjin-sama, are you safe?'[204] and 'Damn! Where is the devil?'[205] He sees the lights of lanterns floating in the

---

[203] Author's words.
[204] Ibid.
[205] Ibid.

darkness as if fireflies are flitting around. Adams jumps into his clothes and then orders all his mariners to go back to the ship. In the dim light of lanterns they pick their way cautiously through the undergrowth to Itoh harbour.

At the break of dawn, all of Adams' men, except two he had left to guard the ship, went back to the scene where Adams had been attacked the previous night. They found footprints in a cedar forest some four or five yards away from Adams' spring bath. One of the men picked up a three-inch dart and called the others over. The dart was made with *washi* (lacquered paper made from straw), in which a needle was fitted. Adams warned him not touch the needle; venom had been applied to its tip. In the same area, they found two more darts and a dead wild boar which had probably licked the needle.

Adams must have wondered who could be trying to kill him. It had been nine years since he arrived in Japan, so it would not be surprising if somebody had developed a grudge. The villain might be one of Ieyasu's former enemies in the Sekigahara battle, but they would normally take revenge against Ieyasu directly, so could it be the Portuguese Jesuits? After Ishida Mitsunari was executed, Father João Rodrigues had revealed how much he hated Adams. That look would have flashed into Adams' mind now. But who was the assassin? Ten more mariners had joined Adams' ship in Itō and only one new mariner was employed in Hirado. As they walked back to their ship, Adams suggested the chief mariner should report the attempted assassination to the Mishima Police Office, but the chief, who trusted all his fellows as much as his family, hesitated. Just when the chief was finally persuaded by Adams, somebody in front raised the alarm. Adams and all the mariners saw clouds of smoke billowing from their ship. Adams drew water from the sea into a wooden bucket, poured it over himself and jumped into the ship. His mariners all followed him. They found the fire had started in some cargo, laid at the bottom of the ship's hold. There was the unmistakable smell of burning wool. The walls and ceiling were on fire. All the mariners formed a human chain and passed bucket after bucket to the source of the fire. It took a couple of hours for the flames to die and turn to dense smoke. Inside the flooded, smelly and smoky hold, Adams and the mariners, some of whom had burnt skin, hair and eyebrows, then carried all the merchandise up to the deck and doused it in water.

Back on deck, the chief mariner bowed low to Adams in deep apology for having disagreed to his earlier suggestion. He asked Adams to come to a room used by security guards on the stern deck. There he uncovered the body of the Uraga-born young guard, Chokichi, the white of his eyes showing. A dart tipped with venom had been stabbed deep into the back of Chokichi's neck and then his body had been hidden behind a pile of fishing nets. The other guard, Sōbei, who had been recruited in Hirado, had disappeared, so it was assumed that all the offences had been done by him, including the failure to assassinate Adams earlier. Adams guessed Sōbei could be one of some 500 converted Japanese-Catholics in Hirado, open therefore to manipulation by the Portuguese. He had trusted Sōbei, who had showed great enthusiasm for learning European piloting. His anger welled up at both Sōbei's deceitfulness and his own gullibility.

When the *goyo yakunin* or local police arrived, Adams described all the incidents and surmised that the offences had been done by somebody trying to obstruct new trade between Japan and the Dutch. Sōbei was thought to have escaped by swimming to shore. The senior officer took Sōbei's description and promised to issue copies of it along the highway and arrest him as soon as possible.

In his residence in Sumpu, Ieyasu was surprised at Adams' unexpected visit. Adams reported on all the attacks, to which he felt it was important to alert Ieyasu immediately. When Ieyasu learnt that the villain had disguised himself as a mariner and carried venomous darts, he assumed he was a *Ninja* or Japanese spy, hired perhaps by the Portuguese but equally by Matsura Shigenobu. Adams was struck dumb. Ieyasu said he was almost sure that Shigenobu was annoyed that all his trade vessels had been commandeered by the government and saw Adams as a threat. As a close adviser to the Shogun, who would report to his ruler on all the affairs that Shigenobu was involved in with the Dutch, Adams was dangerous. It would not surprise Ieyasu if Shigenobu had plotted to burn down all the merchandise in Adams' ship to prevent him from opening a rival trade branch at Uraga. Ieyasu guessed that Shigenobu's real target was Adams' master, the Shogun himself. He mentioned a Japanese phrase, which Adams understood to be, in English, 'he who hates Peter harms his dogs'.[206] Adams suggested this might be an exaggeration, but it was clear from Ieyasu's blank expression that he thought he knew better.

Ieyasu was known to be a fearless ruler, but he was often suspicious and cautious of people, particularly from the samurai families older and of higher status than his. He had an analytical personality and often constructed hypotheses. Even if another's evidence was to the contrary, when the hypothesis felt right, he would stick with it. He would now test his hypothesis that Shigenobu was plotting. If it was true, he would be ready.

Adams and his men came back to Itō and burnt all the damaged merchandise on the beach. After work, and in spite of the shocks that Adams had experienced, they spent a leisurely evening soaking in the hot spring bath. This time, Adams wisely bathed with his men: Sōbei was still at large.

---

[206] Ibid.

CHAPTER 11

A TOEHOLD FOR THE SPANISH

చి

On 30 September 1609 (3 September in the Japanese calendar), Ieyasu sent Adams to the Onjuku Harbour, Chiba, about 120 miles from Edo, in territory controlled by Lord Honda. This is the harbour, famous even in modern Japan, in which pearl oysters are collected by women divers, who also provided throughout history a remarkable rescue service for shipwrecked sailors. There Adams saw the wrecked vessel, the *San Francisco*, which had drifted into Japanese waters on 25 July. It had been en route from the Philippines to Acapulco, Nova España, with former Philippine Governor Don Rodrigo de Vivero Velasco and 421 other passengers. Initially Adams was alarmed that, after he had ended the Portuguese trade monopoly, here were the Spanish, close allies of the Portuguese and Catholic to boot, turning up near to Edo and Uraga and not to the western ports, as he would have expected. He reassured himself that the Spanish could do nothing from a shipwreck. For a moment, perhaps, he was forgetting his own experiences!

The Spanish governor and all 371 survivors were under the protection of Lord Honda. The governor stayed in his house, but under close interrogation the governor felt they were being confined rather than protected. He was becoming weary of repeating the same answer that his vessel had been wrecked on the way home after his term as governor had expired in the Philippines.

Ieyasu had told Lord Honda that Adams was to be assigned as interpreter. Lord Honda explained to Adams that when these survivors were rescued, they were almost frozen to death. The women divers had pulled them to shore, stripped them of their wet clothes and enveloped them with their own naked bodies until their body warmth returned. Not surprisingly, Governor Vivero records his intense gratitude for this unusual service.

Adams described Vivero to be in his fifties, rather stout, serious-looking and with a big black moustache. However, in his shabby clothes the governor looked wretched. When Adams introduced himself as Miura Anjin in Japanese and William Adams by birth, Vivero was clearly surprised at an Englishman serving as a close retainer to the Japanese ruler. Although Adams was reluctant to interpret for his enemy, Vivero was so unexpectedly friendly that Adams was embarrassed. Vivero gripped Adams by the shoulders and touched cheeks with Adams several times. Japanese lords and officials would have been astonished at this extraordinary scene. Then Vivero introduced himself as a Spaniard, but now from Nova España. Pleasantries over, he still chose the Jesuit Juna Baptiste Porro as his interpreter, rather than Adams.

At an audience in Sumpu, Ieyasu gave Vivero a warm welcome. Ieyasu, who already knew something from Adams about Nova España, asked Vivero about his country. Vivero explained how in 1492 the Italian explorer Christopher Columbus, with support from the Spanish Queen Isabel, had sailed across the Atlantic and discovered a new continent. Columbus believed that the continent was part of India and it was another Italian explorer Amerigo Vespucci, after whom the new continent was eventually named, who proved him wrong. Since then, the Spanish had set out to explore America. In 1521, the Spanish explorer Hernán Cortés defeated the Aztec tribe and invaded Mexico. Following that triumph, Francisco Pizarro conquered the Inca Empire in Peru in 1532. Eventually his countrymen had succeeded in colonizing vast areas of South America and contributed greatly to his country's wealth, power and prestige.

After Vivero's explanation, Adams sensed a chance to direct Ieyasu to the evidence of Spain's colonizing intentions, but Ieyasu was still very interested in South America and asked Vivero about Mexican products. Vivero answered that the main products were gold and silver, particularly the silver produced from the Potosi Silver Mine. The Mexican coins cast with this silver had a reputation for high quality and many other countries had been using the coins for trade. At this, Ieyasu was seen slightly to raise his thick eyebrows.

Vivero would have noticed this hint of interest. He suddenly started crying, wiping copious tears with a small towel and proclaiming his great appreciation of Ieyasu's generous help. He then begged Ieyasu to give him another favour by helping him and the other passengers to return home. Adams found Vivero's behaviour rather theatrical. The undemonstrative Ieyasu probably felt the same, but to Adams' dismay he willingly agreed to help.

However, before helping, Ieyasu said he would have some questions about the gold and silver mines in Nova España. He first asked how gold and silver were refined in his country. Vivero proudly answered by the amalgam technique, where the gold and silver present in ores were extracted with mercury. Ieyasu asked how exactly the mercury was used. Vivero had to admit he did not know; only the mining engineers knew that. Ieyasu asked whether Vivero could send fifty experts in silver mining from Mexico to Japan. Vivero abruptly became a completely different person, from the man who had cried so dramatically ten minutes before. He would require some things in exchange... protection for Spanish Catholic priests in Japan, support for the shipwrecked *San Francisco* and her sister ship the *Santa Ana*, and finally the expulsion of the Dutch trading company from Japan. Ieyasu calmly accepted his requests, except the last. He additionally offered to lend him a Japanese vessel for his return to Nova España. He also invited Vivero to stay in Japan as long as he wished. Vivero asked Ieyasu for permission to survey the *Santa Ana*, which lay at anchor in the Usuki Harbour. If he found the ship unrepairable for a homeward voyage, he would take up Ieyasu's offer. With this permission, Vivero left for Usuki.

After Vivero had gone, Ieyasu remarked on Adams' morose mood. Adams tried to recover his composure and insist gently that the Spanish were no different from the Portuguese; they were pirates who intended to conquer the whole world, under the cloak of a religious mission. Ieyasu patiently explained his decision to hire the Mexican experts in silver mining. He was concerned that the yield of gold and silver had decreased recently, despite Japan's many gold and silver mines in Sado-Aikawa, Iwami, Tajima-Ikuno, Izu, Hitachi and elsewhere. The Japanese techniques of refining, called *Seikan* and *Haisui* and invented in the Muromachi era, were limited and had not improved at all since 1573. Lord Honda, sitting beside Ieyasu, made the additional comment that although the Portuguese monopoly had ended, a Dutch monopoly had begun. According to Adams' own advice, he gently reminded him, any monopoly would cause corruption. Ieyasu felt sorry to disappoint Adams, so he asked Adams to trust him and that he still respected Adams' advice and efforts.

Vivero travelled south down the Tōkai-dō on a horse, through Kyoto, Fushimi and Osaka and then to Usuki by sea. There he confirmed that the wrecked *Santa Ana* was irreparable and returned to Sumpu and reported as much to Ieyasu. Taking Ieyasu up on his invitation, Vivero decided to stay in Japan for a few months. During Vivero's travelling, Luis Sotelo, the Jesuit missionary aboard the *San Francisco*, was summoned to an audience with Ieyasu. Ieyasu had made a signed protocol to the King of Spain and wanted Sotelo to arrange for translation. The two manuals were then entrusted to the Catholic priest Alonzo Muños to pass on to the king. In the protocol, Ieyasu stated that he had lent the former Governor of the Philippines a 120-ton vessel (built by Adams) for his return home, and also the equivalent of 4,000 ducats for the voyage. In exchange, he asked the king for his protection of any Japanese trading ship and hospitality for its crew and merchant passengers whenever they arrived in Mexico. Ieyasu was particularly interested to discover how the Spanish had developed trade so successfully and he instructed Tanaka Shōsuke, as head of a trade mission consisting of twenty-three Japanese merchants, to join Vivero aboard the vessel bound for Mexico. The Kyoto-born Tanaka was the first Japanese merchant to sail across the Pacific. When Adams heard that Governor Vivero had renamed his vessel the *San Buena Ventura*, he regretted Ieyasu's decision (see Plate 11).

During Governor Vivero's stay, Sukeji became friends with Alfonso Galcio, one of Vivero's interpreters and Catholic priests, after Sukeji had looked after him when he was sick. Alfonso was impressed by the Japanese landscape and lifestyle. When he stood in front of the magnificent Mt Fuji with the clear blue Ashino Lake below and saw the steam from the hot springs rising from Ōshima Island to the south, he said to Sukeji: 'It is a mysterious and wonderful view.'[207] He admired the five-layered keep of the Edo castle that soared up so beautifully in the sunset. He also praised the wide, clean and tidy streets that he found almost everywhere in Japan. Sukeji heard that Governor Vivero had been particularly amazed at the scale and extravagance of Edo Castle. Although Sukeji realized their compliments were exaggerated, he was proud of his country. Alfonso told Sukeji many stories about the Philippines, Nova España, Luzon, Siam, Cambodia and Cochin China. Sukeji was surprised that there was a Japanese town in each country and about 3000 Japanese in Luzon alone. Former samurai, defeated by Ieyasu in 1600, had escaped there. Alfonso said: 'The Japanese are competing against the Europeans for business in these countries.'[208] After life with the aloof and serious Adams, Alfonso was amusing and fun to be with, but Sukeji's respect lessened somewhat when Alfonso said he would only wish to live in Japan if it was a Catholic country. Vivero recorded in his *Travel Journal to Japan* that he established a good friendship with Lord Honda and that he had never been blessed with as much happiness on his voyages before.

In the middle of December 1609, off the Kami-no (God) island, outside the port of Nagasaki, Lord Arima Harunobu and his troops attacked and sank the 900-ton Portuguese trader, *Madre*

---

[207] Translated by the author from Nishiyama Toshio.
[208] Ibid.

de Deus. On board was the former governor of Macao, André Pessoa. A few months before, Pessoa had had first-hand experience of Governor Hasegawa's duplicity over Portuguese and Dutch trade, when he eventually chose to support the Dutch. When the vessel, *Nossa Senhora da Graça* (Our Lady of Grace) with Pessoa as Captain-Major arrived in Nagasaki, Governor Hasegawa dispatched armed guards to inspect the ship's rich cargo. Pessoa, who was already bitter towards Hasegawa, had arrogantly refused to allow them aboard. Hasegawa tried to come aboard himself, but he, too, was rejected. He was angrier when he learnt that the captain was André Pessoa. It was he who had summarily executed a drunken Japanese crew who had gone on the rampage in Macao a few months before, injuring and murdering many Portuguese crew and Chinese civilians. Others of these drunken Japanese were imprisoned and forced to sign an affidavit declaring that they alone were responsible for their compatriots' deaths in Macao. After they were released, they came back to Japan with terrible tales of misery and suffering. To make matters worse, Pessoa had now demanded that Japanese merchants reduce the quantity of silk directly bought from Chinese merchants.

Ieyasu had not reacted badly when he heard about Pessoa's behaviour in Macao, but he was furious when he heard that Pessoa had shown such disrespect to Governor Hasegawa in Nagasaki. Rather than adopting an extreme policy, killing Pessoa with all the Portuguese, he invited Pessoa to attend his court to receive a full pardon for his role in the Japanese deaths in Macao. Pessoa, smelling a large rat, refused to attend the court and stayed in his secure armed ship. Ieyasu was enraged by this defiance in his own territorial waters, so he had ordered Lord Arima Harunobu to seize Pessoa and his vessel.

Arima was delighted at the chance for revenge, because it was some of his men who had been attacked in Macao. He gathered 1200 samurai warriors and in the first week of December 1609, by which time Pessoa had returned to Nagasaki on the *Madre de Deus*, he attempted a surprise attack against the vessel during the night. His warriors in thirty boats opened fire with their muskets.

Pessoa waited to return fire until the enemy were closer. Just two broadsides from his cannon and the Japanese flotilla was blown out of the water with many deaths. Arima's men repeatedly attempted to attack Pessoa's vessel, rowing bravely out into the bay, but they failed every time. After three nights of fighting, the Japanese retreated and Pessoa escaped to the safety of the open sea. Arima now searched desperately for a different tactic. He built a wooden boarding tower, which was carried by two big boats. The tower was as high as the Portuguese ship's mastheads and was protected by a wet cover against fire bombs. Arima also assembled around 1800 warriors. In January 1610, they began to attack Pessoa's vessel at around nine o'clock at night. Although the fight was horrific, a few Japanese warriors managed to clamber on board from the tower. However, before they could display their proud martial arts, they were chopped to pieces by the Portuguese; Pessoa killed two Japanese samurai with his own hands.

The Portuguese crew had already announced their victory, when all hell broke loose. A musket shot from one of the Japanese warriors hit a grenade that a Spanish guard was about to throw at the enemy. That explosion caused a mighty explosion of all the gunpowder on deck. The mizzen sail was consumed in flames within seconds and soon the whole of the superstructure was on fire. Pessoa immediately realized that his great ship was doomed and that he would have to face death. In a display of great courage, 'he left his sword and shield in his cabin and, without a word, went below taking a crucifix in one hand and a firebrand in another and set fire'[209] to the ship's stock of gunpowder. The explosion was immediate. The *Madre de Deus* split in two and sank in deep water, its captain's body blown to pieces.

In spite of this victory, some Japanese government officials were still indignant over the lack of respect shown to their Shogun and Japanese lords. They advised Ieyasu to kill all Portuguese traders in Nagasaki and exile all Jesuits, but wiser counsels prevailed and Ieyasu, who needed the trade, rejected their advice. However, he did

---

[209] Cooper, Michael.

dismiss his Portuguese interpreter at court, Padre João Rodrigues, and ordered him to pack his belongings and leave Japan. Ieyasu did not need him, because he had William Adams who he now found more trustworthy.

On 1 August 1610, Governor Vivero boarded the *San Buena Ventura* at Uraga Port and set sail for Acapulco. On board were Alonzo Muños, holding various presents in trust from Ieyasu, with Alfonso, Spanish missionaries, Tanaka Shōsuke and twenty-three Japanese merchants with a cargo of selected Japanese products. Adams saw off the vessel, but could not enjoy the familiar sight of the pattern of waves in the ship's wake and the flying fishes flapping their sparkling silver tail fins. He still regretted Ieyasu's decision. He was thinking of how to open trade with the English. He wondered why he had not yet received any reply to his letters from his family and friends.

On 27 October 1610, the *San Buena Ventura* anchored in the Matanchel Port, in the Gulf of California. At the end of the month, they arrived safely in Acapulco. On returning home, Governor Vivero became a retainer to the governor-general Conde (Count) de Curuna. Late in life, he was made a knight of Santiago, Cabellero de Santiago.

For the return mission to Japan, Sebastian Viscaino was appointed envoy. As Admiral of the Nova Espana Gold and Silver mining expedition since 1608, he was the right person for the job* (see page 171).

The new *San Francisco*, captained by Benit de Palacios, set sail for Japan on 22 March 1611, with Viscaino, four or five Spanish missionaries and twenty-three Japanese crew and merchants. Viscaino was tasked to return the 4,000 ducats, to present a Spanish clock to Ieyasu, and to study the 'gold and silver islands', presumably those to the east of Japan. The Japanese merchant Tanaka had failed in his trade negotiations with the Spanish, but was bringing back a map, a clock and a quantity of woollen cloth of five different colours. He was also bringing a large section from a mulberry tree, about 2.7 yards wide and 36 yards long. In those days, a supply of exotic timber was highly prized in Japan and even an object for sightseeing.

When the Spanish vessel reached the eastern coast of Japan, she encountered a typhoon and tidal wave or *tsunami*, which left her battered and drifting. The vessel was eventually surrounded by eight Japanese boats for questioning. When the Japanese guards saw Tanaka Shosuke, they relaxed. The Spanish were even more pleased when the guards guided their vessel to the Iwawada Offing in Chiba Prefecture. The next morning in calmer waters she headed for Uraga. On 10 June 1611 the *San Francisco* arrived safely at the Uraga Port.

Viscaino first presented his credentials to Shogun Hidetada in Edo. He cut an impressive figure, gorgeously attired in a doublet, a jacket, breeches, a ruff and a plumed cap with fine gold trimmings. On the way to one of the churches of the Society of San Francisco[sic.], the Spanish party encountered Lord Date Masamune of the Sendai clan marching with his troops from Sendai in the north-eastern region of Japan. The lord requested the Spanish party to stage a firing of the twenty-four Spanish muskets that Viscaino's retinue had brought. Reluctantly they blasted off the guns. After using up 'a barrel of gunpowder in the hour', the lord was astonished and very excited. At that moment, Viscaino never imagined that this tiresome encounter with this lord was his Karma. The lord would not just save his life later, but help his mission to be successful.

The Spanish party then travelled by land from Uraga to Sumpu for an audience with Ieyasu. When they arrived, they were given a warm welcome by Tanaka Shōsuke and his party. Viscaino solemnly presented Ieyasu with a Madrid-made alarm clock and repaid the 4,000 ducats. The Spanish also paid for the *San Buena Ventura*, which they desired to keep as a talismanic vessel in Nova España. According to Adams' account, *San Buena Ventura* was used by the Spanish as a trading ship, sailing regularly between Acapulco and Manila. After pleading his case with Ieyasu, Viscaino received his support for a gold and silver prospecting expedition.

Viscaino went back to Uraga to meet Mukai Shōgen, the chief of seafaring, with whom he developed a good rapport. With Mukai's assistance, Viscaino had another audience with Shogun Hidetada. When he was given the official permission for his expedition, he handed the Shogun a document setting out the terms. Firstly, he would order from Japanese ship-builders a ship for the expedition, less than 100 ton considering the limited number of crew; secondly, two Japanese controllers should board the ship to control the Japanese crew; thirdly, all the crew would be under the command of Viscaino himself, as Admiral; fourthly, no expense for the ship-building would fall on the Shogun; fifthly, the Red-seal *Shuin-sen* trade licence for the newly-built ship ought to be handed to Viscaino and when the ship arrived in Acapulco, if the governor of that country wanted to buy the ship, the Japanese would sell it at a low price; sixthly, if the Japanese needed a chief of ship-builders, a well-trained Spanish builder would be provided; and seventhly, the Japanese and the Spanish should make a reciprocal agreement under which, when the Japanese paid a salary to Spanish pilots and crew, they would be fully reimbursed by the Governor of Nova España.

Viscaino then visited the Sendai clan, accompanied by Friar Luis Sotelo. They were both given an audience with Lord Date Masamune of the clan who recalled the impressive display of firepower and, with the authorization from Shogun Hidetada, permitted them to prospect for gold and silver in his islands. Viscaino and Sotelo then travelled to Tsuki-no-ura at Okatsu Bay and Kuretsubo Beach in the eastern part of Miyagi Prefecture, north-east of Edo. After inspecting mines, they returned to Uraga.

Meanwhile, William Adams and Jacques Specx devoted much time to trying to convince Ieyasu that the King of Spain 'did not care about trade with Japan'.[210] His Christian majesty's priority, they said, was to save the pagan Japanese from hell, a 'desire that all nations should be taught the Holy Catholic Faith and thus be saved'.[211] So Viscaino's expedition was a precursor to the Spanish King sending a great fleet to colonize Japan. However, Ieyasu was more interested in Viscaino's report on the expedition to the north-eastern coasts of Japan. Viscaino had reported

---

[210] Viscaino, Sebastian.
[211] Ibid.

that the Spanish explorers had discovered a new island of 'Gold and Silver',[212] which, judging from a shipwreck in the vicinity, the Portuguese explorers had failed to find. When he learned he had been accused of preparing for a Spanish invasion, Viscaino told the Shogun and Ieyasu that the Dutch were the real 'devil of hell'[213] and if the Japanese rulers did not believe him, he would personally accompany Japanese officers back to the island to see for themselves.

Adams and Jacques Specx were now more alarmed at this discovery and Ieyasu's evident interest. Adams suggested to Specx that they should urgently provide Ieyasu with Dutch mining engineers. Specx immediately agreed and, as Adams had to remain in Sumpu for his duties to Ieyasu, rushed back to Hirado. There he hired a Chinese ship, *Karabune,* and despatched two staff from the Dutch factory to Pattani, with a request to Victor Sprinckel to arrange for some Dutch mining engineers in Pattani or Bantam to work in Japan for a while.

While Adams and Specx waited and watched events anxiously, another storm of news hit them. They both had felt relief that no Portuguese ship had come from Macao to Japan since the *Madre de Deus* disaster with Captain Pessoa in January 1610. However, Ieyasu was becoming disappointed that alternative trade with the Spanish and the Dutch was so slow to materialize. The Japanese ruler was particularly keen to resume trade with China. So when, in July 1611, a small vessel arrived unexpectedly from Macao with Dom Nuno de Soutomaior as an envoy, Ieyasu saw an opportunity. Soutomaior impressed him. For his part the envoy indicated his silent agreement that the disaster could be blamed on Captain Pessoa's 'mishandling of the situation',[214] while the Japanese on their side dropped the conditions which had been forced on the Macao merchants at Nagasaki in 1610. Japan's trade with the Portuguese would be resumed and the Great Ship could visit Nagasaki as before.

---

[212] Ibid.
[213] Ibid.
[214] Rodrigo, Don.

At the end of August 1611, a Dutch trading vessel arrived at Hirado with Dutch merchants and a Dutch mining engineer. The engineer, Van Andreezon, had been working near Bantam as an expert in gold and silver mining and as a master of the amalgam technique. He was professional enough to bring a lot of mercury with him. In an accompanying letter, however, Sprinckel said Andreezen was the only experienced mining engineer in Bantam and informed Specx that he could only be hired for a couple of months. He asked Specx to have Andreezen board the Dutch ship due to leave Japan for Pattani in October. Adams immediately took Andreezen to Sumpu for an audience with Ieyasu. Afterwards, with Honda Masazumi as a go-between, Adams introduced Andreezen to Ōkubo Nagayasu, director of the government's Mining Department.

Although Ieyasu did not reveal how pleased he was to have the Dutch mining engineer, he wanted him to get to work as soon as he could. He was frustrated that it had been three months since Viscaino's 'discovery' of the island and there was no report as yet of the actual discovery of gold and silver. His intelligence, from the Japanese officers accompanying the Spanish, was that the expedition had spent much more time on surveying the island rather than searching for gold and silver. Ieyasu initially wanted Andreezen to work in the highest yielding gold and silver mines in Sado in the north-east or Iwami to the west of Edo, but when he was informed that Andreezen would only be able to stay in Japan for two months, he chose the gold mine of Toi on the west coast of the Izu Peninsula, the nearest to Edo and which could be reached in half a day.

The gold mine of Toi had been discovered in 1577. Since then the mine had been controlled by the Hōjō clan. After the fall of the clan, the mine was taken over by the Toyotomi clan and was now under Ieyasu's control. The mine had greatly enriched the three rulers, as most of the gold produced was used to make *Koban*, the oval-shaped gold Japanese coins.

The harbour in Toi flourished with the comings and goings of its single-sail ships. Merchants, mariners, engineers, fishermen, farriers, peddlers and many others thronged the pebbled street, with its inns, tea-houses, pubs, old clothes shops, blacksmiths and other shops. Inn-owners calling out the dish of the day struggled to make themselves heard above the general hubbub and the sound of horses' hooves. Adams and his party climbed the rugged path to the mine. They chose an appropriate place where Andreezen would be able to demonstrate the amalgam technique. Andreezen gathered his 'pupils' around him. He crushed a piece of ore, washed it in cold water, collected the mineral powder from the ore and poured mercury into it. The mercury was then well blended with the metal. An alloy could be solid or liquid depending on the amount of mercury. Andreezen then distilled the mercury, evaporated it and abstracted the gold present in the ore.

Ōkubo and the speculators who had watched the demonstration were impressed at the use of mercury. Adams asked Ōkubo whether mercury could be found in Japan. When Ōkubo shook his head, Adams found himself planning how to bring mercury into Japan, before laughing at how the pilot was now playing the market. However, after receiving a satisfactory report on Andreezen's demonstration, Ieyasu did present Jacques Specx with *Shuin-jō*, the Red-seal certificate, which permitted the Dutch to send Dutch mining engineers to Japan and import mercury into the country.

* Don Rodrigo de Vivero Velasco was born and brought up in Kingdom of Castilla (Spain). He had worked as a page for Princess Reina Ana in his childhood. In the course of time, he sailed across to Nova España. In 1595, he became a chateau-guard of San Juan de Ulna. In 1599, he was appointed Director-General of Nova Vizcaya. In 1600, he became Director-General of Tasco Mining Town. In 1606, when Governor Petro of the Philippines suddenly died and the successor Silva had not returned from his exploratory voyage by the due time of 1608, Vivero temporarily became the successor. Late in his life, he became a distinguished member of the nobility.

 Sebastian *Viscaino* was born at Huelva in Spain. In 1567, he fought in a war against Portugal. In the course of time, he sailed across to Nova España. Between 1589 and 1595, he resided in the Philippines. In 1595, he was appointed as head of explorers with three ships for the South of California. For one year in 1596, Viscaino sailed to explore around Cedros (Cerros) Island, at latitude

29°N off California. In 1602, he commanded four ships and reached Cape Mendocino, and subsequently sailed on to Cape Sebastian, at latitude 43°N. In 1604, as Admiral of a Spanish fleet, Viscaino navigated from Acapulco to the Philippines. Late in his life, he was appointed Lord of the Avolos County in Nova Espana.

CHAPTER 12

BETRAYED

~

Since his arrival in Japan in August 1611, the Dutch mining engineer Van Andreezen, under Adams' supervision, had
been daily hard at work teaching Japanese engineers the amalgam technique. Adams had more of an affinity with this skilled
professional than with merchants. So in the evening after work,
he often took Andreezen to a hot spring bath in a valley very
similar to his favourite bathing place in Itō. One evening, they
were casually chatting as usual, soaking in the steaming bath,
when Andreezen mentioned something unexpected. He said that
in 1602 the English East India Company had established a permanent base in the Java Port of Bantam and English ships had
been sailing there for nearly a decade. Initially Adams wondered
what Andreezen was talking about. Andreezen explained that
the English East India Company had been formed in London
in December 1600 and the first branch for trading with the East
set up in India. They had now increased the number of branches,
including one in Bantam.

Adams was stunned and felt as if the steam all around him was
more like a suffocating fog. The year 1600 was when *De Liefde* first
drifted into Usuki Bay. Adams understood that nobody might have
heard about him in England for some time after, but wasn't it odd
that in 1609 when the Dutch vessel *Roode Leeuw met Pylen* arrived
from Bantam, neither Cornelis Matelieff nor Jacques Specx nor any

of the other Dutchmen had ever mentioned the English East India Company there?

Gradually and cruelly the fog lifted. He had been betrayed and on an unspeakable, massive scale for more than a decade. He realized that none of his letters to his wife and friends in England, which were entrusted to Captain Quackernaeck in 1605, would ever have reached England. Adams was on fire with fury, but he managed to control his emotion, so Andreezen, unaware, continued to talk. Looking at him, Adams for a moment saw a clone of his betrayers and came very close to striking him dead.

On the way home, Adams managed to look detached and dignified, but as soon as he entered his private room he exploded with fury. We can assume from Sukeji's description of his mood that Adams banged the table, smashed ornaments, tore bamboo screens off the windows, scattered papers and beat his fists on the floor, and eventually broke down. In his position as a feudal lord, several young mistresses would have been summoned to console and look after him, but this breakdown caused bouts of chronic depression for the rest of his life. In his log book, the style of his handwriting changed dramatically after this shock discovery.

The origins of this betrayal must have gone back further, but we do know that in 1605 in Pattani, Victor Sprinckel of the Dutch East India Company hatched the same plot. Sprinckel had been amazed to learn from Captain Quackernaeck that Adams, a mere English crew member, had succeeded in becoming a lord in Japan. He immediately saw advantages for the English East India Company, established by then and with a base in Bombay. England was a religious and military ally of the Netherlands, but in trade a rival. After giving careful consideration to all the circumstances, Sprinckel took the letters brought by Captain Quaeckernaeck, and pulled out all those from William Adams. Without Quaeckernaeck's and Santvoort's consent, Sprinckel proceeded to open and read Adams' letters, saying: '…. because of my administrative duties, I must open it. You are witnesses.'[215] Quaeckernaeck and Santvoort wondered

---

[215] Translated by the author from Oshima Masahiro.

what would happen to Adams' letters, but they were not allowed to ask any questions and had to go and dress up for a welcome party organized for the evening. Sprinckel was the host at the party and in front of twenty compatriots and guests cheerfully proposed a toast to goodwill between Japan and the Dutch East India Company (VOC) and to the VOC's success. He reported what he had learnt from Ieyasu's and Adams' official letters and expressed his gratitude for the efforts of Adams and Captain Quaeckernaeck's men, which had contributed so much to the VOC. Following the speech, Captain Quaeckernaeck too made a speech and expressed how delightful it was to be reunited with his compatriots some seven years since he had left Rotterdam. Nagai Rokuemon, Lord Matsura Shigenobu's retainer, also stood up to convey Lord Matsura's enthusiasm for future trade with the VOC. After applause and loud cheers, the feast began. For Quaeckernaeck and Santvoort there would have been much smacking of lips, particularly over the beef, which they had not eaten for a long time. They noticed with pride (see Plate 9) that the initials VOC were engraved on all the dishes, knives and forks and stirred by the food and wine dreamed of great things for their country in the land that had held them prisoner.

A few days later, Sprinckel took Quaeckernaeck with Santvoort down for a meeting with Admiral Cornelis Matelieff at the Dutch East India Company base in Johor. Although Matelieff had already learnt about the voyage that *De Liefde* had made to Japan between 1598 and 1600, he went through the motions of questioning Quaeckernaeck and Santvoort about the voyage. Sprinckel passed on to Matelieff the Red-seal certificate from Ieyasu, its translation and the bunch of private letters from *De Liefde*'s crew, requesting safe delivery of all of them to the Netherlands by the Dutch navy.

After Quaeckernaeck and Santvoort had left the room, Matelieff said to Sprinckel that he was sorry that his cousin Quaeckernaeck had returned instead of Adams. One of his twelve vessels required a replacement captain. He put a high value on Adams' talent, ability and skills and 'he wished Adams would have been the captain'.[216]

---

[216] Author's words.

Sprinckel hesitated and finally interrupted Matelieff, saying '.... Sir, I need to consult with you.'[217] He produced a letter from his breast pocket and put it on the table in front of Matelieff. Matelieff wondered what kind of letter it was. He asked whether the letter should be included with those he was given before. Then he was surprised to see that the letter was from William Adams and it had been opened. Sprinckel looked nervous and said that, after long deliberation, he had decided not to send the letter to Holland. He now wanted Matelieff to support his decision.

Adams' success in Japan was already known among Dutch mariners and Sprinckel guessed that rumours must have spread to England. However, if Adams' letter reached his wife and daughter, rumours would become facts, facts that would interest the English East India Company. The content of his letter was only news of where he was and what he did, but when the company learnt that Adams was now Lord Miura Anjin and a close adviser to the Shogun, they would be certain to act. They would send Adams' letter to their base in Bombay and then the director of the base would despatch a trading ship to Japan. If the English ship arrived in Japan before the Dutch, then, such was Adams' power to control trade, the Portuguese monopoly would be replaced by an English one. It was clear to Sprinckel that they should take advantage of the good fortune that Adams' letter had fallen into their hands.

At first, Matelieff disagreed with Sprinckel because it was against the law to destroy another's personal letters and he had no desire to be Sprinckel's co-conspirator. However, eventually he had to agree that, though they personally bore Adams no malice, their first priority must be to beat the English and any other countries in trade. So Adams' letters, written from his heart and soul, were thrown into the South China Sea.

It took almost a month for Adams to regain his composure. Gradually, he accepted that the Dutch were only protecting their national interests. If he or other English merchants were in their position, they would do the same thing. Adams acknowledged

---

[217] Ibid.

that his work for the Dutch East India Company and also his obedience to the Shogun of Japan were in part self-protection and self-promotion.

In the middle of September 1611, before Andreezen left Toi, Adams and Andreezen took a final hot spring bath together in the valley. Andreezen mentioned an Englishman, one of the crew members of the Dutch ship he would be joining in October. Seeing Adams was interested, Andreezen suggested he could arrange a meeting. Adams wondered whether Jacques Specx might object, but with a warm wink Andreezen promised that, as a gesture of friendship, he would ensure the meeting would be secret from Specx.

Andreezen was rewarded for his services with a great sum of gold coins by Lord Ōkubo Nagayasu, a government officer in mining development. Nagayasu also requested Adams to take charge of importing mercury for the Shogunate. Earlier, Nagayasu had served Ieyasu as *Sarugaku*, a Japanese theatre actor. Later, Ieyasu appointed him *Kinsaku-tsukasa*, an accomplished practitioner in mining gold and silver. He had been enobled not for his acting ability, but for his tremendous achievements in developing the gold and silver mines, particularly in Sado in Niigata Prefecture, at Izu in Shizuoka Prefecture and at Iwami in Shimane Prefecture.

Adams had found a new motivation to beat away his angry but sorrowful thoughts over the Dutch betrayal. The information he had had from Andreezen should rather be a beam of hope to brighten his life. He would now be able to use his ability, skills, knowledge, experience and privileged position to the advantage of the English East India Company. Adams' desire to return home had faded. If he left Japan permanently, he would lose all the wealth and status he had gained there. Rather, he wished to serve the English East India Company by sailing regularly to England and back. With the thought of seeing his English wife and daughter again, his drive and ambition revived.

Before going to Hirado with Andreezen, Adams called at his estate in Hemi. Yuki, her father and the servants bowed low as both men passed through the gate. Yuki would have been pleased to see her long-absent husband, but when Adams says that he will stay only for a few days, Yuki pulls a long face, like Mary Hyn used to do. She pushes baby Joseph against Adams' chest, hoping that the baby's father might put off his plan, but to Joseph the absent father is a stranger. He becomes fretful and tries to escape from Adams' arms. When Adams rubs his rough beard on the baby's smooth, pinkish white cheek and kisses him in the Western way, the baby becomes more agitated and starts crying. Although everyone present finds the scene awkward, nobody is allowed to humiliate their lord by showing sympathy to the baby. So they all burst into embarrassed cheers!

In the sitting-room, Father Miura Joshin introduced Chōbei, a young dealer in porcelain china in his late twenties, and trusted by the Shogunate. (Like all servants he had no surname.) It would be the first time for Chōbei to deal in Dutch commodities, but he convinced Adams that he would come up to his expectations. Adams decided to leave seventy per cent of his Dutch consignment with Chōbei and thirty per cent with Magome, Yuki's father. The two dealers were instructed by Adams to negotiate hard over the prices for commodities such as Dutch wool, porcelain and diamonds, Chinese silk and other fabrics, Molucca cloves and sesame; also over sharkskin and the ivory-type mammal teeth and tusks from the South Sea Islands that the Japanese loved to carve into exquisite clasps for the hair or garments [*netsuke*] or into a plectrum for musical instruments.

In the evening, Adams gave a banquet. Many of his retainers and husbandmen would have attended in formal costume. On entering, they would all crouch low in deep obeisance to Adams, seated at the head of the hall. Every single guest said 'Welcome back, Anjin-sama.'[218] The scene greatly impressed Andreezen; Adams' prestige was more than he imagined.

In the middle of October 1611, Adams and Andreezen arrived at Hirado. They were informed that the Dutch vessel would set sail for Pattani via Bantam on 25 October. They were expected to

---

[218] Ibid.

attend a banquet to be held by the Dutch East India Company on 23 October and Andreezen promised to introduce Adams to the Englishman there. It was Adams' intention to pass to the Englishman the same letter that he wrote in 1605.

With jaunty steps Adams would have climbed up from the beach at Sakikata in Hirado to Kida Yajiuemon's house[219] on the hill. Yajiuemon had put his house at Adams' disposal whenever he was in Hirado (see Plate 17). When he opened the wooden sliding door, Yajiuemon and his wife would bow and follow their master into the sitting room. His bath would be ready and after a long journey, Adams was happy to have a leisurely soak. Yajiuemon's wife would have heated the bath one or two hours before Adams arrived, putting wood on the fire to the side of the tub and occasionally, when the water got lukewarm and from behind a screen, blowing through a hollow piece of bamboo to stoke up the fire.

This time, while Adams is sinking shoulder-deep into the hot bath, he hears a girl's voice outside the bathroom door. Adams assumes the girl might be the housemaid he had asked Yajiuemon to find for him. The door slides gently and slowly open. A girl is pushed into the bathroom by Yajiuemon's wife. She bows: 'I am Taki,'[220] she says softly, 'I alone will look after you from today.'[221] Adams peers at her through the steam. He guesses she is a fisherman's daughter. She has dark, yellowish skin, a strong frame, unusually long arms and legs and smooth not folded eyelids. Her eyes are so widely separated, she looks like an alien. Adams finds her quite sweet, but Taki is obviously expecting him to do something. Adams says to her, 'I leave that entirely to you.'[222] Taki continues to stare at him unblinking, holding a towel. In a long and awkward silence Yajiuemon's wife sees things are not going well, so she says: 'If Anjin-sama will please stand, I brought Taki to let

---

[219] The house is preserved today as the place where Miura Anjin resided and died in Hirado, under the trust of the Hirado district council.

[220] Translated by the author from Oshima Masahiro.

[221] Ibid.

[222] Ibid.

her wash your back.'[223] Now it is Adams' turn to feel awkward. He protests that he does not need anybody to wash his back and wants them to leave him alone. After the two women leave, a rather dizzy Adams steps out onto the bathroom floor. The incident has held him in the bath too long. His face and body are as red as a boiled octopus!

Once Adams is seated at the dining table, Yajiuemon comes to ask him if he likes Taki or not. Adams asks why the girl had been introduced in the bathroom, of all places. Yajiuemon answers that in Japan it is common for a housemaid to serve her master in the bathroom, so it is an appropriate time for his wife to arrange the service. Yajiuemon tells him that Taki is one of the slaves sold by the Chosŏn dynasty in Korea and traded by Portuguese, Dutch or Japanese merchants. An endless number of men and women, boys and girls of every age are sold as slaves at very low prices there. He had carefully chosen Taki because she is not a Catholic. Although she is a masculine girl, she will serve not only as a maid but also as a taster to check Adams' food for poison. Adams explains that he is not shy to be washed by a girl, but he is wary of being intimate with a complete stranger. However, because Hirado is an international region and he can expect more risks than in other regions, Adams accepts Taki to be a taster and a maid for him for a while.

In the evening, Adams started writing the same letter to his English compatriots in Bantam as he had written in 1605, informing them about the twenty-month voyage on *De Liefde* from Rotterdam, his life in Japan since the ship drifted there and how much he was concerned about his wife and daughter. As he had no idea to whom he should write, he addressed it to 'My Unknown friends and countrymen.'[224] This time it began differently:

On the occasion of my hearing that a number of English ships, the names of which I do not know, are anchored at the island of

---

[223] Ibid.
[224] Adams, William.

Java, I have boldly decided to write this letter, even though we are not acquainted. ..... My reason for writing such a letter is that my conscience is family bound by the love I feel for my country and its people. .... I had long a-troubled you with writing, but the Hollanders have kept it most secret from me till the year 1611, which was the first news that I heard.

It concluded:

..... I hope that somehow one or another one of my good acquaintances will get news of my wife and daughter to me. I wait patiently for Almighty God to answer this wish. ..... I hope that before I die in this land I will hear news about some of my dear friends, or even meet with them again. For this all must be given to the glory of God. Amen
October 23, 1611. From Japan
Your unworthy friend and servant who will do everything to fulfill your commands.

William Adams

Perhaps because Adams was trying to control his emotion and write in a matter-of-fact way, the letter took three days to complete and ran to 5,960 words.

That evening, the banquet held by the Dutch was lively and cheerful with a feast probably of plaice, mackerel, dried flying fish (*Tobiuo*), roasted thrush meat, boiled-taro with soy sauce and much else. Andreezen came over to introduce a young Englishman with a dark brown beard, called Thomas Hill. Hill greeted Adams respectfully; he had heard of Adams' honour in Japan and he was proud of it as his compatriot. Adams thought Hill an honest man and both men felt some affinity to each other. Hill proudly introduced himself as a Warwickshire man, born in Stratford-upon-Avon, Shakespeare's birthplace. Adams had never heard of Shakespeare and when he learnt that Queen Elizabeth I had died in 1603 and been succeeded by her distant relative, Scottish-born James I, he realized how long he had been away from his motherland. When Hill complained about the new taxes and tolls imposed by the King, including when crossing bridges and using roads, Adams joked that he might, after all, be in a better place.

During the general conversation, Adams was watching for a chance when he and Hill could be alone. When it came, he caught his eye and whispered that he wanted to talk to him privately. Hill nodded as if he knew it was something important. Outside the room Adams explained to Hill why his letters to England had never arrived. Hill's first reaction was a daze of disbelief, but when Adams took the letter out of his pocket, Hill saw the sadness in his eyes and readily agreed to deliver the letter to the English East India Company in Bantam. Adams grasped Hill's hand in gratitude.

On the morning of 25 October, Adams, Matsura Shigenobu and the Dutch merchants came to see off the Dutch ship at Hirado pier. When Adams saw Hill carrying his luggage on board, he was anxious about his letter. Hill was sensitive enough to tap his breast pocket in a sign that his letter was secure.

As the ship sailed away, Adams recalled to mind part of his letter where he had urged the English to come to Japan. He had described Japan as one of the best countries in the world for trading; its people were good natured and courteous; there was little problem with crime and cheating and there was not a better governed country in the world. He had warned his countrymen about the treachery of the Dutch towards the English, but also tempted them to trade with Japan, which their rivals had found was 'an island of silver'![225] Moreover, the Portuguese and the Spanish were dishonoured and the Hollanders were suffering from a shortage of staff. So, all England's enemies and rivals were experiencing difficulties. Adams was confident that it was the best possible time for the English to establish their factory for their future prosperity in Japan.

---

[225] Adams, William.

CHAPTER 13

A WELCOME FOR THE ENGLISH

కం

In February 1612, the Dutch vessel arrived in Bantam and discharged Andreezen and Hill. Bantam was a heaven on earth for Westerners to buy spices, but it also held the horrors of hell. The native Javanese were as expert at chopping up human bodies, as they were chasing game. Severe tropical diseases such as dysentery, cholera and malaria were ever-present dangers.

It was truly a place of extremes, from the burning orange of sunrise to the ebony black of night. The sudden descent of night frightened men who were used to a twilight but, for Hill, it must have been rather convenient to make his secret visit to the English East India Company.

It was on 16 December 1602, that Admiral Sir James Lancaster, commanding a fleet of five ships, had established the English East India Company in Bantam. He left eleven men and ordered them to buy and stock spices. However, within a few months, the factory chief and his deputy had died of tropical disease and several other men were sick with life-threatening conditions. The factory was not much more than a hut, built with frail wood and cane and roofed with thin thatch. It looked thoroughly shabby. Because of the terrible heat, they had to keep all the windows open all day long, but this brought in constant damp from the monsoon rains; filthy muddy water soaked through the wall and bacteria thrived in the humid air. The poor men were attacked by the burning heat in the day and by a cloud of mosquitoes in the hut at night. Even with all this, there were many worse places where the English chose to settle in the East.

In the darkness, Hill quietly knocked on the factory's flimsy door. It was opened with extreme caution, for the Englishmen lived with fear. When Hill introduced himself, he was allowed in with some suspicion and found several miserable Englishmen there. They told Hill that they could hardly sleep for fear of being attacked with darts and flaming arrows by the Javanese terrorists. Their thatched roof had been set alight several times. The chief factor came to shake hands with Hill and introduced himself as Augustine Spalding. When Hill explained to Spalding the background and purpose of his visit, the chief's suspicions of an 'Englishman' from a Dutch vessel were dispelled. Spalding promised to deliver Adams' letter to Sir Thomas Smythe, the governor of the East India Company in London, and carefully put it into a secure drawer. Hill was a sincere man and Adams had been right to trust him. That same month, Spalding handed Adams' letter to a Dutch ship to deliver to the East India Company in London, wisely substituting his name as the sender.

In March 1612, Adams was surprised to hear that Ieyasu and the Shogun had issued a decree forbidding Christianity in all areas of Japan under the direct control of the government. Ieyasu had ordered Itakura Katsushige, Chief of Military Defence in Kyoto, and the Nagasaki Governor Hasegawa to destroy all Catholic churches and exile all Catholic missionaries. Adams wondered why Ieyasu, who had been tolerant towards Christianity so far, had suddenly changed his mind. He learnt from Lord Honda that one of the reasons was the Okamoto Daihachi affair, in the previous year.

The government had sent Okamoto as an investigator to meet Arima Harunobu, after Arima's success in burning and defeating the Portuguese ship *Madre de Deus* in 1609. As a reward, the investigator, a close retainer of Lord Honda, promised Arima he could get Ieyasu's consent to his repossessing the Bizen domain, then owned by the Nabeshima clan. Because Arima felt he could trust a man of Okamoto's status, he gave him money and gifts. However, when he heard nothing more, Arima made an enquiry of Lord

Honda. Lord Honda answered that Ieyasu and he had never heard about such a reward. So Ieyasu and Lord Honda cross-examined Okamoto, who confessed his guilt. Okamoto was sent to prison, where he disclosed that Arima, a Catholic convert, had earlier planned the assassination of Nagasaki Governor Hasegawa, who was anti-Christian. When Ieyasu cross-examined Arima, Arima was unable to prove the accusation false. His domain was confiscated and he was exiled to Kai (today's Ibaragi Prefecture). Later he was ordered to commit *seppuku*, cutting open his own belly before his head was sliced off. Meanwhile, Okamoto was burnt at the stake. It was discovered that Okamoto, too, was a Catholic convert. Ieyasu was further shaken by the report that the number of Japanese who had converted to Catholicism had reached more than seven hundred thousand, including several *uba* or wet nurses in his own castle. Down in Hirado, as Adams secretly knew, Lord Matsura Shigenobu worried about his daughter-in-law who had been christened a Catholic.

Another reason why Ieyasu outlawed Christianity could have been his growing disillusionment with the explorer Sebastian Viscaino, who had not yet delivered on the promised Gold and Silver Island. Ieyasu did not know that Viscaino was in trouble from a delay in the building of his ship. Ieyasu had agreed that the ship would be built by Japanese ship-builders under Mukai's control and up to 100-ton weight. Collusion between Mukai and Adams is thought to be behind the lack of urgency. Adams also took the opportunity of Ieyasu's worry over Catholics to suggest again to Ieyasu that the Spanish would not be trying to find a Gold and Silver Island for Ieyasu, but for the King of Spain and that Viscaino's expedition was a preparation for invading Japan.

So, in April, Ieyasu summoned the Spaniard. Viscaino had just arrived at the Itoh beach at that time in order to inspect the progress in building his ship, but he had to turn back on account of the audience with Ieyasu in Sumpu, which eventually took place on 18 May. Viscaino vehemently denied that the Spanish would invade Japan and promised again to try to discover a Gold and Silver Island for Ieyasu. However, he would need Ieyasu to give him expenses for the expedition and *shuin-jō*, the Red-seal licence, which would guarantee him safe passage on land and sea.

While waiting for Ieyasu's decision, Viscaino travelled to the Sakai port in Osaka. To his chagrin, he heard that this was where most Japanese ships were built, not at Itoh beach. By chance, Viscaino met the Spanish pilot Lorenzo Baskel, who kindly provided him with rations and a valuable chart of the Japanese coastline. On 16 July, Viscaino returned to Uraga, where he was shocked to hear that his expedition would not now be permitted. He immediately sought an audience with Ieyasu. At the audience, Viscaino again demanded permission for the expedition, but offered to make do with a loan of 2,000 taize. Reluctantly, Ieyasu gave Viscaino the permission, but he declined to lend the money and, in an uncharacteristic display of his feelings, returned all the presents Viscaino had brought for him. Behind the scene, Adams' repeated warnings about the true intentions of the Spanish were beginning to be effective.

Viscaino was obliged to sell his own possessions, including some silver dishes, to raise the 2,000 taize. In July, he returned to Uraga and sent several of his men to the Itoh beach to check how the ship-building was going on. Later, they informed him that the ship was rigged out, but the size of the ship was over 100-tons and it would be impossible to sail it with the less than ten crew members stipulated by Ieyasu. Viscaino was furious about what he saw as the Japanese ship-builders' crooked business. 'Japanese were the worst evil nation in the world,'[226] he later reported to Spanish missionaries in Acapulco. 'They think of nothing but making money.' But Viscaino did not appeal against this sharp practice to Ieyasu and Shogun Hidetada, as he knew that they were not in a mood to help Catholics. What he did not know was that the ruse with the Japanese ship-builders was devised by Mukai, on the advice of his good friend Miura Anjin.

Viscaino was now obliged to repair his old ship, the *San Francisco*, and on 20 August, he and twenty-five of his men finally

---

[226] Viscaino, Sebastian.

departed on their expedition to the north-eastern coast. The party reached the supposed location of a Gold and Silver Island on 25 September. For twenty days, they struggled to find the island and on 14 October a typhoon hit the area. As the waves rose higher, the explorers were forced to throw most of the ship's load into the sea to lighten the ship. When the typhoon relented, the weakened men were down to their last rations and eventually they abandoned the expedition.

Soon after the *San Francisco* returned to the Uraga Port, the ship which Mukai had built at the Itoh Beach also arrived at the port. Viscaino was delighted at the smart, European-style ship and promptly named it *San Sebastian,* after himself. However, what happened next was another blow to his already battered hopes. As Viscaino records in his diary: 'The ship was loaded and sailed off by its Japanese crew, disregarding the Spanish instruction. In one legwa (one league is three miles) the ship sank. Mukai admitted the Japanese fault.' Again, some people see the hand of William Adams behind this unfortunate accident.

One day, Viscaino heard that Ieyasu was in Edo. He visited Edo Castle, but he was not received in audience because Ieyasu had gone to falconry. So Viscaino, shivering in a cold waiting room, waited until Ieyasu came back. However, Ieyasu declined to meet Viscaino and for a full five months, Viscaino heard nothing from Ieyasu.

Ieyasu's reason was not only because of Adams' warnings. He had lost trust in Viscaino after receiving a letter from missionaries of the Society of Saint Francis, as they were called, in Nagasaki. In the letter, they reported that Viscaino had borrowed from Japanese merchants the large sum of 6,000 peso without formal authority from the Spanish King or the governor-general of Nova Espãnia. Personally, he did not have the resources to repay and the Society was not going to be responsible for honouring Viscaino's debt.

Viscaino then sent urgent letters to his merchant friend Capitão (Captain) Uniãno and to some Spanish acquaintances residing in Nagasaki. He asked them to lend money for rations and expenses for him and his men to return to Acapulco, promising to pay interest and with his property and income as security. Nobody agreed to lend him money, because they were afraid of censure from the Society of Saint Francis. Viscaino then suggested to his men that they should sell as many of their own possessions as possible, so they could repair the old *San Francisco* and return home. Most of the men disagreed with that suggestion and deserted. Missionary Luis Sotelo came to visit him and offered to help. He visited all the wealthy Japanese merchants he knew, to ask them to lend Viscaino money. All of them had heard the rumour that Viscaino was Ieyasu's enemy and refused to help him. Viscaino was disconsolate and fell seriously ill.

Meanwhile, Lord Date Masamune in the Sendai Domain, who had met Viscaino by chance in the summer of 1611, heard of Viscaino's illness. His messenger called on Viscaino in his sick bed and informed him that Lord Date had obtained permission from Ieyasu to rescue him from his difficulties. The lord would willingly bear all expenses for the building of a new ship, large enough to take twenty-six Spanish men back to Acapulco, on condition that a party of Lord Date's retainers could come too. The lord also promised to feed and accommodate the Spanish, until their departure. To Viscaino, this was evidence of God's grace and he dramatically recovered from his illness. By now, however, his antipathy to all Japanese was visceral and he struggled to behave well to Lord Date and everybody in the Sendai Domain.

The new vessel, called *Rikuo-maru,* eventually departed from Tsuki-no-ura on 14 September 1613. Exactly two months later, she reached Cape Mendocino and, from there, safely to Acapulco.

The following year, Viscaino sent the King of Spain a document dated 20 May. The document tells the story of his involvement with Friar Luis Sotelo:

The old Shogun Tokugawa Ieyasu and Shogun Hidetada had a hatred towards Catholics. In 1612, they ordered the burning of many Catholic churches and exiled its missionaries, including the Portuguese Jesuit Padre João Girão Rodriguez to Macao. Sotelo received an expulsion order, but to Nagasaki. However, he ignored the order and remained in Edo to bear witness for the Catholic Faith. This rebellious action infuriated the Shogun and he sentenced twenty-eight of Sotelo's Catholic followers to death by execution. Although Sotelo was expected to be burnt at the stake, the Shogun decided to exile him to Macao. In great secrecy, I took Sotelo and two other Catholic missionaries back to Acapulco. In Japan, it was believed that the Spanish would invade their country, so all the Catholics of the nation were punished.

Viscaino also mentions William Adams, an English pilot, 'who had by now (1613) become the confidential adviser of Ieyasu on foreign affairs'.[227] Adams was 'a strong Protestant and used his position to foster Japanese fears of the subversive activities of the Roman Catholic missionaries. This was the more unfortunate for the Portuguese and Spaniards.'[228]

Back in April 1612, in Bantam, the chief factor, Augustine Spalding, was delighted to see an English vessel anchoring at the bay, the first for more than one year. The name of the vessel was the *Globe*. She had left England's south coast early in February 1611. The captain was Anthony Hippon, highly respected as an intelligent and wise leader. Sir Thomas Smythe, governor of the East India Company in London, had nicknamed him 'good shepherd'. But when the *Globe* arrived in Bantam, the captain contracted a tropical disease, so, in an echo of the *De Liefde* episode, the Dutch pilot Peter Floris took charge.

During Floris' stay in Bantam, he managed to sell some of the cottons in his cargo and was wondering where to sail next. Spalding recommended Japan and mentioned William Adams, whose letter of invitation would have been recently delivered by a Dutch ship to the East India Company in London. Floris was interested and offered to deliver any correspondence from Spalding to Adams. His first priority was to head north to Pattani to sell his cottons, and

---

[227] Ibid.
[228] Ibid.

then he would sail to Japan. Spalding handed Floris a letter for Adams.

In May 1612, the *Globe* set sail again, but on arrival in Pattani, their fortunes fell sharply. Captain Hippon died and many other crew members were weak from dysentery. The twin evils of drink and disease were sapping their confidence to continue to explore. In any case, the advice to Floris from merchants of Pattani was not to go to Japan, because Japanese pirates had attacked the merchants six or seven times before and proved to be a fearsome foe. Floris decided not to sail for Japan, but when Pattani was stricken by a large forest fire, he had to abandon his attempts to sell his remaining cottons and to return to India.

Before leaving Pattani in October, Floris happened to meet a Dutch adventurer, Peter Johnsoon, who had just delivered to Augustine Spalding Adams' letter to his wife, which was the same as he wrote in 1605. When Floris learnt that Johnsoon knew Adams personally and was preparing to sail for Japan, he judged Johnsoon was the right person to ask to deliver Spalding's letter to Adams. Johnsoon willingly undertook the task, saying that he would be 'very glad at having an occasion to do a kindness to Mr Adams, to whom he was beholding'.[229]

□

Meanwhile, in the same year, confident that an English ship would arrive in Japan soon, Adams requested Ieyasu to allow him to return home temporarily. Ieyasu again rejected the request. However, Adams' confidence was not misplaced. On 24 October 1612, the English ship *Clove* sailed into Bantam. The captain was John Saris, who had been there before, between 1605 and 1608. Saris was not planning to be stationed again on this tropical island, where the burning temperature and unhealthy life had made him weak and miserable. The purpose of his visit this time was to research the pros-

---

[229] Translated by the author form Oshima Masahiro.

pects for trade with Japan. He already knew that luxury goods such as silk, satin, sugar-candies, sandalwood and others could make a man a fortune in Japan, but his interest seems also to have been in the private trade of erotic, pornographic paintings including some very explicit ones. It seems he had long dreamed of going to Japan, after he obtained the information from Dutch acquaintances that the Japanese were passionate about erotic paintings.

John Saris was born in 1579 or 1580. He came from a well-known South Yorkshire family. He was a son of Thomas Saris and his great-grandfather, Humphrey Saris, was particularly highly respected around Doncaster. On his letters, John Saris often proudly used seals imprinted with his family coat of arms. Five of these letters are maintained in the India Office. John Saris had an unhappy childhood. His father died in 1588. On coming of age, Saris sought his fortune in the East. On 25 March 1604, he joined a fleet of six ships under Captain (afterwards Sir) Henry Middleton, bound for Bantam. On 24 July 1605, the fleet arrived at its destination. It lay at anchor in the port until October 1605, when Middleton sailed back to England. Saris remained and during his sweaty sojourn compiled a diary of events and other reports, of which the most interesting were details of the goods which should be sent out from England for trade in the Far East. His reports to the English East India Company in 1608 were highly regarded and in December 1608 he was promoted to Bantam's Chief Factor, as 'Master Saris, merchant'. Promotion achieved, he began to seek some respite from his debilitating work. He petitioned the company and in October 1609 he handed over charge to Augustine Spalding. On 10 May 1610, after settling in his successor, Saris returned to England.

Saris was not much respected among his fellows, although it is clear from his diary he was pleased with himself. He was a disciplinarian, but also rather peculiar. He had not married and most people did not realize that his peculiarity was partly down to problems with sex. A locked chest in his cabin held his secret ... an extensive private collection of pornographic paintings. No one had seen them, but Saris had occasionally boasted about the collection to his close friends. He had seen some Japanese paintings which vividly depicted both men's and women's private parts and their sexual intercourse and he was keen to add to his collection.

The East India Company in London had no idea in 1610 that Saris was building this collection. Sir Thomas Smythe was impressed at Saris' confident, sophisticated and flamboyant manner. He thought that he would make a good ' ambassador ' for England. It mattered not that Saris' crew complained about his 'tyrannical' character, his physical and verbal abuse. He was said to have 'much stormed' and to hate any criticism. If his crew complained to him, he punished them. Saris' position was unshakeable, because of his background and the governor's strong support.

Sir Thomas had willingly agreed to Saris leading a voyage to Japan, although it would be a fact-finding one, rather than to open up trade. When the *Clove* anchored in Bantam in October 1612, after eighteen months at sea, Saris was already planning how to use 'Master' William Adams' assistance as soon as the ship arrived in Japan. On 28 October, he read a letter from Adams to all the English merchants, which filled everyone with hope for their company and country. The *Clove* finally embarked with seventy-four crew members, mostly English but one Spaniard, one Japanese and five Indians and, after loading 700 bags of sesame, departed from Bantam on 15 January 1613.

Coincidentally, three days before their departure, Adams replied to a letter from Augustine Spalding 'delivered by my good friend Thomas Hill, who God shall preserve'. When Hill arrived at Hirado port, he had approached Adams and pretended to ask Adams to give him a light for his pipe. Then Hill had secretely handed him Spalding's letter.

Adams had to read Spalding's letter several times, so great was his emotion. He was thrilled that the English East India Company had made faster progress in coming to Japan than he expected. Hill was the first to benefit from his merry mood. When Adams handed Hill his reply to Spalding, complete with a map of Japan he had drawn, he tipped Hill one gold *Koban*.

In Adams' letter to Spalding, he mentioned that 'I was glad that you received my letter through Peter Johnsoon. In truth, my wife and my friends in England and Holland have sent my letters by these two ships, but only a small number of them have reached me,'[230] he explained. 'One of them was from Sir Thomas Smythe and the other was from my good friend John Stokle. These two letters were not opened by anyone, but they were held from me for forty or fifty days.'[231] Adams advised the English crew to ask for him: 'I am called Anjin *Sama*, in the Japanese language, and am known by that name all down the coast. So please approach the mainland without any fear, for I will arrange for barks with pilots to escort you to where you want to go.'[232]

On 2 June 1613, Saris sighted a triangle-shaped land called Miyako-jima in the outer Ryukyu Islands (today's Okinawa). The *Clove* had intended to anchor there, but they were blown away by a gale. So they continued north, past the great island of Amakusa and into the Strait of Arima. At the approaches to Nagasaki, the *Clove* met four Japanese fishing vessels and contracted two of them to provide food and pilot the *Clove* into Hirado.

At three o'clock in the afternoon of 12 June 1613, after more than two years of voyage, the *Clove* finally arrived at Hirado Port, the first English ship to make land in Japan.

Captain Saris and all the crew were welcomed with great respect by Lord Matsura Shigenobu, his younger brother Nobusane, and Shigenobu's senior retainer Sagawa Shuma. Since this lord retired and became a Buddhist priest in 1589, his son Takanobu had officially succeeded, but in fact Shigenobu continued to hold the real power in Hirado. Shigenobu and Nobusane were dressed in luxurious silk gowns and breeches and wearing *katana* and *wakizashi*, a pair of long swords in lacquered cases, which were elaborately and exquisitely decorated. The courtesy of their greeting was far beyond the Englishmen's expectation. They took off their Japanese shoes, called *zōri*, kneeled down and made countless bows to the important visitors. The lord and

---

[230] Ibid.
[231] Ibid.
[232] Translated by the author from Miura Joshin.

his brother were impressed at Captain Saris' appearance, wearing a broadcloth decorated with silks and satins. They treated him as a lord. They were still bowing as Saris led them to his cabin, where he had prepared a banquet and some simple music from his crew.

After the banquet, Saris flourished a letter from King James I and said: 'I would not open it till Ange (Anjin) had come, who could interpret it.'[233] Saris was intrigued to discover what kind of man his compatriot was. He asked Shigenobu about him and was delighted to hear that Adams was a man exactly as Sir Thomas Smythe had described, being 'in great favour with the King',[234] although he already had a measure of Adams' fame when he had mentioned his name as the *Clove* arrived at Hirado.

Smythe's instructions to Saris had been thorough: to ask Adams to give the English advice on all aspects of trade with Japan; on 'what course should be held for the delivery of His Majestie's letter' to the Shogun and on what gifts should be given and in what manner. Saris was further instructed to offer Adams a passage home with 'as convenient a cabben as you may'[235] and 'all other necessaries which your shipp may afford him'.[236]

Saris' banquet ended just as it was getting dark. Shigenobu was anxious about rowing back to shore, so he expressed his great thanks to the captain for his hospitality and promised that he would invite Saris to a 'kind and free entertainement'.[237] As the lord's and his brother's boat was pushed off, a ship carrying ten or more soldiers approached the *Clove*. To everyone's dismay and then delight, these soldiers clambered aboard the ship and left gifts of beef, venison, chickens, wild boar, with baskets of fruits and specialities of local fish. Saris was at first suspicious of such generous presents. He wondered what Lord Matsura was after, but when he saw the lord's

---

[233] Saris, John.
[234] Ibid.
[235] Ibid.
[236] Ibid.
[237] Satow, Sir Ernest.

and his brother's genial smiles and frequent bows as their boat was rowed away, he realized that the gifts were a genuine token of their gratitude.

The next day, Lord Matsura Shigenobu came aboard the *Clove* again. This time he brought his retainers, their wives and daughters. Saris found the wives and daughters delightfully bashfull and he became excited about inviting them to his private cabin, 'where the picture of the goddess Venus hung, very lasciviously set out'.[238] Eventually, Saris succeeded in enticing the Japanese ladies into the cabin, where to his great surprise the ladies fell immediately to their knees and worshipped the picture of Venus. They had all secretly converted to Christianity and thought it was a portrait of Our Lady. When Saris saw their innocent and total devotion to the naked object of his sexual pleasure, he probably felt a bit awkward but showed no embarrassment.

Saris illuminated the Japanese ladies' figures with a lamp and stared at their sweet faces and elegantly long necks. Their ivory skin was silky, smooth and unblemished. Movement in their loose silk *kimono* revealed delicate hands, forearms and ankles. Saris' sexual desire would have surged up within him. This kind of woman was certainly to his taste.

Lord Matsura noticed that the English captain was interested, but he was embarrassed about the incident. He tried to shepherd the women out of Saris' cabin, but this annoyed the captain. His mood brightened when the lord, mindful of future profit, endeavoured to rescue the situation by urging the women, in Saris own words, 'to be frollicke'.[239] The women sang merrily, played the *shamisen*, similar to the European lute, and danced without inhibition for their English guests. Lord Matsura chuckled at the successful event and began planning his next treat for this strange English captain.

Captain Saris then requested Lord Matsura Shigenobu to recommend convenient accommodation in Hirado for the Englishmen. Two of Saris' men, Richard Cocks and Tempest Peacock, were

---

[238] Ibid.
[239] Saris, John.

shown several appropriate houses including one with a warehouse, owned by Li Tan, the chief of the local Chinese community. Li agreed to redecorate, furnish all rooms with *tatami* mats and to provide food and drink. Saris and his men moved in and, on 19 June, Saris visited Lord Matsura to express gratitude for his assistance.

According to local Dutch advice on Japanese custom, Saris had learnt that presents were very important. So he presented to Lord Matsura Shigenobu a huge number of gifts, such as silk, jewellery, ivory and animal skins. Shigenobu was delighted and made a great show of unwrapping each of the presents. Saris also gave woollen cloth and cotton to all members of the lord's household. When the young lord Matsura Takanobu asked for 'a gold-fringed parasol'[240] he had set his eyes on, Saris was less willing. He had not yet realized there would be a big pay back later. On being given the parasol, Takanobu made 'a million of compliment' with an extravagant number of bows to the English captain.

After visiting the lords of Hirado, Captain Saris called in on the Dutch East India factory in Hirado to show his thanks to the deputy chief factor, Captain Hendrick Brouwer, for welcoming the *Clove* when she arrived at Hirado Port. The chief factor, Jacques Specx, was temporarily absent. Saris presented 'a pot of English butter',[241] which would have been an exclusive gift if it had not been on the high seas for more than two years.

The English captain sensed some rivalry with the Dutch, as Adams had warned in his letter.[242] However, Saris tried to be friendly to Brouwer and suggested a trade agreement that would prohibit each factory from underselling the other. The next day, the Dutch captain rejected that agreement. He seemed less cooperative than the day before; perhaps he did not like Saris' forwardness or even felt insulted by a present of rotten English butter. Brou-

---

[240] Ibid.

[241] Ibid.

[242] Adams had also advised Augustine Spalding in his letter of January 1611 that an English ship should not come to the area (Hirado) where the Dutch were, because it was not a good place for selling merchandise….; they should come to the city of Edo at thirty-six degrees north. The advice was disregarded.

wer told Saris that the Dutch already had successful trade between
Japan and the other countries of the East and they would like to
continue operating independently. Saris resented this rejection and
the incident caused a crack in the relationship between the Dutch
and the English.

On 21 June, Lord Matsura Shigenobu brought several young
girls and women, called *Geiko,* on board the *Clove.* The *Geiko*
was also used as dancers for *Kabuki* comedy plays. They were well
trained in dancing, singing, acting and playing musical instruments such as *Shamisen, tsuzumi* (a kind of small shoulder drum)
and the flute. They created poems and paintings and had per-
fected the etiquette on how to pour drinks and the art of flatter-
ing men.

Because these women were colourfully dressed and sexually forward, Saris initially thought that the lord had brought prostitutes
or sex slaves. However, the *Geiko* were different from the local prostitutes or *Yūjo,* who were used as sex slaves, disposable commodities any time men requested with payment. Many prostitutes were
under sixteen years old. They were sexually and brutally abused in
a cage before giving their services. Often, when they failed to please
their clients, they were punished or killed. Sometimes, prostitute-
mothers killed their baby girls rather than have them inducted into
this hell. According to the record of Richard Cocks, a merchant
aboard the *Clove,* he saw part of a girl's body without legs which
had been fed to dogs in a street. Later, he heard that the girl, aged
fifteen or sixteen, had displeased a Portuguese client.

It was common for *samurai* to test the sharpness of their swords
by cutting into pieces criminals and those prostitutes who had
displeased their clients. Adams, Saris, Cocks, João Rodrigues and
many other foreign residents were witnesses to this, seeing many
heads and body parts in the streets, which had been cut off in this
way. The disgrace and humiliation was part of the punishment.

John Saris was from a very different social background to William Adams. Saris was accustomed to hiring and buying servants
and slaves. He liked the Japanese culture, where, ethically and reli-
giously, there was nothing wrong with men hiring or purchasing

girl-slaves. Saris was keen to get involved in trading girls, including those from Korea and China. This additional prospect must have made him even more eager to establish a factory for the English East India Company in Hirado.

CHAPTER 14

AN AGONIZING DECISION

❧

The Englishmen, who had perhaps become accustomed to Lord Matsura's generous hospitality and his Japanese feasts, now began to complain about poor quality Chinese food and cheap drink in their own factory. For one man, called Jasper, the frustration boiled over and he hurled abuse at the Chinese housekeeper Li. When Li told Saris, the martinet captain ordered a boatman to punish Jasper with a whipping. However, the boatman neglected to carry out the order because he was much the worse for cheap drink. So the captain flogged both men himself. Perhaps Saris regretted his excessive severity. A few days later, he sent the men wines and cider from his private store, an inappropriate gesture in the circumstances.

On 2 July 1613, Richard Cocks visited the Dutch East India factory to try again to negotiate a fixed selling price for woollen cloth by the Dutch and the English. But Deputy Chief Factor Brouwer rejected his treaty. Now Saris was becoming frustrated and impatient for the arrival of William Adams. Saris had passed a letter for Adams to Lord Matsura's close retainer Sagawa Shuma and asked him to deliver it urgently. Sagawa Shuma had handed the letter to a messenger with instructions to deliver it to Adams, whether he was in Hemi or Edo. When the messenger left Hirado, Adams was in Hemi to celebrate the birth of his second child Susanna, or *Kiku* in Japanese. However, by the time the messenger arrived at Hemi,

Anjin's family informed him that Ieyasu had summoned their lord to Sumpu. Curiously, the messenger did not leave Saris' letter at Anjin's estate, nor did he call in at Sumpu. Instead, he went to Edo to report the *Clove*'s arrival to Shogun Hidetada and then returned to Hirado. It was Anjin's family who sent Adams an urgent message about an English ship's arrival at Hirado. Adams was annoyed that the messenger had not come to Sumpu on the way back to Hirado. Japanese sources suggest the messenger was instructed by Lord Matsura not to go to Sumpu, even though it was where Adams was most likely to be. On 12 July, Adams hurried out of Sumpu and headed for Hirado. By horse and ship he feared it would take more than a couple of weeks to reach his destination, some 750 miles from Sumpu.

On 20 July, Sagawa Shuma returned the undelivered letter for Adams to a disappointed Saris. So it was perhaps unfortunate that, on that same day, Jan Jeosten came to greet the English Captain. Saris was in no mood to meet a Dutchman who he had heard from Lord Matsura was a worthless cheater, who had also fallen deeply into debt, and he treated Jeosten with contempt, which would not have improved his reputation with the Dutch.

On 25 July, it was formally announced that Matsura Takanobu was to succeed his father as the lord of the Hirado Castle. At the official ceremony, Captain Saris celebrated Takanobu's succession by firing his cannon eleven times. He also visited the new lord in the evening to congratulate him. Takanobu was very pleased at Saris' respectful manners and presented him with a suit of armour, which his family had treasured since their ancestors had used it in wars against Korea in 1591 and 1596. The next day, in high spirits, Takanobu visited Saris and declared how delightful it was to share company with him. Saris shared with him his anxiety at Adams' non-arrival, but the Matsura clan were in no hurry to have the Shogun's adviser in on their trade negotiations. Takanobu feigned concern and suggested sending a boat to the Shimonoseki Strait to search for Adams' boat, but took no action.

At last, at 10 o'clock on the morning of 27 July, a somewhat embarrassed Adams arrived at Hirado. It had taken seventeen days from Sumpu and it had been forty-seven days since the *Clove* itself arrived. After fifteen years, we can only imagine his feelings when he saw the *Clove*, flying the flag of St George. He alighted from his ship to be greeted, at Saris' instructions, by a nine-gun salute, befitting the Shogun's representative. Richard Cocks and Tempest Peacock were there to welcome him ashore and invite him to the English East India factory, where Captain Saris was waiting to meet his compatriot.

As Adams entered the room, Saris was surprised at the strange-looking Englishman – tall, long haired, blue-eyed and aloof and dressed in rough and modest Western clothes, but still wearing two long Japanese swords. Saris hid his awkwardness with a smile and made to shake Adams hand in the English way, but Adams only bowed solemnly to the English captain. This was of course the best of manners in the samurai world. Adams remembered not to touch his swords, again a gesture of friendship. To Saris, who had no knowledge of Japanese manners and had expected Adams to be just like one of his own men, that greeting seemed cold and arrogant. During their subsequent conversations, Saris records in his diary that Adams made 'so admirable and affectionated commendations of the country (Japan) as it is generally thought amongst us that he is a naturalized Japanese'.[243] For a man from much humbler origins than Saris, William Adams would have seemed remarkably intelligent, knowledgeable, talented at languages, and certainly now more powerful and wealthier than the English captain. So it would not be surprising if to the perceived put-down on first meeting was added a touch of jealousy. For his part, Adams found the young, short, chubby-faced English captain charming and flamboyant, but also bizarre, as it was not long before Saris was asking Adams to provide him with some erotic paintings. Sadly, Saris was definitely not the kind of man to impress Adams.

However, Captain Saris entreated Adams to stay at any chamber in the house of the English East India factory. He would arrange to provide his favourite English meals and give him as comfortable

---

[243] Saris, John.

a life as possible. Adams bowed again and expressed his thanks to Saris for his kindness and generosity, but explained he had a Japanese friend's house, where he normally stayed, and was happy to be on his own. Doggedly Saris persevered. He could arrange for Richard Cocks or any of the English merchants to accompany Adams, at his pleasure, in the Hirado town whenever he felt like some fresh air. Again Adams refused, informing him that he did not wish 'any merchant or other to accompany me'. Saris, who had expected to have the warmest of company with his compatriot and who hated rejection and criticism, resented Adams' behaviour and told him to 'do what he thought best'. Adams took his leave and walked to Yajiuemon's house, where outside a small window another flag of St. George was displayed. Even though the flag was small and made with humble cloth, it was a reminder, poignant at that moment, that Adams had never lost his loyalty to his mother country.

Adams learnt later that Saris had been offended at his apparent discourtesy and had felt humiliated by a lower-class Englishman. Adams felt sorry for Saris, but he did not regret having rejected Saris' offers. He decided to write to Saris to explain why he wished to stay in Yajiuemon's house and why he did not wish Saris and his men to visit him there, where the Portuguese and Spanish would freely come and go. Instead, he would meet the Englishmen at the Dutch house. The letter only increased Saris anger, as he remembered how Brouwer had rejected cooperation with the English. Several crew members of the *Clove* were also upset and thought Adams was a snob, 'who thought the English not good enough to walk with him'.[244] Saris now concluded that Adams' belated arrival at Hirado was out of disrespect for the English.

The first meeting between Englishmen on Japanese soil had not gone well and Adams' letter was now to make things worse. There are no recorded reasons for Adams' distant and formal behaviour. Some historians have assumed that, accustomed as he was to the strict rules of polite Japanese society, Adams might have been embarrassed at the rough English crew, who were as wild, impolite

---

[244] Ibid.

and sexually shameless as they were in other countries. We know Adams advised the Englishmen to learn the local rules and manners, but their lack of experience and a certain over-confidence that they would easily be able to establish the English East India Company in Japan with Adams' name, meant they largely ignored this advice. Adams was disappointed that the compatriots, who he had so looked forward to meeting, were that kind of men.

Although it was not exactly Saris' nature to be tolerant to anyone who had displeased him, he needed Adams and still tried to win his favour. On 2 August, he sent Adams fourteen generous presents, costing 114 reals or about £500 today. They included Turkish rugs, silk sashes and suspenders, shirts, leather slippers, an extravagant white hat and a pair of fine cuffs. Adams was pleased with the presents and a couple of hours later sent Saris a salve of soothing balm from Macao with a handcrafted container, in all worth six shillings or £30 today. Saris grumbled about a mean response.

On the same day, Saris visited the Dutch East India factory to thank Adams for his present, although in fact he wanted to discover how much Adams was respected by the Dutch. Later, he wrote in his diary that Adams was not respected by the Dutch as much as he had thought. However, he also took the opportunity to discuss a plan of action and informed Adams that he had brought presents and a letter from His Majesty King James I for Ieyasu and Shogun Hidetada. They both agreed that they should immediately visit the two authorities in Sumpu and Edo to give these things, 'for the honour of our king and the country of England',[245] and to request permission to sell the English merchandise and establish an English trading house in Japan.

This mood of patriotic agreement did not last long. Adams asked Saris what merchandise his ship had brought. As Saris listed the items, Adams' heart sank. He knew that these would not be profitable. He records how he told Saris that he was grateful the captain had come, but 'I could not think of any way that the large amount of money spent by the company on his voyage could be recovered

---

[245] Ibid.

in this country.'[246] Painfully, he listed the reasons. The price of cloth had become very cheap over the last four years, due to the fact that it had been brought from New Spain (Mexico), Manila and Holland. The Dutch had brought in large quantities of elephant tusks, but the price had fallen dramatically and most of them had been shipped off to Siam (Thailand). Lead, tin and metal bars for spears, which were not in much demand, were selling cheaply in Japan. There was absolutely no demand for calico or fine canequim, because an abundance of cotton was already produced in the country. Regarding the pepper and cloves, which Captain Saris had carefully selected in India, Adams regretted these goods were not used very much in Japan, where their staple foods were rice, fish and vegetables.

Saris took this helpful advice as personal criticism, which he bitterly resented. He decided that Adams was intent on ruining his reputation. Travelling together to Sumpu and Edo was shaping up to be a tense affair, but they both knew they needed each other's assistance. Saris suggested that they should avoid further fault-finding on their journey, to which Adams agreed.

On 7 August 1613, in downbeat mood, the English pair departed from Hirado by a galley, lent by Lord Matsura Takanobu and rowed by forty men. Saris took with him ten Englishmen and his Japanese interpreter, Adams his two Japanese retainers, and there was an escort of a samurai officer plus three guards provided by Takanobu. In addition, 'according to the custome of the country',[247] there was a splendid pike-bearing officer called *yari-mochi*, who walked in front of VIPs in ceremonial attire.

The party chose the quickest and safest route, rowing to Hakata around the northern coast of Kyushu and through the Kanmon Channel, which led into the Inland Sea and on to Osaka. On 27 August, the party arrived offshore at Osaka, where they would transfer from their galley to a small boat to proceed up the river to Fushimi. Saris was impressed at the Osaka Castle, writing 'it was

---

[246] Adams, William.
[247] Satow, Sir Ernest.

as great as London within the walls'. Next day, on the eve of their departure, the host of the house where they had stayed in Osaka entertained them to a banquet of wine and salt fruits (or herbal food), as required by his loyalty to Lord Matsura.

Two days later, they were in Fushimi. Adams had sent a letter to Ieyasu, informing him that he would be arriving in Sumpu in a week with a small group of English visitors. When Ieyasu received the letter, he sent a palanquin carried by six men with nineteen horses so Captain Saris could travel more comfortably for the rest of his journey. Saris was very pleased at this honour and the arrival of Ieyasu's own *yari-mochi*, a fine figure of a man, to lead their procession. He expressed himself less impressed when the party crossed the borderline between each town, where the dead corpses of executed thieves and murderers had been left to decompose.

Every night, the party stopped at an inn or *yado-ya*. They were provided with rice, soup, fish, pickled herbs (*tsuke-mono*), beans, radishes and other roots. Saris particularly enjoyed bean-curd (*tofu*), which he thought was a kind of cheese.

Early on the morning of 6 September, almost a month after setting out, the original odd couple eventually reached Sumpu. The next day, informed by Adams that the captain was now in the city, Ieyasu sent word that, whenever the captain was ready, Adams should escort him to the court.

On 8 September, at the gate to Sumpu Castle, Adams and Saris were met by Lord Honda Masazumi, whose title was *Kōzuke-no-suke* or Chief Secretary, and by Mukai Shōgen as the second of Ieyasu's secretaries. Before their audience with Ieyasu, Adams had spent many hours explaining how important it was to learn the basic etiquette at the Japanese court, but Captain Saris was only half listening. He ordered Adams to inform Lord Honda that he wished to hand over his King's letter to Ieyasu himself. Lord Honda answered that, in his country, foreign people were not allowed to give the Shogun letters with their own hands; the captain could hold onto the letter until he came before Ieyasu, at which time he should hand it to the secretary (Lord Honda) for the official presentation. Then Saris replied that 'if he couldn't deliver the letter himself he would return to his accommodations, which the secretary should be informed of'.[248] After hearing of this, the lord was now offended with Adams. He assumed he had not explained the Japanese custom to the captain well enough, expressing' his displeasure that I (Adams) had not properly instructed him about this issue'. It was an impasse. At that moment, as Adams anxiety peaked, Ieyasu appeared in the chamber. Adams then records in his log book: 'The captain went before him to express his respect and then the secretary (Honda) took the letter from his hand and passed it on to Ieyasu.'[249] Saris, by contrast, wrote in his diary that he stepped forward to Ieyasu and 'delivered our king's letter unto his majestie, who took it in his hand, and put it up towards his forehead'.[250]

Adams and Lord Honda were relieved that Ieyasu seemed unaware of Saris' unruly behaviour. Saris' gifts were presented and he went back to his accommodation, while Adams was called back in to read and interpret the king's letter. After Ieyasu had fully understood the contents, 'He said that he would consent to any request the captain had,'[251] Adams wrote, 'and that these should be made through either the secretary or myself.'[252] Adams reported back to Saris, who then wrote down a list of the items and conditions that he felt the English East India Company needed.

The following day, Adams and Saris visited Lord Honda's residence. Saris presented several gifts, but the lord again refused to receive any gifts worth more than a few pounds, according to his own policy. Saris handed over his list of requests, which Adams later translated into Japanese and took to the Court.

When Adams arrived at the Court, Ieyasu called him in immediately. At the end of the conversation, Ieyasu said almost dismissively that he would grant Saris' requests. He seemed far more interested in whether the English would be able to find the North-west Pas-

---

248 Adams, William.
249 Ibid.
250 Satow, Sir Ernest.
251 Adams, William.
252 Ibid.

sage. Adams answered that the English had not found it yet, but his countrymen were great explorers. Ieyasu mentioned a country called Ezo (today's Hokkaido), approximately three miles off the northern tip of his country. His vassals had travelled to the country for thirty days to promote diplomatic relations. Ieyasu guessed that this was part of the great country of the Tatar. Adams' diary notes his own belief that this was 'a promontory sticked out like an elbow from the coast of Korea, jutting north-eastward toward Cathy or the Great Cam (Mongolia)'.[253] Ieyasu asked whether, if the English East India Company dispatched a ship for this exploration, Adams would be interested in taking part. Adams answered that he would be glad to participate in such an honourable undertaking. Then Ieyasu offered to provide signed letters, which would be very useful for the English to take to Matsumae and Ezo countries. In these countries, Ieyasu had vassals who could speak Korean and Tatar languages and who had towns and castles at which the Tatar and the Japanese were engaged in trade. Thus, in December 1613, Adams writes to the English East India Company suggesting they send a ship for this exploration: 'My own opinion that if we are to find a north-west passage, it will be by exploring the sea route from Japan.'[254]

After taking care of Saris' business, Adams turned his thoughts to the possibility of returning home by the *Clove*. He asked Honda Masanobu and Mukai Shōgen to speak to Ieyasu about his wish to return home, but both declined: the request had been rejected so many times and they were afraid of offending Ieyasu with an endless petition.

However, one day, Adams was summoned by Ieyasu and found him in a very good mood. Adams took a document from his pocket and presented it respectfully to Ieyasu, 'thanking him sincerely for the kindness and love he had shown to me up until then'.[255] Ieyasu stared at Adams in surprise for a moment. The document was the

---

[253] Ibid.
[254] Ibid.
[255] Ibid.

signed certificate of land ownership at Hemi and the lordship that Ieyasu had granted him. Ieyasu realized what Adams was asking for by returning these two great gifts. 'Do you really want to go back to your country so badly?'[256] he asked. Adams answered: 'It is my heart's deepest desire.'[257] Ieyasu then said that it would not be fair if he refused this request, after all the fine work and loyal service Adams had given him. So he granted Adams permission to leave Japan or to stay, whichever he liked. Then, sharp as ever, he asked Adams, if he ever decided to come back to Japan, to bring him from England the commodities he most desired, such as cannon and large woollen rugs. Then, gracious as ever, Ieyasu returned the signed document to his English falcon.

On the way back to his accommodation, Adams felt as if he could indeed fly with joy. Saris showed no interest in Adams' happiness. He was ready to visit Shogun Hidetada in Edo, so they departed at once.

On the way to Edo, Adams and Saris stopped off at the ancient city of Kamakura, about eighty miles from Sumpu. Saris noted the city was four times bigger than Edo and used to be 'the greatest city in Japan'.[258] Adams took him to several Shinto shrines and Buddhist temples. Saris was particularly impressed at the enormous bronze statue *Daibutsu* (Great Buddha) forty feet high, which had stood in its sacred temple since 1252. In hushed tones, Adams explained that visitors were expected to move quietly out of respect for the Buddha, but this seemed to goad Saris to shout, swear and insult this 'heathen' god.[259] A sorely embarrassed Anjin-sama had great difficulty in coaxing Saris out of the temple and not before his compatriots had carved their names with pride inside the Great Buddha.

The two men arrived in Edo on 14 September. Three days later, they were presented at Court to Shogun Hidetada, who received them warmly. Saris presented his gifts, including a silver gilt 'pro-

---

[256] Ibid.
[257] Ibid.
[258] Satow, Sir Ernest.
[259] Adams, William.

spective glass'[260] or telescope, a very new invention at that time. Hidetada asked Saris to take back to King James two varnished suits of armour and a *tachi* or long sword of the highest quality. It is widely believed that one of those suits of armour can still be seen on display in the Tower of London today.

Adams then invited Saris to his estate in Hemi. He thought it would be a good chance to show him the Uraga Port and to explain why it would be a better place than Hirado for the English factory, located as it was near Edo, where the Shogun's Palace, wealthy lords and merchants now were, and a healthy distance from the rival factories of the Portuguese, Spanish and Dutch.

On 21 September, the two men arrived at Uraga Port by boat. Saris stayed in Adams' estate for three days. He gave one silver and gilt cup and some potatoes to Adams' husbandmen and Indian-made white cotton *Tenjuku-momen* to Adams' wife Yuki, her sister and mother. Saris wrote nothing in his diary about his view of Adams' life, but he was impressed at Uraga. He wrote: 'It is a very good harbour for shipping, where ships may ride as safely as in the river of Thames before London.'[261] Adams told Saris that the Shogun had commissioned him to sell a Spanish vessel and its cargo for a high price, but he could offer it to Saris for £100. It was a bargain, but Saris refused. He had already developed a close business relationship with Lord Matsura Shigenobu, who had offered him better deals, including the means to trade in sexual amusements. We know Adams refused to provide Saris with this kind of dubious business and that Saris was offended and felt humiliated by Adams' attitude.

On 25 September, Adams and Saris departed from Uraga for Sumpu, where they would collect Ieyasu's reply to King James I's letter and a copy of the *Shuin-jo*,[262] red-seal trading licence, for

---

[260] Satow, Sir Ernest.
[261] Ibid.
[262] The licence issued to the English was markedly more favourable than those issued to the Dutch in 1608 and 1609. It covered accommodation, medical care and even burial! The licences can be compared in the excellently recreated Dutch East India Company Factory and Museum in Hirado. The original English licence is preserved in the Bodleian Library, Oxford.

the English East India Company. This time, Adams' brother-in-law (Yuki's sister's husband) who was called Zenroku accompanied the two men. He had converted to Christianity and been given the name Andreas.

They reached Sumpu on 29 September, but had to wait until 8 October when at last Ieyasu handed Saris the *Shuin-jo* and a letter to King James I, which Adams translated. This was the day, in the year 1613, when the English East India Company was formally authorized to trade in Japan. Saris was elated at the success of his mission. In his diary, he expresses his great thanks to Ieyasu and congratulates himself. There is no mention of William Adams.

The following day, the party departed for Hirado via Osaka, finally reaching the Hirado Port at ten o'clock on the morning of 6 November. The English welcomed them back with a volley of cannon-fire.

Saris had been anxious about how his men would behave in an unfamiliar country during his absence. When he saw Richard Cocks' glum face, he feared the worst. Cocks told him that nine members of his crew had escaped from Hirado. Just a few days after Saris left, they had caused considerable trouble to local people with outrageous and drunken behaviour. At the time of their Bon festival, the Japanese believe that the souls of dead ancestors return to earth. Worshippers place money in offering boxes at shrines and Buddhist temples, to thank them for looking after the souls and to pay for incense and flowers. The English mariners took advantage of this devout event to steal the money and spend it at taverns and brothels. One of these hooligans, called Francis Williams, got wildly drunk and attacked one of Lord Matsura's retainers with a cudgel. He should normally have had his head chopped off, as an instant punishment, but he escaped. Saris ordered Adams and Cocks to go to Nagasaki and seek the nine escapees, but later they learned that the men had escaped to Macao by a Portuguese vessel and from there they had fled to Manila on a Spanish vessel.

On top of that, the English house had been badly damaged by an earthquake and typhoon. After the quake, Richard Cocks and the other Englishmen were horrified at the first experience of a *tsunami* or great wall of water, when the *Clove* was nearly swept away. The newly-built kitchen of the English house had been completely wrecked. Saris' mood was not improved when he learned that Cocks had failed to sell almost anything from the English factory: the Japanese merchants would not buy without the *Shuin-jo*.

On 14 November, Saris discovered that a cook, one of Yajiue-mon's men who had acted as an interpreter as well as a commodity buyer, was overcharging for wine bought for the English factory on the black market. The next day, in the presence of Richard Cocks, Saris accused Adams of collusion in the fraud. He referred later to Adams' man's 'dishonnest and villainous dealing, being put in trust and to cheat us so unreasonable'. Saris was verbally abusive and launched a personal attack on Adams. Shocked at this uncontrolled behaviour, Adams said that it was 'very evil that his servant should be so thought of'.[263] The word 'evil' incensed Saris and when both men's tempers erupted, Cocks had to intervene. From that point, a chilly atmosphere pervaded the relationship between Adams and Saris, which was now irreparable.

Even after Adams had walked back to Yajiuemon's house, this normally self-controlled man was still in a whirlpool of fury. He had had enough of these difficulties with Saris and realized that it would be impossible for him to make the long return voyage under this captain. Even if Adams did return to Eng-land, he would now be concerned about his future there – it was more than likely Saris had already reported negatively about him to the English East India Company in London. Adams had no wish to build a new career from Limehouse all over again. 'I was going to return home on the *Clove*, but after the rude treatment I was given by the captain (Saris),'[264] Adams wrote to the English East India Company in London, 'I changed

---

[263] Adams, William.
[264] Ibid.

my mind.'[265] It would have been emotionally too painful for Adams to relate everything, so he wrote simply: 'I will not write about these insults here, but will leave it to others to tell the details after God has brought the ship safely home.'[266] When Captain Saris asked Adams whether he would like to return to England, he responded that he would. Then Saris asked, 'by the *Clove*?'[267] and Adams answered that he wouldn't.

It is hard to imagine what Adams was feeling after this fateful decision. He had the permission to leave Japan which he had craved for thirteen years and, even more extraordinary, an English ship in the harbour, which would depart for his own country soon. Surely the gods were smiling on him, and yet he abandoned the opportunity. Some books say the reason was that Adams had very little money to set himself up again in England. It is true that Adams wrote: 'I had been forced to serve the emperor (Ieyasu) in the country for many years. I had become poor.'[268] However, he also wrote that that was not the real reason. It is certainly true Adams could not bear to deal with Saris any more and that his own pride would not permit putting himself in debt to such a man.

He must surely have looked beyond an unpleasant journey home. He was clearly concerned about the damage done to his reputation by Saris' reports and would have contrasted the respect with which he was held in Japan with his uncertain prospects in King James' England, not exactly a meritocracy. He had also never heard from his wife and daughter in fifteen years and would have been assailed by doubts on that score. Above all, Adams was an adventurer who had already achieved much and was hungry for more. He was excited by the search for the North-west Passage and, as he remained close to Ieyasu, was confident he could promote English trade with Japan. Very cleverly, with gifts and challenging tasks, Ieyasu had got into Adams' mind and made it very difficult to

---

[265] Ibid.
[266–268] Adams, William.

return home. What Adams could not know was that a cruel event would soon remove Ieyasu's patronage.

Captain Saris asked Adams if he would be willing to work for the English East India Company. Adams answered that he was very happy to. Then the captain described the work and conditions and asked him first whether he 'would accept the twenty pounds free of interest that the company had already loaned to his wife (Mary Hyn) for her clothes and living expenses, leaving further payment up to the good will of the company'. Adams replied: 'I am very grateful for the Christian charity that the company showed in lending twenty pounds to my poor wife, and I would like to pay the interest on this, if possible.'[269] Later, Adams did repay the twenty pounds with interest to Richard Cocks and asked the company to lend Mary Hyn 'another twenty or thirty pounds if she was in need of it'.

Realizing that Adams was looking for a guaranteed salary, Captain Saris asked how much he wanted. Adams told Saris that he wanted to be paid twelve pounds per month, even though he had previously received fifteen pounds per month from the Dutch and other nations. Saris asked Adams to leave him alone to think about it for a while. When Adams was called back, Saris 'made an offer to Adams of eighty pounds per year'.[270] Adams rejected the offer: 'I had no interest in working for the company for less than ten pounds per month; I did not want to be paid higher wages when the profits to be made in Japan did not justify them, I would rather be given my freedom.'[271] Adams reminded Saris that the Dutch and the Japanese authorities would offer more: 'I had many better options to choose from, as he (Saris) well knew.'[272] Eventually, Saris offered to pay Adams eighty pounds plus the twenty pounds that had already been loaned to his wife, for which no interest would be charged, but again Adams declined. Instead, he suggested they leave it until the next day, when Saris should make his final offer.

[269-272] Ibid.

The next morning, the captain called Adams in and accused him of excessive demands. Insults were now being added to the tortuous negotiations. At last, the captain increased his offer to a clear one hundred pounds per year, which Adams deliberated on for a moment and accepted. Then Saris asked Adams how he would like to be paid. When Adams answered that he wanted to receive the money in Japan, Saris objected again. There was more argument and more hurt feelings. In the end, Adams records that Saris 'offered to lend me twenty pounds to cover the cost of things such as clothes for a period of two years, and I accepted'.[273]

On 26 November 1613, Captain Saris held a meeting of the factory council. He gave his men a long list of detailed instructions as 'remembarances',[274] including the assigning of duties to each of the Englishmen. The main instruction was to explore all parts of Japan, and possibly some parts of China and Korea, for lucrative trade until the next English vessel arrived. On the appointment of a chief factor, it was clear to everyone that the most eligible was William Adams. However, the Captain chose Richard Cocks. He then assigned Tempest Peacock, Richard Wickham, William Eaton, Walter Carwarden and four other Englishmen to higher posts than Adams. He also employed three Japanese interpreters and two male servants and, in a note to Cocks, described William Adams as lazy, selfish and greedy, 'only fitting to be master of the junk, and to be used as a linguist at court when you have no employment for him at sea'.[275]

Right up to Saris' departure, Adams was still trying to convince him to establish the English factory in Uraga, where he believed they could make more profit than in Hirado, but by now Saris was ignoring Adams' advice completely. He had fallen into Lord Matsura's trap and on 1 December before the *Clove*'s departure, the lord gave the captain a sumptuous feast with prostitutes or

---

[273] Ibid.
[274] Satow, Sir Ernest.
[275] Ibid.

'dancing bears',[276] as the English called them. Saris seems to have been intoxicated with this generous hospitality. Lord Matsura was triumphant.[277]

On 5 December 1613 and without ceremony, the *Clove* sailed out of Hirado Port on a northerly wind. According to contemporary accounts and even before the ship had merged into the sky over the horizon, Adams appeared to sink into a deep and dark depression.

To raise his spirits, Adams decided to start planning the exploration of a north-west passage, as he had promised the English East India Company. However, Ieyasu was having second thoughts. He knew that none of the Japanese would be able to lead the expedition. Adams was the only one who could possibly succeed, but it would be at very high risk. Could he risk sending his falcon to his death? At length Ieyasu decided and Adams received the kind of carrot-and-stick order, with which he was now familiar: 'You have to remain in Japan. You are not allowed to make expeditions. If you are not satisfied with the estate of Hemi and the income from its rice field, I will increase the size of your domain.'[278]

Battered by another disappointment, Adams came back to Yajiuemon's house. Yajiuemon, sometimes known as Sanzaburo or Zenzaburo, was also a matchmaker who traded women for foreign sailors or merchants. He had arranged for Richard Cocks to marry a Japanese servant called Matsuko, and other English and Dutch men to marry oriental women or be provided with concubines. Whether arranged by Yajiuemon or not, a Japanese woman called Coshuro is thought to have been Adams' concubine in Hirado. She was a Christian and worked as an interpreter. This time, as so often before in Yajiuemon's house, Adams would have sought solace in

---

[276] Ibid.

[277] His triumph increased Ieyasu's suspicions of the Matsura clan, who had provided him with less than full support at the Battle of Sekigahara. Later in 1613, the clan's *Hinotake* Castle was burned to the ground and this is widely believed to have been an extreme gesture by the clan itself to gain the trust of the Tokugawa Shogunate.

[278] Author's words - according to a description from Uchiyama Hitoshi.

her young breasts and in the total abandonment of his mind and body to sex.

Coshuro was to bear Adams a second son. He was stronger than Joseph and his father had high hopes for him. In time, however, mother and child would be separated when, only a few years after Adams' death, all children with foreign blood were expelled to Indonesia and Japan's long period of isolation began.

CHAPTER 15

A POLITICAL EARTHQUAKE

∂◦

In January 1614, the English East India factory in Bantam received a long letter from William Adams, written in December. The English were very pleased to hear that the Japanese ruler had accepted they could establish a base in Japan, at Uraga or Hirado or wherever they wished. They appreciated Adams' advice on choosing Uraga and were inclined to follow it. However, in his report to both the factory in Bantam and the company in London, Saris dismissed Adams' letter asserting that William Adams was unable to read Japanese and was entirely ignorant about the business of trade. Eventually, the company took Saris' advice. It was an epic mistake. They were rejecting an opportunity to outflank the Dutch East India Company, who had invested nearly four times as much as the English in establishing a foothold in Japan. Most of the English investment in establishing their factory in Hirado would in time be lost.

Meanwhile, following Captain Saris' last instructions, Tempest Peacock and his deputy Walter Carwarden hired two junks in Manila and Pattani. Adams was posted as captain of the junks and interpreter. Richard Wickham was assigned together with an interpreter to the Edo branch of the English East India Company. Captain Saris had designated him as chief factor in the event of Richard Cocks' death. In December 1613, Adams, Wickham and Eaton loaded goods onto a junk and sailed first for Osaka. Eaton was dropped off in Osaka, where he was to be in charge of a branch of the Company. When Adams and Wickham arrived in Edo, Adams left Wickham with all responsibilities at the Edo branch and returned to his house in Hemi to spend New Year's Day with his family, as was the custom in Japan.

In April 1614, Adams visited Ieyasu in Sumpu to request a Red Seal licence or *Shuin* for a voyage to Siam. To his surprise and delight, Ieyasu ordered from the Company three large woollen rugs, one Calverin cannon, one Sacar cannon and 600 cannon shot, at a total cost of £350,000 in today's money. In June, Adams returned to receive the licence, issued by Ieyasu on 16 May. On the way back to Hirado, Adams picked up Eaton in Osaka and on 21 July they arrived safely at the Hirado Port.

Adams evidently enjoyed Eaton's company. He was a diligent, honest and warm-hearted man, a friend to everybody. Richard Wickham, a Wiltshire-born and experienced adventurer, had also become a good friend. What Adams did not know was that Wickham's greedy and unscrupulous character had created bad relationships with Cocks, Captain Saris and all the other English crew members of the *Clove*. When one of Wickham's fellow sailors died, he forged the dead man's will making himself a beneficiary. Although he had done other dubious things, nobody had reported his bad behaviour to the London East India Company; he had an ace of spades, his good friendship with Sir Thomas Smythe. Wickham knew Adams was a useful ally and was careful not to reveal the negative side of his character.

On 26 July, Adams wrote a letter to inform Wickham that he and Eaton had safely returned to Hirado and found Richard Cocks, William Nealson and Edmund Sayers all in good health. Adams did not mention that Nealson was suffering chronic homesickness and had become an alcoholic and a hot-tempered troublemaker among the *Clove's* men, a sign perhaps that he did not think Wickham was entirely to be trusted with incriminating information.

The letter contained three items of news. The first was their tragic conclusion that Tempest Peacock, a well experienced man in merchandising, had likely been killed in Cochinchina. As Peacock, his deputy Carwarden and his junior Sayers needed to supplement their salaries, they had sailed with the Dutchmen to trade in Cochinchina. The king of the land bought all their goods and was particularly interested in cloth. Then, according to the reports, just after sailing away from shore in a small boat, a large ship rammed them. As the boat sank, Peacock, Carwarden and the Dutchmen swam for their lives. It was thought that Carwarden escaped, but all the others were cut to pieces by the Chinese. Sayers had stayed on the mother ship and could only pray to God for survivors, but Carwarden never returned to the ship.

The second news Adams reported was his obtaining a Red Seal licence from Ieyasu for a voyage to Siam and that he hoped to set sail in about three months. He did not mention that the 200-ton junk was dreadfully old. Three months was to prove wishful thinking.

Finally, he reported the death on 26 May 1614 of Lord Matsura Shigenobu, at the age of sixty-six. Adams hoped that the news would reach Captain Saris through the London East India Company, when the captain arrived at Plymouth. Perhaps, Adams wondered, Captain Saris might feel a little less arrogant, on news that his main supporter in Japan had died.

It took more than four months and £1000 for Adams to repair the old junk. Adams named it *Sea Adventure*. He selected Wickham and Sayers to sail with him and employed sixty Japanese sailors. The *Sea Adventure* loaded £720 worth of goods and set off for Siam on 17 December 1614.

Meanwhile, emboldened with his Calverin and Sacar cannons, Ieyasu was planning an attack on the Toyotomi family in their Osaka castle. The family still controlled important areas of Japan and were potentially a focal point for dissent. He instructed all his allies to prepare to go to Osaka and await his orders.

During that summer, Ieyasu heard that the Toyotomi family were preparing a Buddhist inauguration ceremony at the Hōkō-Ji temple in Kyoto. They believed that they would draw the Buddha's soul back there, after they rebuilt its great statue of Buddha. The statue was originally built by Toyotomi Hideyoshi, but it had been damaged. For the ceremony, the Toyotomi family had an uplifting message engraved on the great bell which hung in the temple. A Buddhist priest named Suden and the Confucianist Hayashi Razan, who were both Ieyasu's supporters, had been asked by Ieyasu to find incriminating evidence against the Toyotomi family. Suden and Razan racked their brains. Everything seemed perfect. Eventually, they found that the message could appear sarcastic: 'Wishing the state eternal security and peace,'[279] it said in Chinese characters. The words contained the name Ieyasu. *Ie* means the state and *Yasu* means peace. The letters for eternal security were placed between *Ie* and *Yasu*, so that security could not be achieved for Japan unless the letters became a sword that cut Ieyasu in half. Ieyasu did not take long to agree that this must be treason.

Confused and angry, the Toyotomi family desperately pleaded against this false accusation, but Ieyasu ignored them. He could now put his plan into action, despatching over 200,000 warriors to Osaka. By the middle of November 1614, the Osaka castle and over 100,000 Toyotomi warriors were surrounded and outnumbered by Ieyasu's forces, lined up twenty rows deep. The castle was well protected by tier upon tier of high, thick walls. Ieyasu had decided on a war of attrition. He ordered his warriors to dam up the Yoda River and to build themselves dozens of fortresses, called *Mukai-jo,* around the castle. The *Mukai-jo* were supplied with 1000 six-foot shields against enemy fire. Ieyasu's trump card was the Calverin and Sacar cannons that he had bought from Adams. Remembering Adams' advice about the shooting range, he placed these cannons on the Chausu Mountain, some three miles from the castle, but close enough for the cannonballs to reach their target.

Before firing, Ieyasu was handed the traditional *Saihai,* a tuft of thick papers cut into ribbons, bound to a bamboo stick. It would be the signal to fire. Ieyasu raised the *Saihai* above his head, paused for a moment and brought it down. The Chausu Mountain shook with the first volley. The second, the third, ... until the tenth, one after another these murderous missiles streaked across the sky above Ieyasu's army. Since the Sekigahara War fourteen years earlier, the gunners' skills had greatly improved and they struck with deadly

---

[279] Translated by the author from Nakamura Koya.

accuracy. At the same time, in the equivalent of 'shock and awe' tactics today, Ieyasu signalled to 200 riflemen to fire and 100 others to throw explosives from their positions close to the castle. One by one, the great walls crumbled and, like an onion, peeled away to reveal hundreds of warriors and servants scattering to avoid the gunfire and flames. Many of them jumped into wells, their clothes on fire. For ten days, the Toyotomi family and their vassals endured this hell, from morning until night. Meanwhile, Ieyasu was up to his old tricks. A letter to Sanada Yukimura, the most powerful lord and close retainer of the Toyotomi family, offering a bribe of 100,000 koku, had the desired effect and he deserted.

Early in December, the Toyotomi family pleaded with Ieyasu for peace talks. Ieyasu had two conditions. The castle's second and third citadels must be destroyed. Only the main castle and its separate sanctuary could remain. Two important members of the Toyotomi family must also be surrendered as hostages. On 20 December 1614, Ieyasu halted the bombardment. It was the end of what became known as the Osaka Winter Battle. In seven days, all the walls and citadels, which had protected the castle and sanctuary, disappeared. The onion had been peeled to its core. The secret sanctuary in particular looked like a wrecked ship, hopelessly drifting in the middle of the ocean. Ieyasu gloated over the once impregnable sanctuary, thinking that even a toddler could walk in.

In the same month, Adams sailed his *Sea Adventure* out of Hirado for Siam. The vessel struggled through its first storms off the Amami Ōshima Island, before reaching Ryukyu Island (today's Okinawa) about 500 miles south of Hirado, which at that time was claimed by both the Chinese and Malay. On 27 January 1615, *Sea Adventure* arrived at Naha, the capital of Ryukyu. Adams was given permission by King Shoutei of Ryukyu to undertake repairs to his vessel. While there, he and his men heard that many high-ranking samurai lords loyal to the Toyotomi family had arrived in Ryukyu on 21 January, escaping after a defeat by Ieyasu's army. Like word of an important win for a sailor's favourite team, the news would have been a relief to Adams, although he probably took care to avoid the opposition's exiled fans.

Then Adams encountered some unexpected obstruction from envoys of the local governor, who refused to supply ship-building materials to a foreigner. Adams sent a message to King Shoutei to plead for support. No sooner had he received this support, another problem arose. Many of his crew, fearing things were unravelling, went on strike for immediate payment. There was nothing Adams could do without a crew, so he reluctantly paid them with signed drafts.

On 1 February 1615, a messenger from King Shoutei came to Adams. The king advised Adams that a large trading ship would arrive soon from China and that *Sea Adventure* must surrender its anchorage before then. With no hope of completing all the repairs, a disappointed Adams had to abandon his voyage to Siam, but resourceful as ever, he loaded local produce, including flour and sweet potatoes, before departing for Japan.

Three months after the Osaka Winter Battle ended, Ieyasu heard that the Toyotomi family had started digging fosses at the site of the destroyed second and third citadels. For Ieyasu, this was treachery, a clear sign the family was preparing to rebuild the citadels. He ordered his army to prepare rations for three days. Compared with the Osaka Winter Battle, that stretched over nearly two months, the Osaka Summer Battle was to be completed in three days.

On 5 May, Ieyasu reassembled his Calverin cannon and launched a terrifying barrage on the remaining core of the Osaka Castle. Toyotomi Hideyori, the son of Governor Hideyoshi, Princess Yodo, his mother and all their close retainers took sanctuary in a hiding place, which had been built in the depths of the stronghold. They all, particularly the proud Princess Yodo, preferred double suicide to surrender so, with their short swords or *tan-to*, they stabbed each other to death. Their bodies were subsequently engulfed in a massive blaze, which, on schedule, ended the Osaka Summer Battle at 4 o'clock on 7 May 1615. It is significant date in Japanese history, marking the fall of the Toyotomi family and the establishment of the unshakeable Tokugawa dynasty, which was to last another 253 years.

□

On 10 June 1615, *Sea Adventure* returned from Ryukyu to Hirado and to news of the Osaka Battles, in which the Calverin and Sacar cannon that Adams had sold to Ieyasu had played a star role. When he learned the fate of the Toyotomi family, shivers must have run up Adams' spine. It was pure chance that had originally aligned him with the Tokugawa family and saved him from finishing his life stabbed to death in a blaze in Osaka Castle.

One of Adams' lesser known contributions to Japan was to introduce the sweet potato, called *Kansho* in Japanese. When he brought some back from Ryukyu Island to Hirado in 1615, the English East India Company cultivated them in their vegetable garden. This was called the Hirado Sweet Potato or *Hirado-sho*. By 1620, the potato was commonly grown all over Japan. It was originally discovered by accident on the island in 1606, by Nagumi Sokan, a Chinese minor official stationed at the Ryukyu trading depot. By 1609, it was well established in the Ryukyu economy. Then the Japanese Satsuma clan, who occupied Shuri Castle in Ryukyu Island, imported the potato into Satsuma (today's Kogoshima Prefecture), but kept it to themselves. Adams' achievement was to make it widely available. However, history has not been kind to either Adams or Hirado as the sweet potato or *Hirado-sho* is commonly called *Satsuma-Imo* today.

Adams also brought back from Ryukyu some thin cloth, called *Bashofu,* which looked and felt like linen or calico. The cloth is still used to make summer *kimono*, cushions and mosquito nets. Another souvenir was the potent Ryukyu rice brandy, called *Awamori*, which Adams was careful to give in large measures to the lord and the high-ranking retainers of the Hirado Castle. They were greatly delighted.

On 4 September 1615, the English ship *Hoseander* arrived at Hirado. Adams was put in charge of looking after its captain, Ralph Coppindall. Assuming that Ieyasu was in the Fushimi Castle after his victory in the Osaka Summer Battle, he took the captain there, only to be informed by Hidetada that his father had gone back to Sumpu, eight days earlier. Hidetada then ordered Adams to go urgently to Edo to deal with the ambassador from Nova España.

Adams' instructions were to reject all presents from the ambassador. Adams did not have enough time to explain to Cocks why he had to hurry to Edo alone. Cocks assumed that Adams had wantonly abandoned Captain Coppindall and the other Englishmen. He wrote angrily in his diary: 'I suspect it was a plot laid before Captain Adams himself and the Dutch, to the extent he might go up to serve their turnes. ... truly I esteem he loves them much better than us that are of his own nation.'[280] On this and other occasions, Cocks and his colleagues failed to understand the pressures Adams was under, the alliances he needed and the compromises he had to make to survive. Of course, Adams had never forgotten for how long and how badly he had been betrayed by the Dutch, and he remained hostile towards the Portuguese and Spanish. If Cocks had paused to imagine what it would be like to be quite alone in an unknown land, in effect to be cast adrift in a hostile ocean, he might have reacted differently.

Cocks, Captain Coppindall and the other Englishmen decided to make their own way to Sumpu. They were delayed by a leaking ship, but eventually, on 10 October, Captain Coppindall was received in audience with Ieyasu. Two days later, the English party departed for Edo to pay their respects to Hidetada. Adams stayed at his estate in Hemi until 13 October, returning to Hirado on 27 November, just one day before the English party arrived back there.

On 7 December 1615, Adams departed from Hirado for a voyage to Siam, by order of Richard Cocks. Cocks handed £500 to Adams for business and voyage expenditure. Adams reached the Maenam estuary on 10 January 1616 and Bangkok the next day. He was granted an audience with the King of Siam and succeeded in obtaining a trading licence for the English East India Company. He bought 2350 sections of *Suou* wood, which produced a red dye used in textiles, and 3700 deer skins. Adams and his crew were in high spirits. Before leaving Bangkok on 5 June, Adams heard a rumour that the Japanese ruler had died, but he did not believe it. He arrived safely at Hirado on 22 July 1616.

---

[280] Cocks, Richard.

When Richard Cocks gave him the news of Ieyasu's death three months earlier, Adams must have felt as if he had been hit in the chest. His mind goes blank. He is so shocked that he can find no words to express his mixed emotions, of grief, disappointment and anxiety. Typically, Adams puts his grief on hold and tries to distract himself. He has noticed that an English ship is anchored at the Hirado Port and asks Cocks about her. Cocks replies that she arrived on 12 July and is called *Advice*. A despondent Adams wonders aloud, 'What advice did she bring to us?'[281] and Cocks grins at Adams' wit, but soon realizes that the humour springs from a very dark mood, so he quickly changes the subject.

The *Advice* was in fact one of two vessels which the English East India Company merchants had sent to Hirado, after Captain Saris returned to England in the *Clove*. Saris had arrived in Plymouth at the end of September 1614. It was common for long-distance English vessels to make a short-term anchorage at one of the ports on the south coast to take on fresh water before sailing on to London. The London merchants had expected her in London within a few days, but she had remained at anchor in Plymouth for more than six weeks. Captain Saris made excuses that his vessel had been hit by fierce storms, 'tempestuous .... our lives more endangered than upon the whole voyage'.[282] However, the merchants did not believe Saris. They feared that he would unload some cargo and try to sell it privately. Their suspicions seemed to be confirmed when they were shown two secret letters from Saris to his brother and cousin. In the letters Saris asked them to send 'two trustworthy watermen',[283] surely men who could sell cargo on the black market.

As the evidence mounted that Saris 'had used very great private trade for himself',[284] the company's directors sent two of their agents to Plymouth with orders to protect the cargo. They sent a third official to the postmaster's house to intercept Saris' letters and

---

[281–284] Ibid.

ordered a fourth official to pick up gossip about Saris in the Star Inn in Bread Street, where many mariners stayed.

Captain Saris would certainly have been alarmed to hear of his employer's suspicions, but he had many supporters in the East India Company. They advocated that Saris should not be condemned on slight evidence and succeeded in convincing the directors to repeal an order to summon and accuse Saris in London.

Nevertheless, the directors soon received information from the four officials sent to Plymouth. They had discovered not a secret about Saris but a letter from William Adams, found among a parcel of letters deposited at the postmaster's house. So they learnt that seven Englishmen had been stationed in Hirado and Shogun Ieyasu had offered generous trading privileges. The letter also mentioned that Japan was as rich as the rumours had implied, as well as an ideal country for repairing vessels battered by the long sea voyage; the carpenters, timbers, planking and iron were as good and as cheap as in England.

After his six-week anchorage in Plymouth, Captain Saris set sail for London, arriving in the middle of November. Many merchants were still suspicious of his time in Plymouth, but at a merchant council Captain Saris played to his strengths. In his most charming and persuasive tones, he presented such a glowing report on Japan's highly profitable market that all the merchants were caught up in his fantasy. Their suspicions were forgotten and the discussion turned to joyful anticipation of their future prosperity. Saris encouraged the merchants to prepare brightly coloured broadcloth, baize (a cotton or woollen material resembling felt), linen and Indian cloth, for which the Japanese would willingly pay large sums of money, although Cocks had informed Saris earlier that it would be almost impossible to sell colourful cloth to the Japanese, because they generally prefer sober colours like black or brown. Saris also reported much higher selling prices than the actual prices for cloth, sugar candy and soap. Saris must have been well aware of his over-optimism, but he was desperate to restore his honour and reputation. His cause was helped by word that the Dutch had invested £1500 on repairing and extending their Hirado factory, so the English merchants knew that the Dutch must be confident of profitable trade.

Finally, the merchants decided to trust Saris and so it was that the two vessels, the *Advice* and the *Attendant*, were despatched to Japan in 1615.

Adams' contract with the English East India factory in Hirado had officially come to an end in November 1615. However, after Ieyasu's death the following April, Adams was still concerning himself with the threat to the company's prospects, if Shogun Hidetada was not inclined to renew their trading licences. Adams would have to visit Hidetada anyway to present his condolences on his father's death; so on 30 July 1616 Adams, Cocks and twenty-three other crew members set out from Hirado for Edo. William Eaton joined up with them in Osaka. On the way, at Odawara in Sumpu, Adams had arranged a treat. Two of his servants brought a generous amount of grilled pork, rice wine, grapes and bread. The large party travelled on in good spirits and arrived in Edo on 27 August. Adams lodged everyone at his mansion at Nihonbashi. Later Richard Wickham joined the party.

When Adams met Matsura Takanobu in Edo, he asked him how Ieyasu had died. Takanobu explained that at the end of January 1616, after one of his regular falconry tours, Ieyasu celebrated with a banquet. That night, he suffered acute stomach pain and his throat filled with mucus. The sea-bream cooked in oil from the berries of the Nutmeg Yew (Japanese *torreya*) was thought to be the cause. After treatment from his court physician, Ieyasu recovered and went back to Sumpu. At the end of February, the severe pain returned. He became so ill that he completely lost his appetite. The court people, powerful lords, Buddhist and Shinto priests and many other supporters hurried to Sumpu to try to help. Every day the priests prayed for his recovery. Then, in March, Ieyasu received a notification from the Emperor in Kyoto. The Royal Court had decided to give him the honorific title of Minister President, *Dajo-Daijin*. Ieyasu was still frail and racked with pain, but he dressed up for the ceremony and expressed his gratitude to the Emperor.

At the end of March, his condition worsened. Everybody expected the worst. Ieyasu gathered his close retainers to his bedside and told them he was not afraid of dying. If somebody were to seize power from his successor Hidetada, he would bear them no grudge. The world did not belong to one person. However, while his son reigned, and in the interests of peace and security, he would expect them all to deal with any rebels with the utmost ruthlessness.

On 15 April, Ieyasu got up from his bed and grabbed a long sword handed to him by Miike Norihiro, his closest aide. He then ordered a retainer to test it on a convicted criminal and report back on the quality of the blade. The retainer severed several parts of the unfortunate man's body and reported that the sword was as sharp as it had ever been. Then Ieyasu said: 'With this sword, I will guard and protect my descendants for many ages.'[285] Two days later, Tokugawa Ieyasu died at the age of seventy-five.

Matsura Takanobu had told the story of his Shogun's death with due respect, but when he described the wealth that Ieyasu had amassed for his descendants, his countenance changed. He called Ieyasu a greedy fox, who had owned at least 1.7 million ryō (around £1.4 billion in today's money). He had left 700,000 ryō to Hidetada and over 500,000 ryō to other descendants. For Adams, the most interesting things found among Ieyasu's possessions were over 1000 bars of soap. He imagined the King of Japan bathing every night in a mountain of bubbles, but realized it was more likely the wily fox was attempting to corner the soap market and drive up the price.

Adams found himself recalling his Shogun jailor with respect and affection. He had certainly taken advantage of Adams' weak position but, in asking ever more of him, Ieyasu had challenged him to achieve more than he had ever dreamed.

Adams was astonished and impressed that, after Ieyasu died, two loyal retainers committed *seppuku,* or suicide, to accompany Ieyasu's soul on its journey. Their bodies were buried near Ieyasu's tomb and a monument erected in their honour. He still had much

---

[285] Translated by the author from Nakamura Koya.

to learn about the *Shinto* religion, in which all the souls of the dead became gods and inhabit another world, where gods are counted in the millions.

On 1 September 1616, the Englishmen from the East India Company factory were summoned to meet Hidetada. To his surprise and dismay, the courtiers informed Adams that Hidetada was excluding him from the meeting. Hidetada and his close retainers were hostile to Adams, partly out of jealousy towards a foreigner who had gained Ieyasu's favour, but also because Hidetada, more strongly anti-Christian than Ieyasu, had heard that Adams' wife had secretly converted to Christianity and that she and Adams had hidden and protected exiled Jesuits. Hidetada was far less tolerant than Ieyasu and had little of his father's intellectual curiosity. He was simply not interested, for example, in the differences between Protestants and Catholics.

After Ieyasu's death, Hidetada meeted out harsh treatment to his half-brother Matsudaira Tadateru. During the Osaka Winter Battle, Ieyasu had been furious at Tadateru's negligence. After the battle, Ieyasu ordered Tadateru to remain under house arrest at Ueno Fujioka in Mie Prefecture, in the middle of Honshu. When Hidetada learnt that Tadateru too had embraced Christianity, he exiled him to the island of Ise, off the Shima Peninsula on the east coast. He confiscated his domain and stripped him of his title and samurai status.

Hidetada was revealing himself as a nervous and fearful character, still troubled by guilt at how he had disgraced his family at the Battle of Sekigahara. Since then, he had frequently disappointed his father and one reason why Ieyasu resigned as Shogun early was probably to train Hidetada to become a worthy successor. Excluded from the audience with Hidetada, Adams advised Richard Cocks on the complicated rules of etiquette and respect at the Shogun's court. Unlike Saris, Cocks willingly took Adams' advice. Hidetada accepted the Company's presents, such as silk, animal skins and ivory. He also listened politely to Cocks' request to renew their licence and trading privileges, but declined to give him a response at that time. It was becoming clear to all members of the English

East India Company factory that they faced an uncertain future, now Adams had lost his protector.

The next day, Adams decided to visit Edo castle himself to plead with Hidetada for the trading privileges. The courtiers told Adams that Hidetada had gone for falconry, which Adams suspected was an excuse to avoid meeting him. Next day, he visited the castle again, but received the same excuse. Every day and all day for three weeks, Adams waited in an anteroom alone with no tea or food. Adams wrote that he was 'racked and tormented very much'. Some courtiers would probably have observed that torment with satisfaction. The blue-eyed samurai was receiving his come-uppance.

After three weeks, Hidetada probably thought that his ill treatment of Adams was enough and granted him an audience. While Hidetada still stalled on the English trade privileges, he showed Adams respect and asked him to become his master-pilot on a mission to explore the legendary North-west Passage. Adams answered that, as he was still assisting the English East India Company, he was unable to serve two masters. However, he promised to do what he could to investigate for the Shogun those islands to the north of Japan which were thought to have rich mines of gold and silver. Hidetada's mood improved and eventually, on 23 September, he gave Adams the Red Seal licence and trading privileges for the English East India Company.

Adams and Cocks decided to hurry to Adams' estate at Hemi to celebrate their success. All Adams' husbandmen lined the road and bowed deeply. Like a returning hero, Adams' arrival prompted joy and respect. They brought him fresh fruit such as oranges, figs, pears, chestnuts and grapes. Cocks was impressed at Adams' status. He wrote that he had never seen such numbers of husbandmen and servants for those English lords he knew back home.

Their joy was short-lived. On 30 September, Adams received an express letter from Richard Wickham in Edo. The contents sent Adams into a state of shock. Wickham reported that Hidetada had issued a new decree forbidding Japanese merchants to buy merchandise from any foreigners who resided in Osaka and Kyoto. When Adams reread the documents that Hidetada had given him, he found that the English trading areas were indeed limited to Hirado and Nagasaki.

Adams, Cocks and Wickham dashed straight back to Edo castle to plead with Hidetada to alter the documents and revoke his decree. On arrival, they were largely ignored. None of the courtiers came to greet them. When they eventually met Sakai, a senior courtier, Cocks pleaded that the Shogun 'might as well banish us right out of Japan as bind us to such an order, for that we could make no sales at that place'.[286] Sakai's response was crushing; 'You cannot expect favours from the Shogun if you address him by the wrong name.'[287] It appeared that the English East India Company's petition to Hidetada had been addressed to his dead father, an error not picked up by their translator or subsequently by Adams.

It wasn't until 14 October that they were seen by Hidetada and Cocks' diary records how he told the Shogun: 'King James would think it to be our misbehaviours that caused our privileges to be taken from us. It stood me upon as much as my life was worth to get it amended, otherwise, I knew not how to show my face in England.'[288]

Hidetada remained unimpressed. The English would be confined to their isolated factory in Hirado. Hidetada agreed only that the stock already stored in their branches could be sold off under the terms of the original agreement. All future trade must be confined to Hirado. On the other hand, William Adams was to be exempted from the new decree. One of the reasons Hidetada was jealous of Adams was possibly because he admired and respected him so highly. He also needed the exceptional knowledge and skills that Adams had shared with his father. To protect his own power, Hidetada decided to protect Adams. He reaffirmed Lord Miura Anjin's status as *hatamoto*.

The despondent Englishmen set off for Hirado on 17 October 1616. A few days later, after staying at an inn at Yui town in Sumpu,

---

[286] Cocks, Richard.
[287] Ibid.
[288] Ibid.

they were at full gallop when a crow flew out of the hedgerow startling Adams' horse. Thrown to the ground, Adams found his right shoulder-bone was out of joint and he had ricked his neck. The local medical treatment set him back 300 silver coins, much more than he expected. The following day, Adams felt a little better, but fearing his shoulder would slip out of joint again, he decided to stay behind in Sumpu for five more days.

Adams realized it was not just his physical power that was weaker now. It was clear for all to see that his political power was a shadow of what it had been, but it seems his thoughts were still on protecting his countrymen. On 30 October, on the way to Osaka, Cocks received a message from one of Adams' servants. Adams advised Cocks not to stay in the inn where they planned to stay at Ôtsu, Shiga Prefecture, because the Japanese staff there could no longer be trusted to treat them well. It would be safer to find another inn.

Although still suffering pains in his shoulder and neck, on 15 November, Adams managed to catch up with the Englishmen at Sakai Port, Osaka. William Eaton had joined them, but it was not a happy group. A deep sense of failure and foreboding hung like a black cloud over their ten days together in Osaka and on the voyage back to Hirado.

Brighter news greeted Cocks on his return to Hirado on 3 December. During his absence, the sale of their sapwood had made a large sum of money for his factory, sufficient to stave off bankruptcy. All the Englishmen decided to count their blessings and hold a lavish Christmas banquet, spiced up with dancing girls, and before 21 December, the day when they were due to set sail for Siam for trade. This time, William Adams did not join the Englishmen, either for the party or the voyage. After he returned to Hirado, it is believed he suffered some kind of mental breakdown from the succession of painful events, both physical and psychological. Certainly Cocks' diary reveals serious concern over his health and self-imposed isolation. The steely determination that had seen him through so much was beginning to crack.

CHAPTER 16

PRIVATE DISGRACE AND COMPANY DEBT

∂∾

In the meantime, after his narrow escape from prosecution, Captain Saris was back in favour. The London merchants had received many letters from the Englishmen in Hirado, pleading with them to send the silks that the Japanese craved rather than the colourful Indian cloth, baize and others that Saris had recommended, but they were ignored.

Sir Thomas Smythe became more supportive of Captain Saris. He even lent him a room in his house, to store his personal belongings. Then, just a few days before Christmas, Sir Thomas heard a rumour that Saris had collected on his voyages a large number of pornographic and erotic books and paintings and secreted them among his effects. One evening after work, he opened one of the boxes, not wanting to believe this of his favourite captain. He was horrified to find a vast amount of 'lascivious books and pictures'.[289] When he informed the senior merchants of the company, they felt physically sick, knowing that the disgraceful discovery would be 'held to be a great scandal onto this (their) company'.[290]

For Sir Thomas, it was doubly embarrassing that the lascivious things had been found in his house. He convinced his merchants

---

[289] Keay, John.
[290] Ibid.

that he had had no knowledge and would never have countenanced such trade, but the gossip spread with much mirth. 'Derogatory speeches'[291] were made about it in the London Exchange. Smythe decided he must destroy all the books and pictures in a public burning ceremony, with Saris present. On 10 January 1615, Saris' precious international collection was piled up outside the offices of the company. Sir Thomas himself 'put them into the fire, where they continued till they were burnt and turned into smoke'.[292] The black ashes blew away and with them went Captain Saris' career.

Unknown to the London merchants, there was another scandal brewing. Richard Cocks was becoming increasingly anxious about a large deficit that Captain Saris and the other Englishmen in Hirado had run up on dancing girls or prostitutes, servants and extravagant building work. To hide these expenses in his profit, Cocks desperately needed to sell his cargo to, as he wrote, 'turn all into ready money before any other ship come out of England'.[293]

Captain Saris had taken a mistress called Oman. He would have had to give her generous presents such as silk, satin and jewellery from the company's cargo and, according to Cocks, he put almost all the payments for her on the company's expense account. However, Oman found Saris, who may have been infertile, an unsatisfactory lover and eventually rejected the captain and transferred her favours to the junior crew member, William Eaton. Later, they produced two children called William and Helen. Not surprisingly perhaps, there is no mention of any of this in Saris' letters or diary.

All the other Englishmen in Hirado had mistresses, whose willingness owed something to the prospect of creating a family that would be the financial responsibility of the husband and the company. Cocks was provided at first with a twelve-year-old dancing girl, but he complained she was too young for intercourse. The girl was replaced with an older dancer called Mitinga, or Oharu in

---

[291] Ibid.
[292] Keay, John and Wilbur, Marguerite.
[293] Cocks, Richard.

Japanese records. Cocks was very satisfied with her and showered her with presents and even a house in Hirado with maids and servants. All the bills were paid from his own pocket. Later, Cocks learnt that Mitinga had been diversifying her portfolio. Cocks wrote of her 'villany' and how she had 'abused herself with six or seven persons'.[294] Like Captain Saris, Cocks too was thought to be infertile and the 'infidelity'[295] seems to have hit him hard. Mitinga on the other hand had been a prostitute and may not have thought that sleeping with six other men was unfaithful. By contrast, Edmond Sayers had a good mistress, called Maria. She was faithful to Sayers and gave birth to a daughter.

Back in London, after salvaging some honour by burning Saris' pornography, Sir Thomas Smythe had gone back to normal life in his busy office at Philpot Lane, where he received regular guests such as merchants, sailors and explorers. Among his more unusual guests, on the morning of 13 April 1615, was a haggard and shabby-looking female with dry, grey hair. This was Mrs Mary-Hyn Adams. She was now desperately short of money. Her living expenses had risen sharply and her small savings had been consumed a long time ago. She had had to leave Limehouse for a vagrant life of begging. It was now impossible for her to support her seventeen-year-old daughter Deliverance. The company's records show that poor Mary-Hyn pleaded with Sir Thomas Smythe to be 'relieved with £30 out of her husband's wages' for food and clothing.

This was the sum that Adams had already asked the East India Company in London to provide for his wife, but Sir Thomas seems to have been a parsimonious protector of the company's coffers. The company, he said, would give her £20 at that time and £10 in twelve months. Mrs Adams protested and eventually was given most of the £30 that day, but the experience taught her not to trust the company and that she would have to persist with her claims if she was to receive the remaining money. We don't know what the company told her about her husband's life in Japan, but we do

---

294 Ibid.
295 Ibid.

know that Adams' carefully written letters had never reached her. It must have been distressing, even for a sailor's wife.

When Christmas was over in 1616, Adams, who had not changed his mind about ending his contract with the East India Company, turned his thoughts to operating his own private trade. He asked Cocks to sell him at half price the junk that the company had bought in Siam. Cocks agreed and Adams decided to sail for Cochinchina. First the junk needed some repairs; so, on the first day of the new year, Adams made a trip to Nagasaki to buy timber and masts. He named his junk the *Gift of God* after one of the fleet, with its flagship the *Duffield*, on which he had worked before in England. Not everyone was pleased about *the Gift of God*. The young Lord Matsura Takanobu had wanted Adams to spend his money on the repairs in Hirado rather than in Nagasaki, where Adams had found the wood cheaper. The angry lord let it be known that Adams was not allowed to use any carpenters in Hirado. So Adams had to hire several men from the English East India Company to complete the repairs. Then, when Adams was making final preparations for the voyage, three rough men clambered aboard the ship and, in Cox's words, 'held Adams, and before he was aware, they wrung him and punched him'.[296] His arm, still recovering from the fall, was wrenched almost out of its socket. When Adams cried out in pain, Edmond Sayers and the English boatman John Phebie rushed to the rescue. Then Adams remembered to reach inside his breast pocket and pull out a document, 'kissed it and held it up over his head'.[297] As soon as the violent men saw that it was the Red Seal licence from Shogun Hidetada, denoting Adams still had access to the court, they scattered like rabbits. Later, Adams asked Cocks to report the incident to Lord Matsura Takanobu.

It turned out the rough men were henchmen working for the Hirado port's principal merchants. The merchants had objected to the English Company's recent sale of Siamese sapwood and were still in dispute over it. Some of the merchants were hot-blooded

---

[296] Ibid.
[297] Author's words.

and prejudiced against Adams, as a favoured foreigner. When they also heard that Adams had made all his equipment purchases in Nagasaki, they chose three of the wildest among their henchmen to exact their revenge.

Apparently unfazed by the incident, Adams refocused on the voyage and asked Cocks whether there was anything he could do to help the company. Cocks mentioned that he had heard nothing more on Tempest Peacock and Walter Carwarden, who had sailed to Cochinchina in the spring of 1614 and had been expected to return in four or five months. There had been rumours that the two men had been killed, captured or drowned, but over the last two years Cocks had done nothing to confirm them. Here was a good opportunity to ask Adams to find out what had really happened. Adams readily agreed and also offered to help in trading goods in the English Hirado factory for the Chinese silks and animal skins, which were to have been brought back by the two missing men. Cocks volunteered Sayers to accompany Adams and on 23 March 1617, the *Gift of God* loaded up and sailed out of Hirado.

The *Gift of God* anchored at the mouth of the vast Quang Nam River, its waters as dark as a forest. The local officials in charge of the river were puzzled at the unexpected vessel. They questioned Adams about the purpose of his visit. Adams explained to them that he came on behalf of the chief factor at the English factory in Japan to find out what happened to the two Englishmen, Peacock and Carwarden. The official looked a bit awkward and mumbled something. When the local governor's secretary arrived, Adams answered the same way to the same question, but this time added: 'We heard they were killed here.'[298] With what Adams took to be feigned politeness and sympathy, the secretary answered that Peacock and Carwarden 'were drowned by mischance in a small boat'.[299] He warned Adams to pursue the case no more and attempted to silence him with the words: 'That is gone and past, and is not needful for

---

[298] Cocks, Richard.
[299] Ibid.

to speak of this now.'[300] Adams realized that he knew more than he was letting on.

During Adams' stay in Cochinchina, he quizzed many local traders about the missing seamen. After much reliable evidence, he concluded that Peacock was murdered by a Japanese hired-killer called Mangosa, who had been paid by local officials, possibly even the secretary whom Adams had met. Mangosa had disguised himself as a merchant and Peacock was tempted with the promise of trade and trusted him enough to lodge together. The trigger for the killing was that the drunken Peacock had offended the Cochin Chinese with his boast that the 'superior'[301] English could blockade all the coastal ports of Cochinchina to cripple their trade. It was never known quite how Peacock died, but it is said that he was probably strangled 'in the water with harping irons, like fishes'.[302]

Carwarden's death was less of a puzzle. He had waited for Peacock in the river estuary, while his friend was meeting Mangosa. When he heard from local people that his friend was in trouble, he would have sped there in a small boat. While frantically rowing, the boat overturned in a storm. Carwarden was probably drowned before he could reach the shore.

Adams had threatened the Chinese he would take revenge if either of the Englishmen were found to have been murdered. It was an empty threat. He was in no position to carry it out, nor was he able to recover the silver they had carried or the money that Sayers had to buy silk. Although his own trade had been successful, it was with a heavy heart that Adams returned to Hirado by the *Gift of God* on 9 August 1617.

On 13 August, the fifteen Japanese crew members, who had been aboard the *Clove*, returned to Hirado from southern countries such as Java and Pattani. They put in a claim for more wages, because it had taken longer to return than they expected. Then, when Cocks

---

[300] Ibid.
[301] Ibid.
[302] Ibid.

rejected their claim, they raised a riot. Cocks expected to be helped out by Adams, but when Adams ignored the problem Cocks was infuriated. He went to Yajiuemon's house where Adams lodged and gripped Adams by the throat. News of the incident quickly spread around Hirado.

For the first three years, Cocks had suspected that Adams had better friendships with the rival Dutch and the Portuguese and the Spanish enemies than with his compatriots, even that he was secretly working for them. He conceded that his judgement was wrong, when he saw Adams pleading for many days with Hidetada for the English trading privileges. Somehow, with Adams' aloof manner and perhaps condescending way of talking, Cocks' prejudice occasionally resurfaced. Of course, Adams had already resigned his position at the English East India Company, so he had good reason not to involve himself in all their troubles. With his recurring depression, it is also possible that Adams had simply had enough of the disappointment with his drunken, unruly and inefficient compatriots.

Cocks' fury towards Adams was also caused by stress. During Adams' absence in Cochinchina in the spring of 1617, Cocks was faced with a severe financial crisis at the English factory. Naively, he was still pinning his hopes on making contact with the kings of Ming dynasty China, for trading Chinese silk through middlemen, although everyone knew trade with China was far more difficult than with Siam, Java or Pattani.

When Cocks mentioned this hope to the former Chinese landlord of the English factory, Li Tan, Li offered to help. Cocks knew Li well and trusted him. He had even become godfather to Li's infant daughter. Some people called Li a trickster, who overstated his influence with Chinese merchants and promised more than he could deliver, but Cocks thought that these people were jealous of Li, who owned two splendid houses in Hirado and Nagasaki and lived with 'several pretty wives and children'.[303]

---

[303] Ibid.

So Cocks reported to the London Company directors that he had now 'extraordinary hope to get trade in China'.[304] He was prepared to bet the last resources of his factory on gaining access to these precious silks. Cocks handed Li Tan an advance of £1500. The fabulous amount of money would have surprised Li, and Cocks followed it up with extravagant presents.

A report on these extraordinary dealings reached George Ball, the new chief factor in Bantam, through Richard Wickham, who had sailed to Java on the *Advice*. Cocks had selected Wickham to go there and report on the dire situation in his factory, because he thought Wickham understood it best and would explain it well to their compatriots. He never imagined that Wickham would use his visit to accuse him of causing the crisis by bad management, credulousness and foolishness.

George Ball seems not to have been a team player and to have taken pleasure in undermining his colleagues. He put on a show of dismay and disgust at Cocks' failure and the damage to their company, while figuratively licking his lips. He was obliged, he decided, to write a report to Sir Thomas Smythe in London, and a letter of admonition to Cocks.

When Cocks received his letter, he was absolutely horrified at such an unexpected attack. The letter began with the usual hearty salutations, but the invective quickly followed. He read that he was reported to be 'the loudest liar .... extreme hot in passion, and most miserable cold in reason'. Ball declared that hearing from Wickham the details of Cocks' misconduct was like the worst nightmare. The harshest criticism was heaped on Cocks' mishandling of Chinese trade and being duped by Li Tan, who Ball called 'the father of deceit'. In an even stronger letter to Sir Thomas Smythe, he maintained that Cocks had lost all sense of reality and that such an incompetent man was no longer qualified to be a chief factor.

Ball's letter exaggerated, but held some truth. Cocks had misjudged Li Tan, who would not have been interested in giving a rival

---

[304] Ibid.

an opportunity to set up a trading branch in China. As a result, the English Company gained hardly any benefit from the £1500 given to Li. However, an angry Cocks decided to write a long letter of explanation to Sir Thomas Smythe and warned him not to believe all that Ball described. 'I have ill-willers, which go about to bring me in disgrace with your worships, as Mr Ball by name. His accusations were totally spleene.'[305] He added that he was inclined to return to England to reply to the charges. After his protest, Cocks' fury temporarily subsided and he remained in Hirado. In London, the company directors had put a large question mark over Cocks' leadership, but in Hirado, Cocks was more concerned with how to deal with Wickham on his return.

However, Richard Cocks' life did have its lighter moments. One day, he noticed an amazing ornament that Nealson had brought into the factory. Barely stifling his laughter, Nealson explained it was the giant wooden penis of an ancient Japanese lecherous god. The erect penis was an object of devotion for women who wanted to be blessed with a child and it was their custom to carry the penis tightly clasped in front of their eager eyes and process around the altar. Nealson had observed the ritual entranced, and thought it would be amusing for his colleagues to have it displayed at the Hirado factory. He asked one of the women to give it to him. Somewhat surprised, she agreed, no doubt wondering generally about these strange foreigners and more particularly what good this icon could do for him.

On 26 August 1617, Adams departed from Hirado in the *Gift of God* for Edo, in order to obtain another Red Seal licence. On the way, the ship sprang a leak and the cargo of silk was damaged, but she limped into the Osaka Port on 8 September. After repairs, Adams sailed on to Kyoto, where on 11 September he met Cocks, who had arrived there earlier. Adams was informed that Hidetada was actually at the Fushimi Castle not at the Edo Castle, so the two men climbed the steep steps into Fushimi Castle to plead again with the Shogun to change his mind on the new trade restrictions.

---

[305] Ibid.

Hidetada had an important visitor, an ambassador from King Li in Chosŏn (today's Korea), so their audience was delayed. Adams and Cocks sniffed an opportunity to gain access to trade with Chosŏn. They hurried to the ambassador's accommodation, but when the ambassador returned from the castle, henchmen barred their way. The henchmen were employed by the lord of the Tsushima clan, who monopolized all trade with Chosŏn. He did not want any foreigner muscling in on his territory.

Finally, it was Adams alone that the Shogun invited in, as Lord Miura Anjin in the role of his adviser for the ambassador's audience, so it was not appropriate for Adams to mention trade with Chosŏn. However, Hidetada gave him his Red Seal licences for Siam and Cochinchina and Adams departed on 1 October 1617.

When Adams rejoined Cocks in Hirado, Cocks was delighted to hear that he had obtained some licences. Would Adams, he wondered, sell his own ship, the *Gift of God*, and the Red Seal licences to the English factory? In a decision that was to come back and bite him, Adams consented to the request. And in a further indication of his continuing and now unpaid commitment to the factory, he agreed to assist in collecting the money owed by clients of the company's Osaka branch. It would be a sixteen-day journey to Osaka.

Early in 1618, Richard Wickham arrived back from Bantam with a surprising announcement. He informed Cocks that he had decided to resign from the factory, because he was weary after his five years of work in Japan. Captain Saris had permitted his return home earlier, but he had wanted to earn more money and make a decent saving to give his 'most kind mother'[306] a comfortable life. Wickham then wrote to tell his mother that he had decided to leave Japan because he had been suffering the 'wrongs and crosses that sustained by some enemies',[307] but for reasons that will become clear, it was only after his visit to Bantam, that he suddenly revealed how eager he was to go back home.

---

[306] Ibid.
[307] Ibid.

As an aside, Wickham's 'devotion'[308] to his family seems not to have been reciprocated. Later, he was to complain that he had not heard from them for seven years, 'much marvelling that parents and allied friends can so much forget me'.[309] He assumed that 'they all supposed him dead or else he was hardly induced to believe he could be so forgotten'.[310]

Cocks was deeply anxious about Wickham's planned return to London. He had had enough torment from Wickham's tongue. He knew that Wickham intended to report the same things to his friend Sir Thomas Smythe as he had to Mr Ball in Bantam. Wickham had also promised Ball he would impress on the London merchants that Cocks' gross mismanagement of the Hirado factory had been 'the great hindrance of the East Indies Company and dishonour of our nation'.[311] The plan was to pin the blame for their lost money firmly on an incompetent chief factor. Cocks' nightmare was that he and his men would be recalled by the London company in dishonour.

---

[308] Ibid.
[309] Keay, John.
[310] Ibid.
[311] Cocks, Richard.

CHAPTER 17

WAR AND DEATH

ॐ

This time, fortune smiled on Cocks. As soon as Wickham arrived in Bantam, the first anchorage on his long voyage to England, he fell ill, probably with typhoid, malaria or dysentery. Weak from the high fever, he was given emergency treatment, but soon breathed his last. After a relatively healthy life in Japan for many years, he had possibly not developed enough immunity from tropical diseases. The scandal he was stoking around Cocks was buried with him, in a grave far from home. Later, it emerged he had never intended to return to England after all. His earlier visit to Bantam had convinced him that this was the place, rather than Japan, to make his fortune.

Wickham's death was even better news for his estranged wife. She and his dying mother went into the required mourning, but as soon as they were informed by Wickham's executors that his estate was worth an astonishing £1400 and Mrs Wickham was the chief beneficiary, the now devoted wife hurried to the London East India Company office to claim her dearest husband's bequest. However, the directors refused to pay a single penny. Nobody believed that Wickham, who earned only £40 a year and working for only five years 'in a place where the company lost all',[312] would have been able to make that kind of fortune. They suspected he had focused

---

[312] Keay, John and Wilbur, Marguerite

all his energies on his private trade. In that, they were right, but Mrs Wickham was no pushover. With the whiff of a fortune in her nostrils, she decided to fight. The battle lasted more than six years. She even took her case to Chancery and finally the company handed all the money to her. The scoundrel's wife was now a very rich woman.

With Wickham's death, Cocks mood improved. He threw more parties for his men and local contacts. There were more dancing girls and more alcohol. Occasionally however, the parties yielded useful information. At one, Cocks learnt that the Dutch were starting to occupy their trading areas and becoming increasingly aggressive towards not only the native chieftains but also their trading rivals, the Portuguese, the Spanish and even the English. The Dutch had always admired the Japanese skill in martial arts and now they were employing Japanese samurai warriors to attack rivals on their behalf. In 1617, they attacked an English ship called the *Swan* off the coast of India. According to Cocks' Spanish informer, the attack was ferocious. Samurai swords severed English arms and legs. The lucky ones were shot dead. Most of the English were captured, tortured, starved and kept in chains at the outlet of a Dutch sewer.

Despite this and several other accounts, Cocks remained good friends with the Dutch Chief Factor, Jacques Specx. They both trusted that the English and the Dutch would not attack each other in Hirado. The Shogun had forbidden all foreigners to fight each other in his territory and it would not be in either's interests. The chemistry between them was good and, on an isolated island in a very foreign land, senior personnel would have needed the company of their European peers.

However, in June 1618, Cocks was unsettled by news that Lord Matsura, who until then had treated the English and the Dutch equally, suddenly made over to the Dutch 'a street of fifty houses', together with labourers to demolish these houses and rebuild two large warehouses. Soon after, Cocks was more disturbed by reports that the Dutch were reinforcing their military strength in the East. He was also shocked to hear that the Dutch regularly insulted King James I, calling him a homosexual.

Cocks hid his concern when he went to inspect the Dutch building work. He expressed his admiration to Specx and in his diary described the new factory as a 'mansion house with a great hall, a series of elegant chambers, two warehouses, a gatehouse and a dovecote' (see Plate 8). Cocks looked enviously at the building, which would give the Dutch trade a boost and raise their status in Hirado. His English factory was as different as night is to day.

In July, Specx visited the English factory to ask Cocks to lend him William Adams. The Dutch wanted to take the Dutch envoy called Barkhout and his attendants to the Edo Castle, for an audience with Hidetada. Hidetada no longer trusted Jan Jeosten, so Specx wanted Adams to escort the envoy instead. Cocks and Adams consented and on 31 July 1618, Adams and the Dutch group departed for Edo.

On the night of 8 August, during Adams' absence from Hirado, Cocks was enjoying the gentle breeze on his veranda, when he sighted what he supposed was a Portuguese or Spanish ship, that had been captured by the Dutch. Its mast had snapped and was hanging overboard and much of the ship was in splinters. Why had the Dutch brought their captured ship into harbour? That was a very rare event. Cocks sent Sayers to the Dutch house to ask Specx to investigate and to offer use of the English factory's boat. While Cocks awaited the boat's return, a surgeon who worked for the Dutch visited him and asked to have a private word. The surgeon stunned Cocks with news that the captured ship was an English ship. That night he couldn't sleep at all. The next morning he confirmed that the English ship was the *Attendance*, many of whose crew members had been 'slaughtered, and the rest were taken to prison'.[313] When the English boat was returned by the Dutch, it came with the shocking message that the *Attendance* had been taken 'by order of war'.[314] He was told bluntly that the Dutch had no need, therefore, of English help to bring the ship into the harbour.

---

[313] Cocks, Richard.
[314] Ibid.

With Adams away, Cocks and his men started to panic. Cocks dashed to the office of Doi Toshikatsu, a high-ranking government official, and asked him to send Japanese officers and warriors to the *Attendance* 'betime tomorrow'[315] and find 'whether the Hollanders take themselves enemies of the English or no'.[316] Jacques Specx was genuinely as astonished as Cocks by the incident. He was anxious to express his sympathy and remorse, Cocks wrote, 'to certify me he was sorry for what had happened'.[317] Specx also offered the stricken ship to the English factory, an offer brusquely refused. Cocks felt humiliated and any Dutchman was a target for his anger. Specx was also upset, but he visited Cocks at the English house and continued to make efforts at reconciliation. However, he too was provoked to anger at Cocks' next accusation: 'It seems your masters command you to be common thieves, to rob English, Spanish, Portuguese and Chinese ... without respect.'[318] Their friendship was over.

The open hostility between the English and the Dutch dismayed the Japanese in Hirado. At a meeting in the Dutch house, the Dutch sought to explain the cause of their conflict. They had, they said, become increasingly suspicious of the English import of military weapons. Lord Matsura Takanobu's brother, Nobutoki, had realized for some time that the relationship between the two foreign nations would be unstable and, as the Dutch looked more likely to deliver successful and profitable trade, the lord had already decided to support them rather than the English.

In the English factory, Cocks also called a meeting with three colleagues, Nealson, Sayers and Osterwick. He suggested that the factory should make a formal protest to the Shogun about the Dutch bellicose behaviour. After a few small disagreements, they decided unanimously to 'proclaim'[319] against the Dutch offence. Cocks decided to 'take that long and troublesome voyage in hand'[320] himself. He would of course need Adams' linguistic and

---

315–318 Ibid.
319–320 Ibid.

negotiation skills but, as he said the words, all the factory members must have realized their predicament. Adams wasn't just absent, he was well on his way to Edo with a Dutch mission. It was Cocks who had agreed to the assignment to help his friend Specx. Cocks dashed to hire a 'swift bark'[321] to carry his urgent message to Edo, praying it would overtake Adams before he reached the court. His message was 'not to go with them before the emperor'.

Cocks then petitioned Lord Matsura Nobutoki for his support of the English factory. He informed Nobutoki that he was preparing a protest to Hidetada, accusing the Dutch of being 'common thieves and sea robbers'.[322] Wearing his Japanese mask of concern and sympathy, Nobutoki appeared to believe Cocks' story and expressed his good wishes for his success with the Shogun.

Cocks decided to take Nealson with him to Edo and the two men prepared their presents of velvets and satins and set sail on 23 August 1618. When they anchored at the port of Simonoseki on 1 September, Cocks was relieved to be told that his message had reached Adams in Kyoto. His relief evaporated as he read Adams reply. Adams said in his letter that 'he was none of the English Company's servant',[323] he would not take responsibility for any protest at the Dutch offence, so he intended to continue escorting the Dutch mission to the court. Cocks was in a hot temper when he had finished reading the letter. He wrote later that it was 'such an unseasonable and unreasonable letter as I little suspected he would have done'.[324] Cocks was particularly hurt by the words 'none of the Company's servant'[325] and he couldn't get them out of his mind.

Ten days later, Cocks arrived in Osaka and was handed another message from Adams. His letter said it was ludicrous that anyone would plead with the Shogun to punish the Dutch for attacking an English vessel in Malay. Cocks, he said, could

---

[321-323] Ibid.

[324] Cocks, Richard

[325] Adams, William.

cause irrevocable damage to the English side if he annoyed Hidetada with such a nonsensical protest. He had learnt through his experience, and as witness to the Portuguese and Spanish missions, that Hidetada was very impatient at being distracted with foreign affairs or conflicts between foreign residents in Japan.

Cocks was in no mood to absorb this advice and in his diary he vented his spleen. Adams, he said, had pretended to be an English compatriot, but in fact he was a hidden enemy to them, and he prayed that God would save the English from this enemy. It was an echo of his time as a merchant in France, before he joined the English East India Company, when he was doubling as a spy for his country and the Jesuits were the enemy. His mood was not improved by a painful stomach infection when they arrived at the port of Ōiso, Kanagawa Prefecture, which was used by vessels from Osaka as an anchorage. He wrote: 'I verily thought I should have died.'[326] There was no sympathy from the owner of the inn where Cocks and Nealson planned to stay. Like most Japanese at that time and since, he would have been very conscious of hygiene and concerned about the possibility of epidemics. Worried that his other guests might leave in disgust at diseased foreigners being on the premises, he made it clear they were not welcome. So Nealson humped a sick Cocks out into the busy street, where even the cackle of the local seagulls seemed to be mocking them; it was a tough job to find an inn somewhere else. They realized that, without protection, foreigners were likely to be treated worse than animals.

At the end of September, Cocks' condition had begun to improve and they decided to resume their journey to the court. On 3 October, they called at Totsuka, inside today's Yokohama and some ten leagues from Edo, to stay overnight at an inn. Outside the inn, the Englishmen encountered the Dutch mission, returning from their audience with Hidetada in Edo. They managed an icy acknowledgement of their rivals and the Dutch replied with a

---

[326] Cocks, Richard.

'small greeting'[327] before passing quickly on. After the Dutch had gone, they both wondered whether their eyes had deceived them. Adams was with the party, wasn't he, but he was at the margins of the group as if hoping not to be seen. Later, Adams returned to inform them that horses and footmen were prepared for them on their way, allowing Cocks to feel that Adams still cared a little about his compatriots. Adams also told them that he had withdrawn his earlier refusal to support Cocks at the court. He still believed privately that Cocks was digging his own grave, but he had decided it was wiser to try to arrange an audience rather than continue to antagonize such a stubborn character.

The next day, Cocks arrived with Nealson at Adams' house in Nihonbashi, close to Edo castle. On the morning of 6 October, he was escorted by Adams to the court, but an audience was not granted, nor the next day, nor the following day. The Shogun was busy at entertaining others with banquets and falconry, but the Englishmen knew they were being ignored.

On 9 October, Adams was summoned alone. Adams noticed immediately that Hidetada was in a bad mood. Hidetada said that the reason why he had summoned Adams was to demand of him whether he had sold Cocks the Red Seal licence for Cochinchina, that he had granted Adams for his private vessel. Adams confessed that was true. Unknown to Adams, the Japanese crew employed by Cocks had sailed to Cochinchina with the licence and created a disturbance there. Hidetada had received a written protest from the Chinese authorities. In the face of a very annoyed Shogun, Adams thought it best to keep silence. Hidetada's patience with Cocks had snapped and his request for an audience was refused. It seemed now that Hidetada might never grant another Red Seal licence to the English factory.

Cocks was expecting good news after Adams was summoned by the Shogun, but when Adams returned to the house his expression would have told a different story. On receiving such terrible news, Cocks probably did feel as if he was handed a shovel to dig his

---

[327] Ibid.

own grave. On 18 October 1618, all hope lost, Cocks and Nealson left Edo for Hirado. In contrast, Adams visited the court every day petitioning for a Red Seal licence for the English factory. However, Hidetada would not be persuaded and on 11 December Adams gave up and left Edo for Osaka. Adams rested in Osaka for a while, then sailed back to Hirado, saddened by the outcome.

William Adams, as Lord Miura Anjin, was still entitled to his own Red Seal licence, so he decided to make one last voyage for Cochinchina and Tonkin. He rented a vessel from Sagawa Shuma, a close retainer of Lord Matsura, and set sail from Hirado on 16 March 1619.

In August of the same year, during Adams' absence, Cocks and his men received news that confirmed a state of war had indeed been declared, between the English and Dutch in the East, at the end of 1618. A large English fleet under the command of Admiral Sir Thomas Dale had been despatched to Java to engage the Dutch. Sir Thomas was known to be brave and ruthless and when after the first skirmish the Dutch retreated, all seemed to be going well. However, the retreat had been tactical, to regroup with the rest of the Dutch fleet, so they returned in great strength. The English rapidly realized they were heavily outnumbered and outgunned. Much of the famed Admiral's fleet was scattered in all directions. The Dutch chased the most vulnerable ships and captured the English survivors. Sir Thomas managed to escape to India, where he caught malaria and died in the summer of 1619.

Back in Hirado, Cocks and his men saw a Dutch ship called *Angell* sailing into the port. She brought more members of staff to the expanding Dutch factory. Cocks and his men heard that she also carried three English prisoners. The Dutch had picked them out of the sea during battle, shackled them all together and tormented them with beatings. Cocks was afraid they might parade the English prisoners through the streets in Hirado to display their superiority. Cocks and his men knew they should try to rescue their compatriots, but the *Angell* was anchored in the middle of Hirado Bay and the difficulties seemed insuperable.

At the end of August, Adams returned to Hirado, after successful trade in Cochinchina and Tonkin. However, the Englishmen noticed Adams, their protector, had aged dramatically. He was frail, with hollow eyes and cheeks, and his hair and beard had turned grey. He had caught a tropical disease and fought against it all the way back. At home in Yajiuemon's house, the fever overwhelmed him and he sweated it out in bed all day. However, when news of the three English captives reached him, he left the house secretly to attempt a rescue. It is a complete mystery how he managed to board the *Angell* and Adams knew that detection would endanger his good relations with Jacques Specx. That night he succeeded in rescuing two of the three English prisoners, William Gourden and Michael Payne, and bringing them to the English factory. The following night Adams rescued the third, a Welshman called Hugh Williams.

In reporting the rescue, Cocks chose his words carefully. He did not want word to reach London of his own failure to act. In his account to Sir Thomas Smythe, he said simply that the captives 'escaped ashore with the assistance of Mr William Adams'. Mr Adams was not going to publicize his own heroism. As a samurai lord he had learned that actions should speak for themselves.

News of the daring rescue spread among the Dutch. They must have been infuriated that their ship had been infiltrated, not once but twice in the space of twenty-four hours. When their demand to return the captives was summarily refused, a Dutch mob rushed to the English factory. Cocks' diary records that, at first, they were repelled and the factory's strong gates held firm. Eventually, however, the mob broke the tough border fence and surged towards the main house. This was no ordinary mob. The reinforcements the *Angell* had brought for the Dutch factory were a bestial bunch, and the Englishmen feared for their lives.

Deliverance came just in time, in the form of Japanese warriors despatched by the local authorities to quell this violent breach of the peace by the *yaban-jin*, or foreign barbarians. The peace was short-lived. Cox went to bed grateful that the Japanese 'took our parts'[328] but, as another grey dawn broke, he was woken by a volley of gunfire. A small group of Dutchmen, carrying muskets and the Japanese swords *Katana*, had broken into the English house and had 'wounded John Coaker and another'.[329] Cocks feared for his and his men's lives, but remembered he and Adams had set up an alarm system of sorts. Cocks rushed out into the yard and beat the alarm bell with all his strength, so that its clanging rose above the noise of battle. Within a few minutes, Japanese warriors poured into the English factory and scared the Dutch away. Cocks wrote that, if the Japanese had not come, all the English would surely have been killed.

Lord Matsura Takanobu responded to this disorder with a warning to the Dutch that they would be severely punished if they broke the peace again. It was ignored. When another large Dutch fleet arrived at Hirado, the threats against the English factory resumed. Cocks reported to Sir Thomas Smythe that the Dutch had 'proclaimed open war against our English nation, both by sea and land, with fire and sword'. They had threatened 'to take our ships and goods and destroy our persons to the utmost of their power, as to their mortal enemies'.[330] Knowing that the English were employing Japanese guards to protect them, they had even offered a reward for Cocks' head: '50 reals of eight to anyone would kill me and 30 reals of same for each Englishman they could kill.'

Surrounded by his Japanese guards, Cocks came out from the English factory and sailed for Edo. He intended to plead with Hidetada to take the English side or mediate between the English and Dutch. Hidetada seemed sympathetic to the English with 'good words and promise that we should have justice',[331] but the words were meaningless. Hidetada was impatient at being disturbed, both by insignificant matters between foreigners in his land

---

[328] Ibid.
[329] Ibid.
[330] Ibid.
[331] Ibid.

as well as foreign affairs well outside Japanese waters. He refused to side with the English and left all these difficulties to the local lord of Hirado. Not for the first time, Cocks felt powerless. He needed Adams' help and ordered the English factory to send him to Edo. The reply from William Eaton, dated 8 September 1619, reported that Adams was so ill he had been confined to bed. They had no idea when he would recover and be strong enough to sail for Edo.

By that time, news of the dispute between the English and Dutch and of the English losing the Shogun's protection had spread to Macao, where the Portuguese and Spanish were well established. They saw an opportunity to reopen trade with Japan and perhaps to re-establish the Catholic missions and churches banned by Hidetada. Through their extensive Catholic network, they contacted compatriots who had been living secretly in Nagasaki, Kyoto and Osaka and gradually some of the Jesuits, who had been exiled earlier, re-entered Japan stealthily on the trading vessels from Macao. After landing in Japan, it was not difficult for them to hide their identity, protected by the cells of Japanese Christian converts. They stayed in safe accommodation and crept out only at night.

However, they were taking a big risk. As the rumours spread, Hidetada ordered Ōmura Yoshiaki, one of the lords in Nagasaki, to carry out to the letter the penalties he had laid down in his anti-Christian decree. The penalties were torture, death by the sword, being boiled in a large iron pot or burnt alive. Back in 1617, Padre Jean-Baptiste Machado and his fellow priest had been executed in this way. The padre had actually told Lord Ōmura that they longed to be martyred in this brutal manner. Moments before each Jesuit's body was severed with three strokes of the executioner's blade, Padre Machado was heard to call out that he 'thanked Jesus for his plight'.[332] Their corpses were thrown into a common grave, but, as Hidetada's wise father would have anticipated, that was not the end of it.

To command respect for the decree, the execution was held in public. Padre Machado's strong faith and devotion to Jesus

---

[332] Boxer, C.R.

Impressed not only the Catholic priests and their converts, but also a large number of the local Japanese, many of whom subsequently converted to Christianity. Two more Catholic priests challenged the Shogun. One of them, Padre Alphonso, declared that he did not accept 'the emperor of Japan but only the emperor of heaven'.[333] Lord Ōmura had Alphonso and his fellow priest executed and thrown 'into the sea with stones tied about their necks'.[334] Each martyrdom seemed to give the Christians greater courage.

For their part, the Jesuits seemed to have believed that all their troubles were caused by William Adams. They wrote privately about his 'malicious and most vile reports'[335] to the Shogun. Later in one of their books, they described how the Shogun and Japanese authorities were 'incited by the words of an English pilot, who spoke most bitterly against religious men and Spaniards',[336] how the authorities were 'not a little provoked by the foolish words of a certain pilot',[337] and how Adams had informed Hidetada that the Portuguese and Spanish priests were actually soldiers, who intend to 'make war against' Japan and invade the land.

It is true that Adams had made critical reports on the Catholics to the Shogun, but he was only giving as good as he got. He was nearly crucified after the Jesuits had given the Shogun hostile reports about him. Hidetada's anti-Christian actions were more likely down to his sense of inferiority in foreign relations and the impatience with foreigners and their conflicts, which Adams had noticed. Hidetada failed to understand what drove the Catholic missionaries – conversion not invasion. Hidetada had been infuriated when the Portuguese and Spanish led a protest against his edict in Osaka, but the majority of the Portuguese and Spanish Christians did not support the extreme fundamentalists.[338] They pleaded with Hidetada not to punish all Christians, when only a

---

[333] Shioda, Takashi.
[334] Boxer, C.R.
[335] Ibid.
[336] Ibid.
[337] Ibid.
[338] See 'China and Macao' (also Japan), Willis, R.C., (ed).

small group had caused the disturbances, and most Christians were living under Japanese rule with respect and no thought of invasion. It is possible the courtiers never passed on this plea to Hidetada or Hidetada simply ignored it. It is also true there was something of a north/south split among the Japanese, with the former less inclined to accept moral instruction from foreign religions.

The Portuguese and Spanish too had failed to understand Adams and why, so exceptionally, he had been accepted into the samurai class. He was a pragmatic not a deeply-religious man and, just to survive in those early days and later to maintain his influence, he had cultivated a reputation for neutrality. In public at least, he had learned not to carry the flag for only one nation.

The growth of Christian converts in his fiefdom alarmed Lord Ōmura and he ordered all the remaining churches and towers in Nagasaki to be demolished. The English and Dutch observed the plight of the Catholics with mixed feelings. It seemed to be the end of Catholicism in Japan, but who would be next? Hidetada's punishment of Catholics intensified after he received a letter from the Dutch. The letter reported that the Dutch had discovered a confidential letter from the Portuguese authorities, when they boarded a Portuguese vessel, which recommended that the Portuguese and Spanish should 'make war'[339] against Japan and invade the country on the Pope's authority. For an already prejudiced Shogun, this was convincing evidence.

There is no Portuguese record of such a recommendation and it is more likely to have been a Dutch forgery, prompted perhaps by Adams' hardening attitude. He certainly wrote around that time to Jacques Specx that '... all our trouble is the fault of the Portuguese missionaries, for it is because the emperor (Hidetada) is afraid of his citizens being made Christians that he will not let foreign people trade in the upper part of the country. .... all our problems can be blamed totally on the Catholics.'

One of the most horrific mass punishments took place in Kyoto, by the Kamo River on an autumn evening in 1619. Over

---

[339] Boxer, C.R.

fifty local Christians, including mothers and children, were burnt at the stake. 'Amongst them,' Cocks recorded in amazement, 'were little children of five or six years old.'[340] He was even more amazed at what the world now knows as a peculiarly Japanese form of stoicism, as the intense heat and flames enveloped their bodies. 'They would not forsake their Christian faith,'[341] wrote Cocks, with the children 'burned in their mothers' arms'.[342] It was no wonder that many in the large crowd of ordinary Japanese were moved to tears.

The horrors continued in Nagasaki, where sixteen more Christians were martyred. Cocks wrote that five of them 'were burnt and the rest beheaded and cut in pieces and cast into the sea in sacks at thirty fathom deep'.[343] Despite all these brutal executions, the Christians appear not to have been intimidated. Risking all, they went to collect some of the bloated corpses that had been dumped in the sea and kept them secretly for relics. Their faith in Jesus and a place in heaven was unshaken.

All this time, the English were left unscathed, protected by Lord Miura Anjin, who had succeeded in convincing the Shogun of their antipathy towards Catholics, in spite of Hidetada's general impatience with foreigners. The Dutch, as loyal informers, were of course judged to be innocent. The main English fear now was of another attack from the Dutch, emboldened by their new support from the Shogun.

Cocks was also facing severe financial difficulties at the English factory. He could not find buyers for his goods in Japan and, without a Red Seal license, he could not trade with neighbouring countries. The three Englishmen Adams had saved from the *Angell* were still under the care of the factory. They were all too frail to work, so the factory's living costs kept piling up. Cocks again turned to Adams for help. Adams allowed the English factory to trade lead shot with Governor Hasegawa in Nagasaki, through Adams' own agency. We know the trade brought in a decent sum of money because, on 18

---

[340] Cocks, Richard.
[341–343] Ibid.

February 1620, Cocks reported to John Osterwich, one of the staff in Adams' agency, that it had been of great financial help.

The hostility between the English and Dutch rumbled on, but this time there was no help from Adams. News came to Cocks that their protector was seriously ill, a recurrence it seemed of the tropical disease that had laid him low on his return from Cochinchina. If it was malaria, it is likely that Adams had been gradually weakened by a series of recurrences. At first, Cocks hoped he would recover, not least because he and Adams had enjoyed a 'longboat race'[344] only a few weeks before.

The English pilot, however, seemed to know he was nearing his last port. On 16 May 1620, he called Cocks and Eaton to be witnesses to his last Will and Testament. The two Englishmen hurried to Yajiuemon's house, outside which a flag of St George was still fluttering in the breeze. When the men entered his room they found Adams confined to bed with a high fever. They sat at his bedside and it is said Adams asked Eaton to take dictation of his Will. It began with modesty, as befits a samurai lord in front of those of lesser rank. 'I, William Adams, mariner, that have been resident in Japan the space of some eighteen or twenty years, being sick of body but of a perfect remembrance – laude and praise be to Almighty God – make and ordeine this my present testament.'[345] His will is now preserved in the library of the London City Hall.

Adams had always lived prudently. Since he started trading in Japan and later working for the English factory at Hirado, he had saved £600 (£119,500 in today's money).[346] Additionally, the rice-fields of his Hemi estate produced an income of 88 ryō per annum (around £70,000 in today's money), although most of this was paid out in salaries for his ninety servants and husbandmen and for maintenance. Adams decided to divide his savings in half between

---

[344] Ibid.
[345] Adams, William.
[346] The average house price and also the average annual living expense in England in this period was £30 (£5,586 in today's money).

his English family and his Anglo-Japanese children Joseph and
Susanna. It is thought that he produced a third child by his maid
at Hirado and more children by a Japanese interpreter at Hirado
and a mistress in Edo, but not one of them is included in his Will.

Adams wanted his English daughter, Deliverance, to be the main
beneficiary in England, so the Will makes clear that his wife Mary
Hyn should not receive more than half of the money. 'For it was
not his mind (that) his wife should have all in regard she might
marry another husband and carry all from his child.'

As was the custom in Japan, Adams gave his son Joseph his
set of ceremonial swords, *katana* and *wakizashi*. Richard Cocks
was left Adams' precious celestial globe, his sea-charts and another
fine sword. Eaton was given all his books and navigation equipment. John Osterwick, Richard King, Abram Smart and Richard Hudson, were each given one of his best kimono. Antony,
his servant was given five tayes in money and released from his
debts. Jugasa, his maid servant, was given a dressing table, a linen
summer *kimono* and '2 bars of silver qt (sic) containing eight tayes
six mas'.[347] John Phebe, his servant, was given four tayes three mas
and exempted from his debt. Yajiuemon and his wife were given
sixty tayes. After all his accusations about favouring the Dutch,
Cocks must have been surprised that Adams left nothing to his
Dutch friends.

'And so hereunto I have set my hand, these whose names are
hereunder being witnesses.'[348] Dictating the will and signing it with
a shaky hand had taken an immense effort. His last task completed,
his great strength drained away and within hours the blue-eyed
samurai was dead.

This time, in his report home, Richard Cocks paid unbridled
tribute:

> I cannot but be sorrofull for the losse of such a man as Captain
> William Adams; he, having been in such favour with two emperors

---

[347] Cocks, Richard.
[348] Ibid.

of Japan as never was any Christian in these parts of the worlde [and a man who] might freely have entered and had speech with the emperors, when many Japan Kings stood without and could not be permitted.

Adams' young friend Sukeji saw things differently. Now a foreign language teacher and samurai, he remembered Adams' tales of the sea and wrote how he 'looked at the crystal sea water as blue as Anjin-sama's eyes and felt as if Anjin-sama's spirit would be welcomed into the water'.[349]

Adams' death hit the English factory hard. It seemed to herald the last act of their Japanese drama. Certainly things could never be the same. Cocks wrote to Sir Thomas Smythe that he was 'out of hope of any good to be done in Japan'.[350] We know that he organized the digging of a grave for Adams in a field next to the English factory and over the next two months spent £20 on a stone wall to protect the grave. Exactly where Adams' body lies now is unknown. The execution of fifty- five Christians in 1622 and the massacres of Christians that followed meant that many Westerners were buried in the area.

On the first Christmas after Adams' death, Cocks visited Adams' family at Hemi. He had earlier sent Yuki some simple jewellery; now he was able to hand over to six-year-old Joseph his father's ceremonial swords. Joseph would have been taught that his father's soul resided in these swords and Cocks records that the little boy had tears in his eyes. In 1622, Cocks visited the family again and gave Yuki white silk and silver, Joseph and Susanna damasks and taffeta, and offered to contribute to Joseph's school fees.

Back in August 1620, with Cocks and his men still downhearted after Adams' death, an English ship, *James Royal*, captained by Martin Pring arrived unexpectedly at the Hirado Port. It was followed by two more English vessels, *Moon* and *Elizabeth*, and sev-

---

[349] Translated by the author from Nishiyama Toshio.
[350] Cocks, Richard.

eral Dutch ships, all without a sign of hostility. A year before, on the other side of the world, the English and Dutch had signed a peace treaty and were now allies against the Portuguese and Spanish. For the beleaguered English factory, this was great news and, with the fleet's fresh supplies and chests of silver coins, they could banish all thought of what they had needlessly suffered over that last year.

Not all went well. In a pattern that was becoming familiar, when over 1000 Western sailors disembark, the local Japanese hope for the best but fear the worst. The local prostitutes of course were in great demand. Unlike other Asian prostitutes, these Japanese and Korean girls took time also to bath the client, provide massage, serve *sake* and snacks and show some tender care. However, the inevitable quarrels erupted between the sailors and over the women. Public statues, windows and chairs were smashed and fighting broke out with local Japanese residents. The hooligans were eventually punished by the Japanese authority. After they were beheaded, their corpses were 'left in the fields to be eaten by crows and dogs'.[351] Lord Miura Anjin would have turned in his grave.

In the autumn of 1620, the *James Royal* was ready to sail back to England. Richard Cocks handed Captain Pring a copy of Adams' Will for his English family, together with £100 of silver coins from Adams' savings. Cocks wrote '£200 would be paid'[352] to Adams' family, because silver coin was worth twice as much in England. In seven months, Cocks informed the London Company that he would either take the rest of Adams' money with him when he returned to England or send it when he next had a safe carrier.

In 1622, the *James Royal* returned to England. Captain Pring handed Adams' Will and Testament to the Director of the London East India Company. One of their staff was dispatched to Mrs Adams to hand over both the Will and the £200. Here, at last, was

---

[351] Ibid.
[352] Ibid.

some reward for Mary Hyn's twenty years of patience and suffering, not to mention the great pride she would feel at first-hand accounts of her husband's extraordinary achievements. It was not to be. A neighbour informed the company's envoy that Mary Hyn had died just a few months earlier.

CHAPTER 18

EPILOGUE

჻

Shortly after William Adams' death, his son Joseph was summoned by Shogun Hidetada. Fulfilling his own father's promise to Adams, Hidetada conferred on the young child Adams' title, his samurai privileges and the Hemi estate, including the villages, rice fields and servants.

Adams' illegitimate children fared less well. Richard Cocks records that in February 1621 Coshuro, Adams' interpreter, came with her child Cowjohns to claim financial support. He gave her two tayes and offered to pay school fees, if the child were put under English guardianship. Again, in April of the same year, Cocks paid out two tayes and one mas for a *kimono* each for another who claimed to be Adams' child and again to Cowjohns.

Richard Cocks' nemesis came in the shape of Richard Fursland, a severe disciplinarian who had been posted by the English East India Company to Batavia [today's Jakarta], as President of its Council of Defence. Fursland had been put in charge of dismissing or punishing all incompetent or degenerate employees in the Moluccas and in Banda, Sumatra and Pattani. When Fursland turned his attention to the Hirado factory, he was shocked by the reports of extravagant feasts, dancing girls, concubines and illegitimate children. In the spring of 1622, Fursland recalled Cocks, Eaton and Sayers to Batavia for punishment, but Cocks simply ignored the command. Only Japan's monsoon season prevented a furious Fursland from immediately despatching a vessel to Hirado.

Cocks' reprieve did not last long. In the summer of 1623, one of Fursland's vessels, *the Bull*, captained by Joseph Cockram, sailed into Hirado Port. Captain Cockram handed Cocks a letter from Fursland repeating his order to report to Batavia. The captain had specific orders to inspect the factory's accounts and was astonished at the enormous deficit. He reported back to Fursland that there were no funds to maintain the factory any longer and, on 25 July 1623, the Council of Defence decided to close it down.

Cockram announced the *Bull* would depart for England on 22 December 1623. On the appointed day, the English factors' concubines, illegitimate children, Lord Matsura himself, several Dutch friends and many townsmen with their wives and families all came down to the wooden quayside to say farewell. Many had tears in their eyes. William Eaton's concubine was having to say goodbye to her son, beseeching Cocks 'please be kind enough to take good and gentle care of him', while Eaton himself had to leave his daughter Helen with her mother. Much moved by the personal dramas being played out in front of him, Cockram decided to invite them all onto his ship for a farewell party, but the vessel was too small to have everyone so he allowed the Englishmen to return ashore to spend a little more time with their families and friends. The ship finally departed at noon on Christmas Eve.

After ten years, six months and thirteen days, the English factory had closed in failure. When the *Bull* arrived at Batavia on 27 January 1624, Fursland reported to his London headquarters that it brought only 'trash and lumber' and an unrepayable debt. He was particularly critical of Cocks' mismanagement and considered whether he should seize all his personal possessions and money [some £300] and send him home as a criminal. However, he was concerned about Cocks' age and declining health, so he left it to the English East India Company to make a fair judgement on Cocks' return to England. In London, Cocks' card was already heavily marked and the company might well have agreed to the punishment that Fursland had suggested, but Fate intervened. On 27 March 1624, Cocks passed away before his ship reached London. His body was committed to the waves. Edmond Sayers also died on the voyage. Only William Eaton, of the original Hirado factors, returned to England. No-one understood what happened to him: the naturally warm-hearted gentleman had turned cold and blunt. He had been close to Cocks and may have felt his friend had been unfairly treated. However the Council of the London company was unimpressed and dismissed Eaton in disgrace.

The disgraced John Saris, on the other hand, was ordered to resign from the company, after the events of January 1615. Shortly after leaving the company, Saris married Anne, a daughter of William Meggs of Whitechapel and granddaughter of Sir Thomas Cambell, who had been Lord Mayor of London from 1609 to 1610. She was twenty-nine years old. There were no children and eight years later she was dead, buried in the parish church of St Botolph in Thames Street. Five or six years after her death, Saris moved to Fulham in West London and his name appears on the poor-rate assessments from 1629 until his death on 11 December 1643. His grave might still be seen in All Saints, Fulham. According to Saris' Will, the £30 that he left was to be spent by that church on two penny-worth of loaves to be given to thirty poor people every Sunday, until it was exhausted.

The East India Company placed the blame for the misfortunes of their Hirado factory squarely on John Saris and Richard Cocks. However, the company should have shouldered some of the blame, in selecting two men for tasks that were beyond them and in a subsequent failure of supervision. They had also ignored much of Adams' advice and seriously underestimated Japan's reserves of gold and silver.

The deserted English factory, warehouse and chambers in Hirado did not last long. After a few years of typhoons and probably earthquakes, nothing remained of the Company's presence in Japan. In today's Hirado, there is a branch of a Japanese bank on the factory site, but the local people still display the Union Jack around Yajiuemon's house to honour the English pilot, William

Adams. The current and forty-first Lord Matsura is supporting a renewed search for Adams' grave.[353]

In July 1623, Hidetada was succeeded by his eldest son Iemitsu. The third Shogun had been a disappointment to his parents, who had made no secret of their favouring their third son Tadanaga. A bitter and sadistic man, Iemitsu took revenge on his brother and then turned his anger on foreigners and their foreign religions. He ordered the torture first, and then the expulsion, of Jesuit priests and their converts and finally the Portuguese traders. In 1633, 1635 and 1639 he issued closed-country decrees, *sakoku-rei,* which remained in effect for over 200 years, until in fact 1868 when it was another Englishman, Sir Harry Parkes, who helped the American admiral Matthew Perry to open Japan up again to a very different world.

Even the Dutch were ordered out, but to a small offshore island, reclaimed for the purpose out of the Kawaguchi Bay in 1636. The island was called Dejima, which means 'pushed-out island', referring to the way the island was created, rather than the fate of the Dutch. The Dutch moved to Dejima on 13 February 1641. They were allowed to receive only one Dutch ship a year and the small bridge that linked Dejima to the mainland was heavily guarded. Japan was not in a mood to build more bridges to the Western world.

Hirado was particularly badly affected by the *sakoku* decrees. Before the decrees, its population was around 4500, of which some 2000 were foreigners. Once the decrees were in effect, even those Japanese who shook a foreigner's hand or touched his shoulder faced punishment. All children of mixed race were expelled to Jakarta, including those that Adams, Cocks and Eaton had fathered. When a Japanese woman called Oharu was forced to part from her child in 1639, the local people were moved to erect a statue, *Jakara Musume*

---

[353] Matsura Akira is following the scholarly example of his ancestor Matsura Seizan in running his own museum, preserving and replicating historic buildings, supporting archaeological research and promoting international exchange programmes.

or 'mother of the child', and to compose a song in sympathy for her plight and that of so many others. The statue still stands and the song is still sung today.

Before he died, Joseph Adams is thought to have been responsible for erecting a pair of stone monuments, four yards high and two yards wide, in memory not only of his father but also his mother Yuki, who had died in 1635. They stood on the hilltop at Tsukayama Park in today's Yokusuka City, on what became known as Anjin-*zuka* or Anjin Hill (see Plate 20). According to *Shin'pen Sumō Fudo Ki,* or Edo contemporary topography, it is believed that Joseph built a shrine (today's Kashima Jinja) in 1636. This is thought to be on the site of the main house where Adams and his family resided. Joseph died young, before marrying or producing children. There is no record of any children from his sister Susanna.

With no family to maintain them, the monuments were quickly overgrown; until 1872, when an English merchant called James Walters set out to find them. Walters was residing in Yokosuka, close to Adams' Hemi estate. Tenacious, as if inspired by Adams' spirit, he raised the necessary funds for the search, through a petition in a Yokohama newspaper. Then, with the help of the temple at Hemi, *Jōdo-ji,* he rediscovered the monuments. Today, the city council and local volunteers maintain the site and every year, at cherry blossom time, festivities are held there to honour Adams' memory and to celebrate his contributions to Japan.

Adams' place in Japanese history is secure. He was and is Miura Anjin, *hatamoto,* the only foreigner ever to have been so honoured. He was a close adviser to Japan's most celebrated Shogun, instrumental in his rise to power and in the country's first opening up to the Western world. As we have seen, his achievements are still celebrated in monuments, an annual festival and in the name of a railway station! His name will be familiar to every Japanese child who has worked their way through the school history books. In 1934, the Japanese Government even erected a substantial clocktower in Adams' hometown of Gillingham, Kent. Each day thousands of motorists will pass it on busy Watling Street, quite unaware of its significance.

The Dutch too have every reason to bless the day, in 1600, when the Rotterdam merchants hired a young English pilot, who over the next twenty years would do so much to establish them as favoured trading nation in Japan.

In English history, Adams' achievements have been overshadowed by a trading venture that went disastrously wrong. The English failure to use the status and respect that Adams held in Japan was certainly a missed opportunity. It is at least arguable that they, rather than the Dutch, might have been permitted to remain offshore as the preferred trading partner if they had established their factory at Uraga, close to Edo and the Shogun's power base, as Adams had suggested. However, by keeping Adams in ignorance of his compatriots' arrival in Bantam, the Dutch secured themselves several years to establish their base in Japan and to monopolize Adams' advocacy. They also, it has to be said, put better men in the field, who were more willing to be advised.

There is much debate in Britain today on the obligation on immigrants to adopt or adapt to British culture, but it seems, through much of their history, the English have been unusually suspicious of their own countrymen who adopt, or adapt to, foreign cultures. 'Going native' was the disparaging phrase. Loyalty and objectivity were put in doubt; local knowledge and advice dismissed. The assumption seemed to be that these people had lost something of their essential 'Britishness', rather than added extra layers of perception and understanding. Perhaps William Adams and the many others who have wielded great influence in foreign lands deserve better of us all.

AFTERWORD

&

Western historians researching the Edo Period in Japan face a number of seemingly insurmountable hurdles. First, there is the language, notoriously difficult to master, with classical Japanese in early documents even harder. Second, there is a paucity of accessible primary sources, in some part due to the desire of the great feudal families to keep their family archives 'sacred' or secret [the words are the same in Japanese]. Obtaining permission usually involves the right letter of introduction by someone in the family's circle and the kind of traditional Japanese manners, in making the approach, that have gone out of fashion. I am probably one of the few Japanese of my generation who still write letters using traditional brushstroke calligraphy. Even with permission granted, one invariably finds the archives are neither designed nor staffed to handle scholars' enquiries.

Compounding this, and of course related, is the tendency of even the most respected Japanese historians not to reveal their sources. Naturally, therefore, publications that contain 'new' information without documentary evidence arouse suspicion among those steeped in the Western traditions of scholarship. And yet, in my experience, these accounts are often the product of extensive research.

Much of this research is conducted at the local level, typically on local government records, at libraries and temples, with local historians, amateur and professional, and at historical sites. In some ways, Japan is highly centralized in the way it is governed, but information is maddeningly decentralized. Well-researched history books often have small print runs, whether out of modesty or a determination to keep things local, I do not know. There is of course no centralized national reference library, like the British Library or the Library of Congress in the USA.* In the book, I describe how William Adams was the first to introduce the sweet potato into Japan. In fact, the Satsuma clan found the potato first, but typically kept the information [and the potatoes!] to themselves.

The question of precise authorship of official records at that time is also opaque. At Nikko Tosho Gu and Sanko Library, one of the few family archives open to scholars, no-one can or will tell you whether a particular record was written by Ieyasu himself, or a close retainer, or anyone else.

My own experience reinforced the value of this local 'on the ground' research. Perhaps a few examples will suffice. At the Matsura Historical Museum in Hirado there are over 200 volumes by the scholar Matsura Seizan [1760–1841] who drew on over 100 records from Adams' contemporary Matsura Shigenobu. Ōita and Nagasaki District Councils were able to confirm the authenticity of a contemporary account of life in Usuki, that Makino Tadashi had drawn on in his *Aoime no Samurai*. A visit to today's Hirado Castle revealed the extent to which the Matsura clan had to go to convince Ieyasu of their loyalty. They burned down their castle!

I have no means of verifying this, but time and again I was told I was the first scholar from the West to make these types of visits. If that is true, it is quite extraordinary given the extent of scholarly Western literature on William Adams.

The nature of Japanese historical research is certainly different. After immersing themselves in the evidence and the context, and even oral traditions, there appears to be a greater willingness to

---

* Japan has the National Diet (government) Library, Tokyo, established in 1948 for the benefit of Diet members, but also open to the public and now sourced through the legal deposit system similar to the British Library and Library of Congress. The Nichibunken Library, Kyoto, established by the Japanese government in 1987 to support its new International Centre for Japanese Studies, also contains a significant holding.

explore all possible scenarios and to decide which is the most likely. The culture among historians is also more deferential and there is no system of Peer Review. Validity is assessed by a Ministry of Education committee, who give their seal of approval for use in educational establishments. Committees are not infallible, but 'winners' in non-fiction are sometimes decided by committees in the West!

Clearly both scholastic traditions have their merits and limitations. What is self-evident to me, and which I hope my book goes some way to demonstrate, is that any definitive account of what William Adams achieved in Japan and why he is so revered must take full account of the story as seen through Japanese eyes.

H.T.R.

BIBLIOGRAPHY

ॐ

Adams, William, *The Log Book of William Adams* (preserved on microfiche and at the Bodleian Library, Oxford).

Boxer, Charles R., *The Christian Century in Japan and Jan Compagnie in Japan*, Martinus, Nijhoff, Amsterdam, 1936, and *The Journal of Portuguese Studies*, Portugal, 2004.

Boxer, Charles R., *The Christian Century in Japan:1549–1650*, University of California Press, Berkeley, 1951.

Boxer, Charles R., *The Great Ship from Amacon: Annals of Macao and the Old Japan Trade, 1555–1640*, Centro de Estudios Historicos Ultramarios, Portugal, 1959.

Blusse, Leonard, (ed.), Remmelink, Willem, (ed.) and Smits, Ivo, (ed.), *Nihon Koryū 400 nen no Rekishi to Tenbo (Bridging the Divided 400 years, the Netherlands – Japan)*, Nichi-Ran Gakkai, Amsterdam, 1946, 1947 and 2000.

Caron, Francois, *Nihon Daio Koku Shi*, Tokyo dō, 1946 (translated from Portuguese into Japanese by Kōda Shigetomo).

Caron, Francois, Boxer, Charles, R., (ed.), *A True Description of the mighty Kingdoms of Japan and Siam*, Argonaut Press, Portugal, 1935 (translated from Dutch into English by Capt. Roger Manley with Introduction, Notes and Appendices by C. R. Boxer: reprint of English edition, 1663).

Carletti, Francesco, *My Voyage Around the World: The Chronicles of a 16th Century Florentine Merchant*, Methuen & Co., Ltd., London, 1964.

Cocks, Richard, *Diary of Richard Cocks, 1615 -1622*, 3 volumes, Historiographical Institute, University of Tokyo, 1978 -1981.

Cocks, Richard, *Hirado Eikoku Shōkan Nikki*, Shinozaki Shorin, Tokyo, 1972 (translated into Japanese by Minagawa, Saburō).

Constantine de Rennevill, René Auguste, (ed.), *Recueil des Voyage, account of Specx, vol. 7 of 10,* Amsterdam.

Cooper, Michael, (ed.), *They Came to Japan: An Anthology of European Reports on Japan, 1543 – 1640,* Thames and Hudson, London, 1965.

Cooper, Michael, (ed.), *João Rodrigues's Account of Sixteenth-Century Japan,* Hakluyt Society, London, 2001.

Corr, William, *Adams The Pilot: The Life and Times of Captain William Adams, 1564 – 1620,* Folkestone, Japan Library, 1995.

Corr, William, *Maritime War and Trade before Sakoku,* Osaka International University Journal of International Studies, Osaka, 1991.

Corr, William, *Miura Anjin, The Story of Captain William Adams,* Nara Dawn Press, Nara, 1989.

Corr, William, *The Crew and Cargo of the Liefde,* Himejigakuen Review, Himeji, 1991.

Cortazzi, Sir Hugh, *Higashi no Shima, Nishi no Shima, Adams on De Liefde,* Chūō Kōron Sha, Tokyo, 1986.

Cortazzi, Sir Hugh, *Isles of Gold: Antique Maps of Japan,* Tokyo and New York, Weatherhill International, 1983.

Date-Ke Kiroku-Ki, vol. 2, (the Date family's account), Ojika-cho, Nagasaki.

De Lange, William, *Pars Japonica: The First Dutch Expedition to Reach the Shores of Japan,* Floating World Editions, Warrren, CT, 2006.

Dōmon Fuyuji, *Matsura Seizan Yawa Gatari,* Jitsuyō no Nihonsha, Tokyo, 2006.

Etō Iwao, *Miura Anjin to Hirado Eikoku Shōkan,* Yamaguchi Shoten Kan, Yamaguchi, August 1980, (preserved at Kyushū University).

Gotō Seikichi, *Miura Anjin to Kazoku, vol. 74–75,* Kanagawa Fudoki, Kanagawa, 1983.

Hakluyt, Richard, *The Principal Navigations, Voyages, Traffiques and Discoveries of the English Nation, 1598–1600, vol. 1–12,* Hakluyt Society Extra Series, London, 1903–1905.

Hirado no Taigai Bōeki no Hanashi, Hirado, (preserved at the Matsura Historical Museum).

Houhuijs, J. W. Van, *Het Hekbeeld Van Het Schip De Liefde Ex. Erasmus In. Het Keizerluk Museum Te Tokio,* W. L. D. J. B. Russe, Amsterdam, 1927 (describes the maritime history of Rotterdam and Erasmus).

Iguchi, Kaizen, *Chado Meigen Shū,* Gendai Kyōyō Bunko, Tokyo, 1968.

Inagaki, Nobuo, *Jidai Koshō Jiten,* Shin Jinbutsu Ôraisha, Tokyo, 1971.

Itazawa, Taeko, *Nihon to Oranda (Holland),* Shibun dō, Tokyo, 1958.

Iwao, Seikichi, *Miura Anjin to Kazoku (Family), review, Nichi-Ran Gakkai Sōritsu 10 Shūnen Kinen Shi (The 10th Anniversary of the Founding of the Netherlands and Japan Society),* Nichi-Ran Gakkai, 1985.

Iwao, Shigekatsu, (trans.), *Keigen Igirisu Shōkan,* Yōsho dō, Tokyo, 1928.

Kanai Madoka, *Erasmus to kateki-sama,* Chūnichi Shinbun, Tochigi, 1983.

Kanai Madoka, *Gosso Sama, Miura Anjin, Chisi to Rekishi, No. 34* (Topography and History), 1983.

Kanai Madoka, *Nichiran Kōshō Shi no Kenkyū,* Shibunkaku Shuppan, 1986.

Kanagaki, Robun, Kochōhen Wakana, (ed.), *Tōse Geisha Kabuki, Owari no Senzo Izumo no Okuni,* Shōe dō, 1883.

Katō Sango, *Hirado no Shirabe,* Kyōkō Sha, 1912.

Katō Sango, *Miura no Anjin,* Meisei Kan, Tokyo, 1917.

Kageyama, Hiroshi, *Kateki-sama,* Kyōdo Bunka wo Kangaeru Kai, Tochigi, 2010.

Kawashima, Genjirō, *Shuin sen Bōeki Shi, Vol. 4,* Kōjin Sha, 1942.

Keay, John, *The Honourable Company: A History of the English East India Company,* HarperCollins, New York, 1991.

Keichō Kokushi Taikei, (ed.), *Keichō Kenmon Shū, Vol. 5–9 of 38, the contemporary Japanese historical record,* Kokusho Kankō Kai, Tokyo, 1929, San'ichi Shobō, Tokyo, 1969.

Kikuno, Matsuo, *William Adams no Kōkaishi to Shōkan,* Nagumo dō, 1977.

Kōda, Shigetomo, *Nichiō Tsūkō Shi Hen II, Vol. 4,* Chūō Kōron Sha, Tokyo, 1942.

Kōda, Shigetomo, *Miura Anjin,* Chūō Kōron Sha, Tokyo, 1972.

Kodama, Kōta, *Tokugawa no Subete, Bakkaku, Tokugawa Ieyasu, pp. 64–97,* Shin Jinbutsu Ôrai Sha, Tokyo, 1995.

Kokushi Taikei Shūroku, (ed.), *Tokugawa Gojitsu Ki, Tokugawa Jitsu-Ki, Vol.1, Anthology,* Yoshikawa Kōbun Kan, Tokyo, 1929 and 1930.

Kuwata, Tadachika, and Owada, Tetsuo, (ed.), *Sengoku Bushō no Chanoyu,* Miyaobi Shuppan, Kyoto, 2013.

Levenson, Jay, A., *Encompassing the Globe: Portugal and the World in the 16th and 17th Centuries,* Smithsonian Institution Press, Washington, 2007.

Liefde's arrival in the Travels of Pedro Teixeiro, Hakluyt Society, London, 1902.

Lindschten, John Huyghen van, *Voyage to the East Indies,* Hakluyt Society, London, 1885.

Makino, Tadashi, *Aoime no Samurai, Miura Anjin,* Ito Kanko Kyokai, Ito, 1980 and 1993.

Malucca, Philippine Shotō Shi, Iwanami Shoten, Tokyo.

Massarella, Derek, *A World Elsewhere: Europe's Encounter with Japan in the Sixteenth and Seventeenth Centuries,* Yale University Press, London, 1990.

Matsura, Seizan, *Kasshi Yawa, Vol. 43–49,* Hirado, 1821.

McDermott, James, (ed.), *The Third Voyage of Martin Frobisher to Boffun Island,* Hakluyt Society, London, 2001.

Milton, Giles, *Samurai William, The Adventurer Who Unlocked Japan,* Hodder and Stoughton, London, 2002

Minagawa, Kengo, (trans.), *Saris Nihon Tokō Ki,* 1947.

Minagawa, Saburō, *Elizabeth chō – Nichiei Kankei Bunken to Gengo,* Shinozaki Shorin, Tokyo, 1972.

Minagawa, Saburō, *Keiseiki no Higashi Indo Gaisha to William Adams,* Shinozaki Shorin, Tokyo, 1983.

Minagawa, Saburō, *William Adams Kenkyū, Rekishi teki Tenbō to Ningen Adams,* Taibun dō, Tokyo, 1977.

Miura Anjin to Hirado Eikoku Shōkan, Yamaguchi Shoten Kan, Yamaguchi, 1980.

Miura, Hiroshi, *Zōsen Shiwa,* Shizuoka Shin'bun Sha, Shizuoka.

Miura Jōshin, *Keichō Ken'mon Shū, Vol. 5 of 38,* San'ichi Shobō, Tokyo, 1969 (preserved at Kunaicho Shoryōbu Archives/ Imperial Household Ministry Archives).

Motokiyo, *Keisei Okuni Kabuki,* 1859.

Moran, J.F., *The Japanese and the Jesuits: Alessandro Valignano in Sixteenth-century Japan,* Routledge, London and New York, 1993.

Mutō, Nagazō, *Nichiei Kōtsū Shi no Kenkyū,* Naigai Shuppan, Great Britain, 1937.

Mulder, W.Z., *Hollanders in Hirado,* Fibula van Dishoeck, 1985.

Murakami, Naojirō, (trans.), *Kin Gin tō Tanken Hōkoku (Vizciano, Sebastian's report on the exploration of the islands of gold and silver),* Yūsho dō, Tokyo, 1947.

Murakami, Naojirō, (trans.), *Nihon Kenbun Roku (Rodrigo De Vivelo. An Account of Japan, 1609),* Yūsho dō, Tokyo, 1947.

Murakami, Naojirō, *Shijō no Hirado,* Nihon Gakujitsu Fukyō Kai, Tokyo, 1917.

Nakamura, Kōya, *Tokugawa Ieyasu Bunsho no Kenkyū*, Nihon Gakujitsu Shinkō Kai. Tokyo, 1929 and 1930.

Nakamura, Kōya, (ed.), *Tokugawa Ieyasu Kōden*, Nikko Tōshō Gū Shamusho, Tochigi, 1965.

Nagasaki Shi (prefecture), (ed.), *Nagasaki Ken Shi (History of Nagasaki)*, *Taigai Kōshō Hen*, Yoshikawa Kōbun Kan, Tokyo, 1986.

Nagazumi, Yōko, *Hirado Oranda Shōkan Igirisu Shōkan Nikki: Hekigan no mita Kinsei no Nihon to Sakoku e no michi*, Iwanami Shoten, Tokyo, 1981.

Nichi-Ran Gakkai, and Shohan, (ed.), *Nagasaki Oranda Shōkan Nikki*, *Netherlandshe Oost-Indische Compagnie*, Amsterdam, Yūsho dō Shuppan, Tokyo, 1989.

Nishiyama, Toshio, *Aoime no Sōdan Yaku, Ieyasu to Anjin*, Saera Shobō, Tokyo, 1974 and 1989.

Ogasawara, Kyoko, *Okuni Kabuki Zengo*, Iwata Shoin, Tokyo, 2006.

Okada, Akio, *Chosaku Shū, Miura Anjin, vol. 5*, Shibunkaku Shuppan, Kyoto, 1957.

Okada, Akio, *Miura Anjin*, Sōgen Sha, Osaka, 1944.

Oharu, *Oharu's account*, Hirado Kankō Kyokai, Hirado (describes how her child of mixed parentage was deported to Jakarta, Indonesia in 1639).

Onjuku, Encyclopedia Britannica.

Osawa, Yūhō, Chief Priest *Sōtō-Shū Teiseizan Ryūkō-In, vol. 11, No. 652*, Tochigi Prefecture.

Ōshima, Masahiro, *Umi no Hayato*, Gakuyō Shobō, Tokyo, 1999.

Pourade, Richard F., *The Explorers 1492–1774*, Chapter 5 (Sebastian Vizcaino's account), San Diego History Center, 1960.

Rodrigo de Vivero Y Velasco Aberrucia, *Roderigo De Vivero. An Account of Japan, 1609*, Hardinge Simpole Publishing, Edinburgh, 2015.

Rogers, Philip George, *The First Englishman in Japan: The Story of Williams Adams*, Harvill Press, London, 1956.

Royal Geographical Society, *The First Westward Voyage from Europe to Japan, 1598–1600*, Vol. 68, No.5, Review, *Geographical Journal*, 1926.

Ryūkō-In, (ed.), *Erasmus Ritsuzō*, Sano-Shi, Tochigi, 1950.

Sadler, A. L., *Shogun: The Life of Tokugawa Ieyasu*, George Allen & Unwin, London, 1937.

Saitō, Kumatomo, *Seiyo Bunka no Nihon*, Sōgen Sha, Osaka, 1941.

Satow, Sir Ernest. M., *The Origin of Spanish and Portuguese Rivalry in Japan*, Asiatic Society of Japan, Tokyo, 1890.

Satow, Sir Ernest. M. (ed.), *The Voyage of Captain John Saris to Japan 1613,* Hakluyt Society, London, 1900.

Scammel, G. V. and Hakluyt Society, *Great Age of Discovery, 1400–1650,* Hakluyt Society, London, 1981.

Shioda, Takashi, *Kirisitan Kinkyo to Sakoku* (describes the forbidding of Christianity and national isolation), Taika Shobō, 1947.

Shimada, Taka'aki, *Kiku to Lion – Nichi-Ei ni miru Nihon Jōhō no rūtsu,* Shakai Shisō Sha, Tokyo, 1987.

Shin'pen Sumō Fudoki Kō, Edo contemporary topography, (preserved at the local library in Hemi).

Sito Hirado, (History of Hirado), Matsura Historical Museum, Hirado.

Suganuma, T., *Dai Nippon Shōgyō Shi, Hirado Bōeki Shi,* Iwanami Shoten, Tokyo, 1940.

Suzuki, Kaoru, *Tokugawa Ieyasu no Supein (Spanish) Gaikō – Mukai Shōgen to Miura Anjin,* Shin Jinbutsu Ōrai Sha, Tokyo, 2010.

Takenaka, Yasukazu and Kawakami, Tadashi, *Nihon Shōgyō Shi (Book, 1965),* Mineruva Shobō, Kyoto, 1965.

Tanakamaru, Eiko, (ed.), *The Eleven Letters of William Adams,* Nagasaki Shinbun Sha, Nagasaki, 2010.

Tatsumoto, Kiyotaka, (ed.), *Sen'no Rikyū Rekishi Kaidō, pp. 14 -72,* PHP Kenkyūjo, Tokyo and Kyoto, 2013.

Tames, Richard, *Traveller's History of Japan,* Interlink Publishing Group, United States, 2008.

Tames, Richard, *Japan's Christian Century* (Round the World Histories No. 29), Hulton Educational Publications Ltd., London, 1973.

Tames, Richard, *Servant of the Shogun: Being The True Story of William Adams, Pilot and Samurai, the First Englishman in Japan,* Paul Norbury Publications Ltd, Tenterden, 1981.

Tokyo Historiographical Institute, (ed.), *Nihon Kankei Kaigai Shiryō, Igirisu Shōkanchō Nikki,* Tokyo University Press, 1979–1980.

Tokyo Teikoku Daigaku, Shiryō Hensangakari, (ed.), *Dai Nihon Shiryō, dai 12-hen-Edo jidai,* Tokyo Teokoku Daigaku, Tokyo, 1901<2015>.

Toyoda, Seishū, *Kansho Inyū: Igaku to Seibutsu Gaku, 116 (3), (*on the imported sweet potato*),* 1988.

Tuji, Yoshinosuke, *Edo Jidai Shiron,* Yūshi Sha, 1991.

Uchiyama, Hitoshi, *Adams to Ieyasu,* Isobe Kōyō dō, Tokyo, 1926.

Usuki Shidan, (History of Usuki), Usuki Sidan Kai, Usuki.

Wieder, F. C. (ed.), *De Reis Van Mahu En De Straat. Van Magelraes Haar. Zuidiamerika En Japan 1598–1600,* Martinus Nijhoff, Amsterdam, 1923.

Wilbur, Marguerite, *The East India Company and the British Empire in the Far East,* Stanford University Press, California, 1945.

Willis, Clive, (ed.), *China and Macau: Portuguese Encounters with the World in the Age of Discoveries,* Ashgate Publishing, Aldershot, 2002

Yamaoka, Shōhachi, *Tokugawa Ieyasu, Vol. 4,* Kōdan Sha, Tokyo, 1987.

Yoshimura, Sadaji, *Eccentric Keifu, Rekishi no Nakano Kyojin-tachi,* (describes the English power broker, William Adams, and his influence on forbidding Christianity in Japan), Sakuhin Sha, 1982.

INDEX